GENDER AND ORGANIZATIONS - CHANGING PERSPECTIVES

Gender and Organizations - Changing Perspectives

Theoretical Considerations and Empirical Findings

Jeanne de Bruijn and Eva Cyba (eds.)

VU University Press
Amsterdam 1994

VU University Press is an inprint of:
VU Boekhandel/Uitgeverij bv
De Boelelaan 1105
1081 HV Amsterdam
The Netherlands

tel. (020) - 644 43 55
fax (020) - 646 27 19

cover by Neroc Special Services, Amsterdam
typesetting by Roos Siwalette, Amsterdam
printed by Wilco, Amersfoort

isbn 90-5383-312-9
nugi 665

Acknowledgements

The editors would like to thank the European Group for Organization Studies (EGOS) for offering the opportunity of organizing a Work Group on "Women and organizations" to mark EGOS 10th Anniversary Conference held in Vienna in 1991. This project started there.

We would like to give a special word of thanks to the Coordinator of the Interdisciplinary Center for Women's Studies at the Free University, drs. Marianne Grünell. Without her contribution, it is doubtful this book would ever have been published.

Anne Lavelle corrected some of the chapters.

Manuscript corrections were made by Roos Siwalette (lay-out), Vera Boots, Margriet Lambert en Greet Stolker.

CONTENTS

Introduction

Jeanne de Bruijn

Research group Policy, Culture and Gender Issues
Faculty of Social and Cultural Sciences
Free University Amsterdam, The Netherlands

Eva Cyba

Department of Sociology, Institute for
Advanced Studies, Vienna, Austria

Women are changing the demographics of the workforce. Their increased precence and importance is one of the radical developments organizations have to cope with. Working with and under female managers, flexibility in schedules for combining work and family responsibilities, changing manners between de sexes in the work-place, sexual-harassment policies, changing organizational cultures and equal opportunity legislation - these are some of the issues which have been addressed recently by both research and policy.

These developments in organizational practices have generated new perspectives in the literature on organizations. It began with studies on sex-differences in positions and careers, case-studies on sex-segregation in job structures and studies on combining work and family life. Studies on women's special qualifications became popular in the 'women and management' literature. However, sofar a more profound gender debate in organizational studies was lacking. This lack of new theories and concepts on gender and organization became a bottle-neck for further research and theory development. This volume, comprising both theoretical and empirical papers attempts to contribute to a more profound debate on gender and organization.

The point of departure is the gendered character of organizations. This means not only visible differences between men and women are the subject of research, but also the mechanisms behind these differences and the (re)-production of the meaning of gender differences in organizations.

Approaches to gender in organizations

The first conceptual frameworks on gender and organization were developed in the eighties. These were primarily *person-centred*, which means they approached individual sex differences between women and men. This approach assumes that gender influences the behaviour, the attitudes and treatment of men and women, and it leads to research which accentuates and attempts to explain specific differences between women and men. The differences traced tend to be ascribed to biological inheritance or cultural upbringing. This person-centred approach proves useful for analyzing experiences and attitudes of female and male managers, and the consequences of these differences for the organization. But this approach leads easily to circle reasoning. For example, if one studies sex-differences which can explain why women lag behind men in an organization, one becomes focused on the type of differences in which women differ from men negatively. Some differences, where women differ positively from men in their organization, will not become 'visible' because such differences cannot contribute to the explanation of why women lag behind. In addition, differences between women, for example in skills or training, or differences between men in these same aspects, are 'not seen' or not remarked as relevant, even if they are more significant than the female-male differences. Logically, only negative differences count in an explanation of the women's backlogs. Therefore, this person-centred approach only 'finds' that women are 'behind' men, and in this way reproduces the problems it aimed to solve. The explanation then becomes a circle reasoning.

The *situation-centred* approach assumes that organizational structures and cultures are much more determinant for women's positions in organizations than people's personal characteristics as male or female. This approach explains observable differences between male and female managers through situational, structural and cultural factors.

The *gender organizational system* approach combines both approaches - the person-centred approach and the situation-centred approach - but also has two additional starting points. First, an individual and his or her organization is explicitly part of a historical and cultural context. Second, if the individual, the organization or the system changes, then all the other components change as well. In this approach, the systematic factors which influence individuals and organizations are embedded in laws, policies, sex-role stereotypes, cultural values and historical developments.

In this model, individual differences between men and women could be due simultaneously to individual experiences, organizational context and societal system.

Organizations are gendered and produce gender

Dissatisfied with explanations on the visible level of male/female differences in organizations, feminist researchers look for new approaches (e.g. Hearn et al. 1989, Smith 1990, Acker 1990, 1992, Mills and Tancred 1992). The two approaches mentioned above are already examples of more contextual and reflective approaches. From a so-called gender perspective, feminist researchers are starting to examine organizations as gendered processes. This is a new step. Traditional gender research tends to focus on the visible differences between men and women in the organization, with the aim of reducing or removing these differences. This is to be achieved primarily through women adapting themselves to male norms and male choices in order to get the same chances and positions. The new gender research takes the construction of gender-differences as a starting-point. In this approach, gender differences are historically and culturally produced meanings of maleness and femaleness, interwoven with rules and procedures of organizations and the labour market and with job structures and qualifications. These meanings of maleness and femaleness also underlie organizational theories. It brings central questions to the fore, such as: which gender differences became or become meaningful, where, when and why? In this sense, gender not only applies to people but also to aspects of culture or structure of organizations (re)productions of meanings of maleness and femaleness are part of daily organizational practices.

New insights developed in women's studies on gender as a multi-level concept (e.g. Scott 1986, Butler 1990) have also been applied in the field of organizational studies. A common starting-point is: gender and gender relationships are present in all types of institutions and there is no reason to believe that organizations are an exception. This starting-point does not mean that gender and gender relationships are necessarily the most important structure in a particular case, but it signifies that they are certainly a major structure in most.

Gender is a much debated concept in women's studies. In this volume we recognize the use of gender in a multi-level manner; gender as a *social category* for differences in jobs, wages, positions etc. between men and women, gender on a *symbolic level*, gender on an *interactional level,* and gender as appropriate gender *behaviour* or gender *identity* (e.g. Scott 1986).

Nexo Jensen, who opens this volume, uses the 'structure of gender relationships' concept which signifies a twofold meaning of gender for organizations: organizations have a gender and are gendered. The first refers to gender as a social category, the second to the other three levels of producing gender through symbols, in interaction procedures or in creating gender-appropriate behaviour. These are analytically segregated levels, but in fact interact. Nexo Jensen claims that the concept of the 'structure of gender relations' indicates that we must understand that gender is to be found in the social structures of organizations, *and* we have to understand how human practices in organizations constantly bombard and affect social structures. Even in an organization with personnel only of one sex, the organizational structure, the behaviour, the norms and values are gendered.

If the other sex enters such an organization, one can also study gender relations empirically. The analytically different levels of gender in organizations open an attractive field of research. The apparently gender-neutral practices in organizations especially become of interest for discovering gender production and reproduction. Comparative research can demonstrate how organizations produce gender in different ways, as well as how organizations use gender as an organizational principle.

So far, gender is studied primarily in relation to females, femaleness and femininity or women-friendliness in the organization, and is sometimes related to males and maleness. New gender research looks at variety in maleness and masculinity in organizations.

Content of the book

The *three main parts of the book* are (I) gender and main-stream organizational theories, (II) production and reproduction of gender in organizational contexts, and (III) performance of female management. The *theoretical part* contains two chapters. Nexo Jensen shows us how wide the theoretical gap between gender and organization still is, and at a conceptual level suggests how bridges could be developed between the two. She subjects main-stream organizational literature to a 'gender-test'. Her chapter documents how much - or in fact how little - organization theories deal with the gender dimension, and outlines what she thinks are the reasons for this. She stresses the need for a more differentiated gender concept. Hurst and Usher examine the literature on organizations on the issue of organizations' apparent reluctance to remedy gender inequality in the workplace. They want to know whether current organizations change theories can tell us something about the feasibility of dismantling the gendered structure of labour and achieving gender equality in organizations. This is relevant knowledge particularly for organizations in the process of change.

The *second part* of this volume looks at how *gender is produced and reproduced in an organizational context*. Brumlop presents a critical review of new discourses in management literature. Despite all prognoses on women's entry into management and on new 'feminine' styles of management, she asks if the 'new management culture' really offers women a chance to get at the top and to stay there on the basis of 'femininity' in management. Is the new management culture less gendered than the old? She doubts it, because male management also changes.

A rather different outcome is presented by Maddock on the basis of preliminary findings from an empirical research project looking at gender relationships between managers working in local government in the UK. Maddock shows that, if given the opportunity, women do better, in an organizational style based on cooperation and communication. They support the development of more democratic relationships at work and more flexible management systems. During the public sector expenditure cuts the female managers' 'open management' styles were pulled down with an appeal to discourses on efficiency in organizational restructuring. This restructuring produced a more hierarchical structure once again in which male managers got or took opportunities. Therefore, Maddock put a theoretical statement on the relationships between gender, organizational control, and types of decision processes.

In chapter 5, Kerfoot and Knights do not raise the subject of femininity in management, but look at masculinity. Their point of departure is that there is also diversity in maleness - gender is not a dichotomy between men and women - and therefore they explore to the discourse of masculinity in two predominant forms of management. They identify two different manifestations of masculinity, 'paternalistic masculinity' and 'competitive masculinity', which seem to be concrete manifestations of the interplay between historical shifting forms of management and masculinities in operation. In the historical development of the UK financial services industry the authors found an ideal underpinning of their theoretical analysis.

In her contribution Tijdens attempts to connect different gendered practices in organizations, on a theoretical as well as on an empirical level. Research on these interrelations is new as is research on their combined effects. Tijdens' special interest is in three forms of sex segregation in

14

organizations. Her questions are: how are job segregation, hierarchical segregation and departmental segregation related to each other? Which organizational setting and which characteristics in organizations cause less genderedness in comparison to other types of organizations?

This question also plays a part in Laufer's chapter. She links the question of equality between the sexes in organizations to the compatibility of paid work and household and care tasks. She offers a changing perspective: different discourses of interest groups like the treasury, the unions and the state should be linked to organizational discourses. Each group focuses on different aspects and neglects others.

The *third part* of the volume looks at woman's practical experiences, *in top positions* in organizations or in their own businesses. How do they think they manage, and do they feel there is tension between being professional and being 'a women'. Despite popular portrayals of women's upward mobility and female managers, labour force statistics indicate that few women actually advance to managerial positions and survive as business women. Psychological research on the scarcity of female managers tends to approach this issue from a person-centred perspective, focusing on the characteristics of women as an explanation either for their unsuccessful mobility to prove women managers do better than their male counterparts.

The chapters in this section of the book demonstrate that a situation-centred perspective - the organizational context - provides a more useful contribution to understanding female management as a success or a failure.

Burke examines the context of corporate boards of directors in different firms. He compares how men and women reach these boards and how they perform. The greater success of men in gaining promotion is due to their greater use of informal networks. They use other means more frequently than meritocratic ones to bring their desire for promotion to the attention of superiors, and they ensure that on average the better performance evaluations of women do not offset the lower performance evaluations of men.

Van Mens' case study concerns the business of prostitution. She interviewed female managers who head different types of prostitution organizations. Their styles of management, relationships with personnel and the type of professional status they develop are the topics.

Jungbauer-Gans also takes female entrepreneurs as subject of research. She looks at the means of survival these female entrepreneurs use and analyses the chances of succes. She also compares businesses headed by both male and female owners and asks if their chances of survival differ. She also discusses why some gender-related factors matter while others do not.

Most of the contributions use the situation centredness perspective or a combination of person- and situation centredness. The organization and its characteristics are studied as the main factor in explaining women's positions or inequality between the sexes. If we look back from the perspective of constructions of gender differences, then we find some contributions examining the historically and culturally situated (re)production of meanings of maleness or femaleness. The production of different types of masculinity in the history of London's financial sector is a good example. New types of masculinity with new elements of ascribed meanings of maleness were demonstrated. Among new perspectives in 'gendered organizational analysis' is the use of a multi-level gender concept: gender as a social category, gender at a symbolic level, gender at an interactional level, and gender as (re)production of gender-appropriate behaviour. Although not focused on these levels, several authors gave examples of these analytically distinct gender components. Therefore, the authors help to create conditions for a fundamental reworking of organizational theories.

New perspectives

Today, the concept of *gender subtext* appears on the scene in numerous critical analysis from a gender perspective. The concept is connected to the approach of searching for historically and culturally situated (re)productions of gender differences. The approach stems from the humanities disciplines where it is applied to literary texts, to movie scripts, to mass media, etc. However, in gender studies today gender subtext as an (text) analytical instrument is also applied metaphorically to rules and procedures of organizations, to laws, to technical artefacts or systems. Gender subtext refers to a set or a discourse of assumptions that reproduces meanings of maleness and femaleness in an hierarchical order in any societal setting. As long as most gender issues and the mechanisms which cause them are 'unseen' or are seen as obvious or natural, a need remains for analytical instruments to scan these imperceptible practices. The concept of gender subtext could be one of these instruments. Although the concept of gender subtext is not used in the contributions to this volume, we find the openings for it in several of them; for example, the unwritten rules prescribing workplace behaviour for female managers or business women in the contributions by Brumlop, Maddock, Burke, Van Mens and Jungbauer-Gans. Or, for example, part of the gender subtext is the assumption that work is separate from the rest of life. This gender subtext is encoded in arrangements and rules in organizations and, as such, is discussed implicitly or explicitly in several contributions to this volume.

Developing the concept of gender subtext, as well as the multi-level gender concept will not only produce better answers to questions on the (re)production of gender in organizations, but will also contribute to more sophisticated organizational theories.

The volume is a rich composition of empirical research and theoretical developments in today's research field of gender and organizations.
The gender perspective on organization theory seems to generate a new range of questions, propositions and changing perspectives.
This volume attempts to contribute to this gathering eruption of new perspectives in an old area of scientific research.

References

Acker, J. (1990), 'Hierarchies, Jobs, Bodies; A Theory of Gendered Organizations', in: *Gender & Society 4*, pp. 139-58.

Acker, J. (1992), 'Gendering Organizational Theory', in: A.J. Mills & P. Tancred (eds) (1992), *Gendering Organizational Analysis*, London: Sage, pp. 248-61.

Butler, J. (1990), *Gender Trouble: Feminism and the Subversion of Identity*. New York: Routledge.

Hearn, J., D. Sheppard, P. Tancred-Sheriff, and G. Burrell (eds), (1989), *The Sexuality of Organization*, London: Sage.

Mills, A.J. and P. Tancred (eds), (1992), *Gendering Organizational Analysis*, London: Sage.

Scott, J. (1986), 'Gender: A Useful Category of Historical Analysis', in: *American Historical Review 91*, 1053-75.

Smith, D. (1990), *The Conceptual Practices of Power: A Feminist Sociology of Knowledge*, Toronto: University of Toronto Press.

PART I

Main-Stream Organization Theory and Gender

1   Gendered Theories of Organizations

Hanne Nexø Jensen

Institute of Political Science
University of Copenhagen, Denmark

Can organization theory be of any help when studying women in organizations? This chapter documents how much - or, more precisely, how little - organization theories deal with the gender dimension (section three). The chapter further discusses why gender has such a marginal role in organization theories (section four). Finally, suggestions are made on what we can do to bridge the gap between gender and organizations (section five). However, this chapter starts with a definition of main stream organization theory and of gender (sections one and two).

Main-Stream Organization Theory

In this chapter, theories applied by political science are considered main-stream. Mainstream organization theory examines why public organizations are public, the signficance of environments for organizations and the significance of different institutional norms and values. Of course, main-stream theories also discuss how are defined organizations and under what conditions an organization functions most productively and efficiently. At first glance, there appears to be hardly anything on gender in this area of the literature.

The term 'theories of organizations' is like a general designation covering a large number of theories, concepts or approaches in producing knowledge about organizations. Assessing the whole range of organizational theories is beyond the scope of this chapter. A clear, and in this context, useful classification, has been developed by Scott (1981). He distinguishes between, organizations as rational or natural systems and organizations as open or closed systems (see also table one).

Table one: Scott's classification of organizational theories

	Closed Systems	Open Systems
Rational systems	Classic organizational theory Weber, Taylor	Contingency Theory Mintzberg
Natural systems	Human perspective Human Relations	Loosely Coupled perspective Schein, Meyer & Rowan

Today, the literature seldom discusses the distinction between organizations as open or closed systems because modern organizations define themselves as related to their environments. However, distinguishing between organizations as rational systems (in discussions on organizational efficiency and productivity) and organizations as natural systems (in discussions on organizational culture, symbols etc.) is still relevant.

Concepts of organizations based on the premise that they are rational systems (regardless of whether they are open or closed) seldom concern the actual people who make the organizations work (with the possible exception of Weber and his concept of bureaucrats!). Hence, regardless of gender, people as such are not part of the theories and analysis. Often the central theme is how an organization functions most rationally and most efficiently. But do organizations in general function as rational units?

In many ways the natural perspective on organizations is an elaboration of organizational theory from a critique of the rational perspective. The human-relation perspective criticises classic organizational theory for not including human beings. The Human-relation perspective does comprise research that includes a gender dimension: Gender roles and socialization form one cornerstone and Women in Management research forms another. The research that includes a gender dimension is often criticised for focusing excessively on individuals and roles and too little on organizations. Hence, it is difficult to find inspiration from within the human-relation perspective when developing theories on gender *and* organizations.

The "loosely coupled perspective" - which includes a variety of theories - has been developed partly because the rational perspective can hardly conceive phenomena which do not deal with structures. The concept of culture is central in many of the contributions to the loosely coupled perspective. Here one finds a variety of definitions of culture, the meaning of culture and ways of analyzing organizational culture. Schultz operates with three perspectives on culture: rational, functional and symbolic. The rationalist and functionalist perspectives are inspired by the well-known images: the machine and the organism, while the symbolic perspective is based on sociology and the humanities (Schultz 1990: 19).

Hence, there does seem to be room for human beings, especially when organizations are viewed as natural systems (as in Scott's classification of organizational theory). Why subject main-stream organizational literature to a 'gender-test' when you can find more about gender in *other areas* of the literature on organizations? A simple answer: curiousity, and I want to find out if there really should be areas of the social sciences where gender is not an important factor/element. (But first, let me outline my definition of gender and methodological considerations.)

Concepts and methods

Does gender make a difference? One can make a distinction between such different analytical gender categories as the biological, the social, the psychological, the sexual and the cultural. In this context the differentiation is between the biological and the social aspects: i.e. between sex and gender in order to simplify the description.[1]

The concept 'gender' refers to a social process. Gender is a biological fact, which is given different social interpretations, depending on the historical context. Women and men do exist as gender, and each of them play a dissimilar role in procreation, pregnancy and nursing. We are born either as a girl or a boy, i.e. we have a sex. But we are also born into a structure in which gender already has a special meaning, i.e. we are gendered even though we - as human beings - can also affect the structure, even change it.

Gender is neither exclusively a biological fact nor exclusively a social construction; gender is both/and. Let me give an example. More than a hundred years ago their sex excluded women from studying medicine. Nowadays it is not their sex which prevent women from studying medicine. Today - at least in Denmark - some people talk about medicine as gendered, i.e. dominated by female students (causing problems to the status of doctors according to some men).

In relation to social science it is interesting to examine how biology is handled socially. We must try to understand the correlation between sex and gender, and we must understand that gender and the differences between women and men are changing due to changes in social, cultural, political and economic conditions. Marx reasons similarly, when he distinguishes between social conditions (Verhältnisse) and social behaviour (Verhalten). "The point of departure is recognition that human beings do not exist in isolation. In order to meet their most elementary needs, humans have to make contact with each other. Where such a mutual social behaviour (Verhalten) is at play, then a set of social conditions (Verhältnisse) have been established." (Sørensen 1976, 72). One does find a dialectic between human activity and objective circumstances. Bohr has said the same with reference to Chinese philosophy: "We are facing complementary coherences. In the great drama of life we are both actors and players." (Blædel 1985; 225). Giddens, who represents a newer version, has a theory in which the relationship between structure and actor is labelled as a process of structuration.

Organizations both have genders and are gendered. When organizations have genders, then it is equivalent to the conception of gender as a variable such as age, education and occupation: variables such as are found in questionnaires for example. If I were to discuss in what ways gender as a variable could be included in studies of organizations, it is tantamount to the idea: "Add gender and stir". We keep organizational theory unaltered, and add gender. For example Lysgaard (1976) shows in his book "The Worker's Collective", that organizations both employ women and men. Deal & Kennedy (1982) have a chapter entitled: "Women and minorities" in their book: "Corporate Cultures". Neither of the authors discuss whether a gender dimension would throw a new light on their general discussion.

I found a parallel to the idea that organizations have gender in a management-oriented conception of organizational culture. Here, organizations have culture. Managers use culture as a tool. "Corporate culture can be defined as a set of commonly held attitudes, values, and beliefs that guide the behaviour of an organization's members." (Martin 1985 from Collin, 1987; 49). On the one hand one can say that organizations *have* gender and *have a* culture. On the other hand I think that one can argue that organizations *are* gendered and *are* culture.

The discussion of culture in organizations could be improved by inspiration from anthropology. In anthropology, culture is a macro-concept. Cultures are sluggish and resistant to attempts at (conscious) change. The definition of culture in a symbolic perspective corresponds to the conception that organizations *are* culture. Organizational culture is defined as "a pattern of socially created symbols and the creation of meaning." (Schultz 1990: 19). The symbolic perspective is built on a conception of a human being as an active creator of her and his own reality. In organizations meeting-rituals, myths and sagas or such physical symbols as signs, are examples of culture as a symbol.

Organizations can be said to be gendered because, gender and "gender relations are present in all types of institutions - also organizations. They may not be the most important structure in a particular case, but they are certainly a major structure of most." (Connell 1987: 120). Let me give an example. In some organizations one finds women's and men's qualifications that are somehow frozen in time (Dahlerup 1989: 35). Women are hired as seamstresses, men as blacksmiths, even though one can find men who sew and women who can do the work of a blacksmith. The meaning of gender relations can also be seen in the disparity in wages paid to women and men.

The interplay between the conception that organizations have gender and that organizations are gendered, can be captured through the concept, 'the structure of gender relations', which I introduce with inspiration from Dahlerup (1989) and Connell (1987). The concept, 'the structure of gender relations' emphasizes that genders already *are* embedded in a given structure and processes, for example in structures of organizations and processes in organizations. The concept further highlights that gender is not just a biological fact (sex). Gender is also to be found in our practices and existing structures such as organizations, the family, the school and society as such.

When we want to grasp the meaning of gender for organizations, then we must *both* capture, which gender we have (sex) *and* which gender we are (gender), and especially examine the relation between sex and gender. It is not a question of either - or. The structure of gender relations includes the fact that organizations both have and are gendered, and that the two surfaces interact. I therefore place the structure of gender relations in the middle columns of "have" and "are" in table two.

The concept of the structure of gender relations indicates that we must understand that gender is to be found in the social structures of organizations, *and* we have to understand how human practices in organizations constantly bombard and affect social structures. For example, even though you find only men in barracks or only women in domestic science schools, gender influences the structure, the behaviour etcetera. If the other sex enters the area then we can study gender relations empirically.

Table two. Organizations "have" and "are" gender and culture

Organizations	
Have	Are
Culture, tool of management	**Culture** symbolic, anthropology
Gender, variable	**Gender**, social process
- biological, sex	- social gender
- women's and men's situation	- gender relations
Structure of gender relations	

But how can one grasp gender in other research areas? Here I will focus on main stream organizational research and gender. I studied the use of gender-related concepts by main stream organizational researchers in their scientific productions. A criteria for selecting 34 studies on organizations is that the literature is used and produced within political science. Most conceive organizations as rational systems (both open and closed), and some view organizations as loosely coupled. A few authors deal with the human perspective, but these are of secondary importance in political science. I have omitted literature which deals with such psychological and individual aspects as "how to become a leader.." or "525 ways of Management".

I have studied 34 works, written between 1961 and 1990. Firstly, I went through the indices of the books to see if gender was mentioned in one way or another (see "Main stream organizational research and gender"). Secondly, I went through the text to see how the authors dealt with gender issues (see "Behind the figures"). I studied how many references the different books had to the following concepts: family, women, men, gender difference, sexuality, social gender and to the book by Kanter: "Men and Women of the Corporation" (1977).[2] The concepts were chosen pragmatically since these concepts seemed to be the way organizational researchers operationalised gender. Concepts such as feminine or masculine were too sophisticated and did not show up in the literature.

Main stream organizational research and gender - some results

Altogether I found 256 references unequally distributed (see supplement number one). 17 books did not have any references at all. Two books had more than 70 references to gender-related concepts (see table three and four). In a book about gender and organizations: "The Feminist Case against Bureaucracy" written by Ferguson (1984) one finds 119 references to the same concepts! All things considered, that part of organizational theory used within the field of political science only incorporates a gender dimension to a very limited degree.

Table three. Number of references in books

References	0	1	2	3	.6	7	8	.16	.37	.74	.89
No. of books	17	4	2	1	1	1	2	1	1	1	1

One result of the study is that one can spot a development from an almost total neglect of gender in the literature on organizations to an incorporation - even though very limited - of gender related concepts. But it is especially in three books (Hofstede) 1980, and two by Nystrom & Starbuck 1981), that

Table four: Number of references to gender-related concepts

	All books	Without Hofstede, Nystrom & Starbuck
Family:	125	5
Women:	36	12
Gender difference:	50	2
Kanter (1977):	23	17
Social gender:	11	11
Sexuality:	8	6
Men:	3	3
Total:	256	56

we find the greatest number of references. And those three books are more or less in the periphery of the field of political science. The perspective on organizations found in the three books diverges from the rest of the literature, i.e. the conception of organizations is more related to the Human Relation Perspective (Nystrom & Starbuck) or to a general view on cultures in countries as such (Hofstede, 1980). Column two in table four shows the number of references without these three books. In total we find 56 references to gender-related concepts of which 17 refer to Kanter. 13 of those references do not relate to gender but to Kanter's general discussion of power.

A preliminary conclusion of this study of the indices in organizational literature is that organizational theory only incorporates a gender dimension to a very limited degree. Furthermore it is evident that most of the references are to be found in literature located *outside* the hard core of political science. In recent years, we seem to be returning to the time when gender was totally absent. There is, for example, no reference to gender-related concepts since 1988 (see the supplement).

Including more books would not change the result dramatically. The results of the study underlying this article are supported by the findings of Hearn & Parkin (1983) and Burrell & Hearn (1989), who mention that the "'founding fathers' (of organizational theory, for example Taylor, Weber, Machiavelli, Hobbes and Marx, ed.) and their more modern 'sons' do not do a very good job of gender (relations).....In surveying the treatment of gender within organization theory it is hard to avoid the conclusion that gender has either been ignored, treated implicitly as male, considered an organizational 'variable' reduced to relative stereotypes, or been analysed in a blantantly sexist way." (Burrell & Hearn 1989: 9f).

Behind the figures: Men only!

What do we find behind the figures? I have looked behind the figures in order to evaluate how the literature on organizations deals with a gender dimension. Methodologically, I read the text looking for discussions relating to gender in one way or another.

In 17 books there are *no* references at all to gender related concepts. The authors do not think that gender is relevant at least explicitly. Implicitly many of the authors think of the staff of the organizations in terms of men. This goes for Weber's theory of bureaucracy, which implicitly deals with the bureaucratic man (Burrell & Hearn 1989: 9).

Few of the authors recognize that the staff of organizations can be both men and women, even though there is no reference to gender related concepts. Some authors write for example "he and she", when they talk about the workers or the readers. One example: "The term organization and organization structure are terms everyone understands until he or she is asked to define them" (J.R. Galbraith 1977: 2). But gender is in general neglected in those 17 books that are without reference to gender related concepts.

Outside the organizations

It is obvious that the staff of any organization (even men) have to be maintained and serviced at home in order to work properly in the organization. But organizational theory does not even seem to be aware of this. In all, I found 125 references to the concept of family. Most of the references were found in Nystrom & Starbuch (1981) and refer to a kind of ownership, which is uninteresting in a gender perspective.

Anthropology has influenced organizational theory. Family ties seem to be important in relation to nepotism or as an element which influences the kind of job a person chooses/gets (March & Simon 1965, 72). The differences between women and men are only discussed to a very limited degree, even though family ties and marriage seem to be important networks in society as such. For example Gerlach & Palmer (1981, 351) mention that women and men have different resources, but they hesitate to discuss this further.

A third group of references relate to a worker's family. In a Japanese example it is mentioned, "that the firm almost does not distinguish between the workers private life and worklife. The management is involved in the workers financial circumstances, education of his children, religious activities and the education of his wife." (Blau & Scott 1966, 203).

The last and fourth group of references about the family deals with its influence on the socialization of the workers. According to Danet (1981, 389) the bureaucracy has its own way of socializing. Beyond this Hofstede estimates that a very important part of gender role socialization takes place in the family, and at the same time the family is an important institution which sustains cultural patterns in society as such (Hofstede 1980, 22 and 180).

According to Hofstede the biological roles are changed through the socialization that takes place in the family, the school, among peergroups and in the media. He emphasizes the relation between the family and the organization in this way: "The predominant socialization pattern is for men to be more assertive and for women to be more nurturing. In organizations, there is a relationship between the perceived goals of the organization and the career possibilities for men and women; business organizations have 'masculine' goals and tend to promote men; hospitals have more 'feminine' goals and, at least on the nursing side, tend to promote women" (Hofstede 1980: 176).

Hofstede's book is located in the periphery of main stream political science. No other book in my sample discusses the necessity of reproducing workers outside the organization. One explanation can be found in the division of labour between different branches of science. Organizational theory only deals with the workers at work. Therefore it seems irrelevant for organizational theory to study the workers reproduction outside the organization. Connell makes a point when he states that social sciences have picked "a particular institution as the bearer of gender and sexuality. The family and kinship have usually been elected to this honour.....The flip side of this election was that it allowed other institutions (organizations, ed.) to be analysed as if gender were of no account at all" (Connell 1987: 119).[3]

The references to family are chronologically followed by references to women and men (March 1970). In all there are three references to men, but the concept 'men' is much more common in the literature than the number three indicates. One explanation is that 'men' are synonymous with gender in organizational theory.

There are 36 references to women. Some (nine) of these references deal with which new members a bridge club should choose when somebody leaves, or with the correlation between the wife's occupation and her husband's mobility. The Women's Christian Temperance Union (WCTU) is an example of an organization with great success at the time of birth, but the WCTU was not able to adjust to environmental changes. There are two references to roles and role-conflict, where it is emphasized that women cannot choose their own role, womens' roles are chosen by men. Another author mentions that a woman's role conflict is related to her life cycle position. All these results are interesting, but they are not elaborated on.

There are twelve references to discrimination against women. One author mentions that women in men's jobs have great problems, expressed in gender specific preferences and the degree of job satisfaction (Hukin & Triandis 1981: 349). The rest of the references to discrimination are about minorities. One example is discrimination against women and blacks - as minorities, neither have the same career opportunities as white men. Hall (1987: 14) emphasizes a number of authors (among others Kanter 1977), who write about discrimination against women in organizations. Women are not promoted equally with men. And women, who do get promotion are met by responses which are gender stereotyped. Deal & Kennedy (1982: 98 ff) have devoted a special chapter to groups in organizations which are not adjusted to the organizational culture. The heading of the chapter is 'Women and Minorities'. When groups are not adjusted to the life of an organization, then the organization is not making the most of its potential resources. Deal & Kennedy further discuss how the traditional white, androcentric culture can be adapted to non-white male talent.

Equating women with minority groups is problematic. There are differences between women and minority groups. One is that minority groups are socialized and developed through interaction in their own group, while women both interact with and develop in relation to men and their own group. Furthermore women do mean a lot for the other group (the men). Finally there are a huge number of minority-groups; but only two sexes. This means that you cannot just integrate and make women equal with men: "Women make up half the society and the labour force and women are already integrated, but in an unique and discriminative way." (Ressner 1985, 101ff).

Changes in personnel management are linked to social changes such as feminism in the 1970s (Koimann & Eliassen 1987, 158). Here there is a tendency to expand the conception of organizations as part of the environment in which gender plays an important role. Furthermore there is a tendency towards a recognition that the increase in the employment of women is a long term phenomenon. Hence, it is important for managers and organizational researchers to recognize that the use of resources in an organization are not maximized, as long as some groups are not adjusted to the life of the organization (a meritocratic-perspective[4]. I must conclude that organizational theory - if women are included - treat women in an isolated corner of the subject or in a small, isolated section, which is not unified with the rest of the text or the theoretical discussion as such. To some extent this can be explained by the fact that women are looked on as a variable, as a dimension, which organizations *have* or *do not have*.

Division of labour based on biological differences

There are 50 references to gender differences. The contexts range from the fact that there are both female and male workers to emphasizing some gender differences. Women are often hired as secretaries and work parttime etc., since they just work for fun and luxury goods! Women are not supposed to support their family. These kinds of references are often found in Nystrom & Starbuck, vol. 1 (1981). Scott states that women's and men's different positions in organizations leads to a differentiation in wages between women and men (Scott 1981: 187).

Hofstede (1980) has another view on gender differences. He uses gender differences as a criterion on a par with nation, occupation and age in investigations (Hofstede studies cultural differences between nations). Hofstede continues: "From these, occupation and sex are closely related; only a few occupations have sizable numbers of both men and women." (Hofstede 1980: 52).

Furthermore Hofstede discusses the meaning of gender differences in organizations: "All organizations have a division of labour, and most have members of both sexes. In organizational practice, the division of labour and the division of sex roles tend to be linked ... the 'proper' division of labour over the sexes is largely a matter of convention.... Sex bias which bars women (or men) from certain jobs because of tradition obviously affects the functioning of the organization." (Hofstede 1980: 182f).

Hofstede argues that the social differences between women and men influence the functioning of the organization. This point of view is very different from (almost) any other organizational theorist, but has also been the point of departure for my study, i.e. Hofstede's conception of gender is to some extent based on the perception that organizations *are* gendered.

Sexuality in organizations

I found eight references to the concept of sexuality. In one example sexuality is seen as something 'exotic', something special (Warner 1981, 175). Of course, sexuality can be exotic, but in general, sexuality is much more than that - in organizations (and in society as such[5]

Morgan (1986) discusses the relationship between bureaucracy as a form of organization and repressed sexuality. As with Freud, organizations are not only formed by their environment, but also by the unconscious of their employees i.e. their repressed sexuality and other unconscious forces, which create society (Morgan 1986: 210). Morgan finds that Freud was too fixated on sexuality. Finally Morgan makes a statement on women's role in changing organizations: "The major role that women and gender-related values can play in transforming the corporate world.... that the real challenge facing women who want to succeed in the organizational worlds is to change organizational values in the most fundamental sense." (Morgan 1986; 212).

It seems alluring that women have (or can have) such an important role in changing organizations. Hence, it is problematic that changing organizations seems to be a business for women - as a sex. Women do not form a homogenous group. And in some cases a combination of women and men in a group can be more fruitful than a group of women (or men), only.

Gender makes a difference - even in organizations

Morgan (1986) is the only one referring to gender: "It often makes a great deal of difference if you're a man or a woman! Many organizations are dominated by gender-related values that bias organizational life in favour of one sex over another. Thus, as many feminist writers have emphasized, organizations often segment opportunity structures and job markets in ways that enable men to achieve positions of prestige and power more easily than women, and often operate in ways that produce gender-related biases in the way organizational reality is created and sustained on a day-to-day basis. This is most obvious in situations of open discrimination and various forms of sexual harassment, but often pervades the culture of an organization in a way that is much less visible." (Morgan 1986: 178).

Hofstede finds that gender-bias affects the functioning of organizations. Morgan emphasizes the dominance of male values in organizations. He stresses that each person's possibilities and necessary strategies are dependent on gender. Often, women have to use much more energy than men in order to complete the daily task. Both sexes use conscious or unconscious strategies for "gender management" (Morgan 1986: 179). Morgan includes the social meaning of gender, but relates the consequences of different social genders to the possibilities of a *single* woman or man in the organization. Only at the edge of the main stream do we find an author who emphasizes that gender means something *for* organizations.

Rosabeth Moss Kanter: Men and Women of the Corporation

Most of the references to Kanter (1977) (19 out of 23) are *not* related to gender, even though Kanter stresses that men have another position in the opportunity-structure and can more easily be promoted than women. It is striking that Mintzberg (1983a) in his book "Power in and around Organizations" refers to Kanter's discussions about the power and opportunity structure without mentioning women's and men's different positions in these structures.

One of the references deals with discrimination against women as a minority-group (R. Hall 1987: 14). Scott (1981) emphasizes that men systematically have jobs with an opportunity to get promoted, while women end up in dead end jobs (Scott 1981: 88, 184 and 187). For example, it is easier for men to acquire a mentor. A mentor is a manager who protects and supports mostly, other men. In this way management minimizes future uncertainties. This is also called "homosexual reproduction", i.e. men reproduce the organization in their own image (Kanter 1977: 48).

Organizational theorists' 'gender-consciousness'

As stated above the references to gender related dimensions in organizational theory, embrace a spectrum from no references at all to new concepts. Historically we can trace a qualitative development in gender references: from a focus on the family, men and women towards an incorporation of sex as a social phenomenon ("gender") with influence on organizations (see table five).

Table five: Trends in organizational theorists' use of gender-related concepts

Reference	Degree of 'gender-consciousness'
None	There are only men in organizations
Family	There is a life outside organizations
Women Men	Organizations have both female and male employees. Some refer to the discrimination of women
Gender difference	Gendered division of labour based on the biological differences between men and women
	Sexuality in organizations is discussed in the literature
Sexuality	Gender differences have both biological and social roots that influence organisations and the way they work
Gender	

My investigation shows that a gender dimension - if included - is to be found in books in the periphery of the main stream. Hence one cannot talk about a development of organizational theory as such. The books in the periphery of the main stream are characterized by an interdisciplinary approach, which is parallel to the development in a number of disciplines. First units were in focus (i.e. common features of organizations). The second focus was on ethnocentrism (the family, women and men are explicit categories, but the point of departure is a male-dominated conception of organizations). Finally relations and differences (i.e. gender differences, sexuality and social gender and the meaning in relation to organizations) are brought into focus.

How to explain the treatment of gender in organizational theory

A central conclusion drawn from my investigation is that there are only few references to gender related concepts in organizational literature (main stream political science). And there is no discussion of the meaning of gender within main stream organizational theory. The picture I draw is actually more positive, since I include books which are located in the periphery of main stream organizational theory. There exists no single explanation for this. But a presentation of several partial explanations can throw light on the subject.

Reality - theory time lag

In the last twenty years the number of working women has enormously increased i.e. books written in the beginning of the period under examination cannot be expected to pay attention to gender in the same way as newer books, since the number of women employed was much smaller at that time (The year 1961). Furthermore only a few women worked as organizational theorists at that time, for example Follett and Woodward (see Pugh et.al. 1964). Today this picture has changed, since there are more women employed at institutes of higher education. But these arguments do not help explain why newer organizational literature does not - or only to a very limited degree - include a gender dimension. For example it is remarkable that newer anthologies about the public sector (see Gortner et.al. 1987 and Kooiman & Eliassen 1987) have little or no awareness of a gender dimension.

In the light of the huge number of women on the labour market in the Nordic countries and the intensive attention paid to Women in management in those countries, it is striking that a wellknown and widely used textbook about organizations (Bakka & Fivelsdal 1988) does not mention gender[6]. The third edition of a textbook by Robbins (1990) is also without gender related references. Finally, gender has been left out of Peter's & Waterman's (1984) empirical research.

One cannot expect to find gender or women in organizational theory before women work in organizations. Nowadays, women can be found in organizations but women and gender as dimensions are still neglected in organizational theory. The time lag does not explain the absent of gender in newer organizational literature.

Philosophy of social science - an explanation?

Theories do not seem to be able to keep up with reality. Maybe an explanation for this can be found in the fundamental epistemology of the theories. Hearn & Parkin (1983) have written one of the first, critical analysis on gender and organizations. They state that organizational theory can be categorized in four paradigms. They analyse how gender has been treated in each of the four paradigms.

The *functionalist paradigm* with Parsons in the forefront, has contributed with fundamental assumptions about women and men. The gender division of labour is taken for granted or is viewed as a functional necessity. For example, some sociologist use a job-model to explain men's behaviour, and a gender model to explain working women's behaviour. According to Hearn & Parkin (1983) you find a great deal of the literature about women in management under the rubric of the functionalist paradigm. Especially the literature, which combines "a psychological interpretation of women and sex differences with a managerialist perspective" (Hearn & Parkin 1983: 224). The authors state generally that "the literature on women in management can actually be seen as reinforcing patterns of organization and management that neglect women's interests." (Hearn & Parkin 1983: 224).

Most of the contributions based on the *'interpretative'* paradigm, have neglected gender, even though the phenomenological tradition focuses on the subjective realities of the individuals. A consequence of this is that men's accounts of the organizational reality dominate most interpretative analysis (Hearn & Parkin 1983: 224).

'Radical structuralist' is the third paradigm Hearn & Parkin discuss. They make a distinction between two schools. Russian social theory, which neglects gender totally, since women are liberated through the class struggle. Mediterranean Marxism, especially the Althusser inspired part, which

touches lightly on the gender dimension, but sees class divisions "as having far greater significance than sexual divisions." (Hearn & Parkin 1983: 225).

Finally, there is the *'Radical Humanist'* paradigm, which is an anti-organizational theory. Central here is the actor's subjective perception of reality. The radical humanist paradigm is different from the other paradigms, since it includes a wide range of variations. Implicitly men are the gender of the texts. Furthermore, the interest in small, alternative ways of organizing, is widespread (Hearn & Parkin 1983: 226).

The absence of gender in organizational theory cannot be explained by a brief glance at the philosophy of social science. One paradigm only refers to gender, that is the functionalist paradigm. I found no explanations of the absence of a gender dimension in the three other paradigms, even though the radical humanist paradigm explicitly makes room for a gender dimension.

Viewing the paradigms from a gender perspective, throws light on male dominance in science as such. A separate explanation is that most of the books examined are written by men. My view is supported by Burrell & Hearn (1989), who describe organizational theory as being characterized by "male stream". Hearn & Parkin criticize all four paradigms for male - dominance in relation to how work is organised and related to organizational theory.

I have used the concept male dominance several times. In the following section I elaborate further on this concept. I discuss how the absence of gender in organizational theory can be explained by the perception of male dominance in organizational theory.

Gender neutrality on the surface - male bias below

I mentioned earlier that organizations and organizational theory seem to idealize the exclusion of the personal, in line with Weber's conceptions of bureaucrat[7] This means that organizations and organizational theory, ideally, should be gender neutral. However, this is an ideal conception, but it has not very much to do with reality in organizations and organizational theory. Hearn & Parkin (1983) state that organizational theory is characterized by male dominance. Male dominance or male bias in organizational theory means that men's reality and male values delineate the framework for, and the content of, the theories and the research. Those male values are often characterized as rational, logical, aggressive, exploitative, strategic and competitive (see for example, Morgan 1986, 179).

In over-simplified form one can say that men's behaviour is ruled by a technical-economic rationality, which is different from a female nurturing rationality (see among others A. Boman 1983). The differences illustrate which focus men and women choose: men for example often choose productivity (not reproduction), men more often think in hierarchies than women do, and men are in general better suited to direct attention to them-selves than women are. It is obvious that this is not necessarily a charac-teristic of each individual woman or man.

Using the explanation - that organizational theory is tainted with male bias or male dominance - helps us to explain why everything which does not fit in values, norms and men's reality as such is not made explicit in organizational theory, either. Some organizational theorists mean (maybe) that it is unnecessary to include gender in relation to organizations, since the crux of the matter is how organizations produce most rationally, not whom is producing. I think it is relevant to raise objections to such an answer.

First and foremost it is debatable whether organizations function rationally or not. In organizational theory some approaches have questioned this. The development of new-institutionalism is one example, where a critique of rational values is important (March & Olsen 1989). Weick (1979) makes it explicit that organizations are not technical/rational, but character-ized by disorder. The most important thing, according to Weick, is not production in order to fulfil explicit goals. The important thing is the organizing, the process aspect: "Organizations keep people busy, occasional-ly entertain them, give them a variety of experiences, keep them off the streets, provide pretexts for story-telling, and allow socializing. They haven't anything else to give." (Weick 1979: 264). These views draw attention to the fact that other things than rationality are important for organizations.

Secondly, there is more than one way of producing. It is possible to find examples of methods of production where gender has a special meaning. In industry it is a global phenomenon that (young) women are hired to do work which presupposes nimble fingers and patience because the work is repetitious and monotonous (see for example Elson & Pearson 1981). Women's nurturing rationality is important in jobs where contact with clients is dominant. In a Swedish case (health insurance company) clients prefer the way female employees treat them to the treatment they receive from male employees (Boman 1983).

Thirdly, it is necessary to make explicit that organizations also have to be reproduced. There is a life in organizations which is more than production of goods or services. The creation and maintenance of this part of organizational life is also gendered.

Fourthly, there is a relation between production and reproduction. A bad working climate can affect production negatively, and a good climate can affect production positively. DSB - The Danish State Railways - has hired women as train conductors (today there are 50% women and 50% men in this group). Some of the men think that all the conductors have become more open and service-oriented today, which is different from the previous, more authoritarian profile of the job (Wolthers 1990).

Fifthly, and lastly, one can see organizations, not as objective units, but as socially defined and constructed units. Moreover, it is important in what way gender influences this social construction of an organization. Many organizational conditions cannot be explained by using organizational theory, where gender is not made explicit. We can obtain a more varied and a more comprehensive picture and understanding of organizations by using a gender perspective.

The absence of gender in organizational literature from 1961 to 1971 can partly be explained by 'tradition' since women in huge number first entered the labour market from about 1970. The continuing absence of a gender dimension in newer books, can apparently be explained by a male dominance in organizational theory. Some might argue that all organizational theorists do not need to work with gender. The rise of research on Women in Management covers a gender dimension.

Main-stream organizational theory is also male-stream. We do not find analysis of gender and organizations in male-stream literature. Or, put differently, unfortunately, main-stream organizational theorists do not emphasize how, for analytical purposes, sex is handled socially in organizations.

How to minimize the gap between gender and organizations

Using two examples I will illustrate which possibilities and limitations we face when we want to combine gender and organizations. I have chosen Mintzberg to represent the rational, open systems perspective. And I have selected an organizational-cultural perspective as a representative for organizations seen as open, natural systems.

In order to make the relationship between gender and organizations more fruitful, I think we should ask how each perspective deals with: women's situation, men's situation, gender relations and the structure of gender relations. The idea is to grasp that organizations *have* both gender and *are* gendered.

In Mintzberg's theory of contingency, an organization is structured according to its situation, including conditions of production. He differentiates between five models of organizations. It is possible to include gender as a variable, which might influence the way organizations function. Nevertheless, I think it is questionable whether the theory of contingency looks upon gender as a relevant variable, similar to technology, structure, actors, the age of the organization, and other situational factors.

The concept of an actor can vary, depending on the situation of both women and men. In bureaucracies we often find women at the bottom of the hierarchy, and the gender division of work is mainly vertical. Traditional male values such as production, rationality, efficiency, competition and goal-orientation have much prestige. If one includes female values, then the focus

43

will change, and other parts of the bureaucracy will be relevant: for example, the necessity of cooperation and the ability to understand clients. Furthermore, we can disclose the ways in which a traditional bureaucracy sustains dominant and subordinate relationships between, for example, men and women (but a huge number of men are also subordinated in a bureaucracy, Ferguson, 1984). Many investigations by women researchers indicate that women, but also men, expand their talents much more in an organization characterized by networking (Kvande & Rasmussen, 1990). This is what Mintzberg calls an adhocracy, but he focuses primarily on structure and production.

If organizational culture is the focus, then we can add gender by making a differentiation between feminine and masculine aspects of organizational culture. This applies in both a management-oriented and a symbolic-oriented conceptualization of organizations. In the management-oriented concept, we find examples distinguishing between a female, a male and an androgynous style of management. In the symbolic perspective there are cases where organizational culture is characterized as feminine or masculine. One example is Billing and Alvesson (1989), who investigate three Danish organizations. The Welfare Department *(Socialstyrelsen)* is depicted as feminine, while the Ministry of Foreign Affairs is depicted as a masculine organization. Gender is used as a metaphor analogous to the way Morgan (1986) differentiates between eight organizational metaphors. Instead of adding new metaphors, I think it could be interesting and relevant to reflect on which new dimensions a gender perspective would add *to each of* the existing metaphors, i.e. combine gender and the machine-metaphor, combine gender and the political system metaphor etc., rather than adding a new one.

In the symbolic perspective there is a tendency to focus on the reproductive side of organizations. This relates to the concept that organizations *are* gendered (see table six). One example is the anthology: "The Sexuality of Organization" (Hearn et al., 1989). The aim of the book is to contribute to "a critical reorientation of organization theory towards concerns with gender, reproduction and sexuality rather than just production and productivity." (Burrell & Hearn 1989: 2). The authors state that an understanding of gender - and especially sexuality - should be incorporated into organizational theory and in the reproduction of organizations. Sexuality and gender are rooted in practice and are viewed as processes, expressed in discourses. The definition of sexuality should be broad "in at least two ways: (1) to see sexuality as an ordinary and frequent public process rather than an extraordinary feature of private life; and (2) to see sexuality as one aspect of an all-pervasive 'politics of the body' rather than a separable, discrete set of practices" (Burrell & Hearn 1989: 13, inspired by Foucault). Instead of focusing on 'organization of production', the authors want to contribute to a concept of 'reproduction of organizations'.

The authors concept of gender, sexuality and organizations as alternatives is based on (a) post modernism and that "both organization(s) and sexuality are social constructions, existing within specific historical and spatial relations" (Burrell & Hearn 1989: 18)); (b) actual experiences and (c) a cooperative network. Furthermore, methodological pluralism is important. They aim at developing a discourse about the relationships between sexuality, gender and organizations (Hearn et al. 1989: 179).

Table six. Organizations have and are

Organizations	
Have	Are
Culture, tool of management	**Culture** symbolic, anthropology
Gender, variable	**Gender**, social process
- biological, sex	- social gender
- women's and men's situation	- gender relations
Structure of gender relationships	
Structure	Processes
Production	Reproduction

In contrast to the importance of including both production and reproduction in the study of organizations, there is a tendency to place special emphasis on 'the sexuality of organizing'. Both views are extremes: a rational point of departure and one in which sexuality is crucial both involve omissions.

My point is that we have to both focus on and study organizations as units of production, but also as units of reproduction, where production and reproduction (structure and processes) interact. Organizations do not only carry male values but, to a great extent, also carry female values. We cannot get a balanced picture of organizations without including both sides. It is also important to investigate the interaction between what organizations have and are, that could be gender, culture, female and male values, production and reproduction (see table six). In this connection it can be very helpful and important for organizational research(ers) to abandon concept of either/or in favour of studying organizations as both/and.

Organizational research in itself can come up with examples of using more than one perspective in analyzing organizations. The classical example is Allison, who analysed the Cuban crisis by using three different models (rational choice, organizational process and bureaucratic, political model), ending with three distinct explanations for the Cuban crisis process (Allison 1969). Morgan (1986) emphasizes that you get the most varied picture of an organization when using more than one metaphor in an analysis. Kjell Røvik (1992) discusses the basic values of consultants working within the public sector. He distinguishes between two different types of basic values: the doctor model and the designer's model, reaching the following conclusion: most consultants work within the designer model. Their reports contain advice which is fashionable, and does not necessarily provide an answer to the organization's actual needs . The consultants try to put a scientific veneer on their work by using elements from the doctor model.

The "both/and" concept is not a totally new idea within organizational - and public research. One could speed up the use of "both/and" by asking questions about 'gender'. It should not be a question of "add gender and stir", but a question of "combining gender and organizations" in a way that, hopefully, can later change both gender and organizations.

Supplement number one: References to gender in organizational literature.

	To tal	Fami-ly	Wo-men	Men	Gen-der diff.	Sexu-ality	Gen-der	Kan-ter
1961 Etzioni	-	no indicies						
1962								
1963								
1964 Pugh et.al	0							
Crozier	0							
1965 March & Si	1	1						
1966 Etzioni	0							
Blau & Sco	0							
1967								
1968 Etzioni	-	no indicies						
1969 Weick	0							
1970 March	2		1	1				
1971 Pugh	0							
Weber	0							
1972								
1973 French & B	1	1						
1974								
1975								
1976								
1977 Galbraith	0							
1978								
1979 Meyer	0							
Mintzberg	0							
1980 Hofstede	89	69			20			
1981 Nystrom 1	37	31	4			2		
Starbuch 2	74	20	20		28			6
Scott	6				2			4
1982 Deal & Ken	7		6			1		
1983 Mintzberg,a	8							8
Mintzberg,b	0							
1984 Peters & Wa	0							
1985								
1986 Harmon et.al	0							
Bakka & Fiv	0							
Perrow	3		2	1				
Schein	2	2						
Morgan	16					5	11	
1987 Hall	8	1	2					5
Gortner et	1			1				
Koimann & E	1		1					
1988 Quinn	0							
1989 Heffron	0							
1990 Robbins	0							
Total	256	125	36	3	50	8	11	23

47

Notes

1.   In Danish we do not have two different words for sex and gender.

2.   It is obvious that works dated 1961-1977 cannot make any reference to the work of R.M. Kanter. I do not think that the final result will be changed dramatically, since I only found four references in 13 works in the year before 1977.

3.   There are many examples which emphasize the importance of studying the relationship between working life and family life, when seeking to understand women's and men's position on the labour market. See for example: Veronica F. Nieva (1985): Work and Family Linkages. in Laurie Larwood et.al. (eds): *Women and Work*. An Annual Review, Vol. 1. Sage Publications. London.

4.   Billing & Alvesson (1989b) differentiate between four perspectives in the study of "female managers": Equal Opportunities perspective; Meritocratic-perspective; Women-Can-Contribute Something-Special and Alternative Values perspectives.

5.   Hearn et.al. 1989 underline the necessity of studying sexuality in the study of gender and organisations. The title of their book is: *"The Sexuality of Organization"*.

6.   In the second edition from 1992 Bakka & Fivelsdal include the concepts of feminine and masculine, when referring to Hofstede.

7.   In addition to the exlusion of gender, religion and ethnicity are also excluded.

References

Allison, Graham T. (1969), "Conceptual Models and the Cuban Missill Crisis." in *The American Political Science Review* no. 3.

Billing, Yvonne Due & Alvesson, Mats (1989), *Køn * Ledelse * Organisation. Et studium af tre forskellige organisationer.* (Gender * Management * Organization). Copenhagen. DJØF's forlag.

Blau, P. & Scott, R. (1966), *Formal Organizations. A Comparative Approach.* London. Routledge and Kegan Paul.

Blædel, Niels (1985), *Harmoni og enhed. Niels Bohr. En biografi.* (Harmony and Unity. Niels Bohr. A biography). Copenhagen. Rhodos.

Boman, Ann (1983), *Omsorg och solidaritet ohållbara argument?* (Nurturing and Solidarity, Secure Arguments?) Stockholm, Arbetslivscentrum.

Burrell, Gibson & Hearn, Jeff (1989), "The Sexuality of Organization." in Hearn, Jeff m.fl. (eds), *The Sexuality and Organization.* London. Sage Publications.

Collin, Finn (1987), *Organisationskultur og forandring.* (Organizational Culture and change). Copenhagen. Nyt fra Samfundsvidenskaberne.

Connell, R.W. (1987), *Gender and Power. Society, the Person and Sexual Politics.* Standford University Press.

Crozier, Michel (1964), *The Bureaucratic Phenomenon.* The University of Chicago Press.

Dahlerup, Drude (1989), "Når man ikke kan se skoven for bare træer. Kvinder og køn i forskningen." (When you cannot see the wood for trees. Women and gender in science.) in Steen Brock & Poul Pedersen: *Dømme*kraft. Objektivitet, subjektivitet og videnskab.* Århus. Aarhus Universitetsforlag.

Danet, Brenda (1981), "Client-Organization Relationship" in Nystrom & Starbuck (eds): *Handbook of Organizational Design.* Vol 2. Oxford University Press. p. 382-428.

Deal, T.E. & Kennedy, A. (1982), *Corporate Cultures.* Reading Mass., Addison Wesley.

Elson, Diane & Ruth Pearson (1981), "The Subordination of Women and the Internationalisation of Factory Production" in Kate Young m.fl. (eds): *Of Marriage and the Market. Women's Subordination in International Perspective.* London. CSE Books.

Etzioni, A. (1968)(originally 1964), *Modern Organizations,* Englewood Cliffs, N.J., Prentice Hall.

Etzioni, A. (1966), *Studies in Social Change.* London. Holt, Rinehart and Winston.

Etzioni, A. (1961), *A Sociological Reader on Complex Organizations.* London. Holt, Rinehart and Winston.

Ferguson, Kathy (1984), *The Feminist Case Against Bureaucracy.* Philadelphia. Temple University Press.

French, W.L. & C. H. Bell (1973), *Organizational Development.* Englewood Cliffs, Prentice-Hall.

Galbraith, Jay, R. (1977), *Organization Design.* Publishing. Mass. Addison-Wesley.

Gerlach, Luther P. & Gary B. Palmer (1981), "Adaptation through evolving Interdependence". in Nystrom & Starbuck (eds): *Handbook of Organizational Design*. Vol 1. Oxford University Press. p. 323-384.

Gortner, Harold, Mahler, Julianne & Nicholson, Jeanne Bell (1987), *Organization Theory. A Public Perspective*. Chicago, Illinois. The Dorsey Press.

Hall, Richard (1987), *Organizations, Structures, Processes & Outcomes*. 4. ed. Englewood Cliffs. N.J. Prentice-Hall International.

Harmon, Michael M. & Mayer, Richard T. (1986), *Organization Theory for Public Administration*. Boston.

Hearn, Jeff m.fl. (eds)(1989), *The Sexuality of Organization*, London, Sage Publ.

Hearn, Jeff & Parkin, Wendy P. (1983), "Gender and Organizations: A Selective Review and a Critique of a Neglected Area", in *Organizations Studies*, vol 4, no. 3, p. 219-242.

Heffron, Florence (1968/1982/1989 Reprinted), *Organization Theory & Public Organizations. The Political Connection*. Englewood Cliffs. New Jersey, Prentice Hall.

Hukin, Charles L. & Harry C. Triandis (1981), "Meanings of Work in Different Organizational Environment" in Nystrom & Starbuck (eds): *Handbook of Organizational Design*. Vol 2. Oxford University Press. p. 336-357.

Jensen, Hanne Nexø (1993), *Køn og organisationer under forandring*. (Gender and Organizations under Change). Institut for Statskundskabs Licentiatserie nr. 1. Copenhagen.

Kanter, Rosabeth Moss (1977), *Men and Women of the Corporation*. New York, Basic Books.

Kooiman, Jan & Eliassen, Kjell A. (eds)(1987), *Managing Public Organizations. Lessons from Contemporary European Experience*. London. Sage Publications.

Kvande, Elin & Rasmussen, Bente (1990), *Nye kvinneliv. Kvinner i menns organisasjoner*. (New Women lives. Women in mens Organizations). Oslo. Ad Notam. Arbeidslivsbiblioteket.

Lysgaard, Sverre (1976), *Arbeiderkollektivet*. (The Workers Collective). Oslo. Universitetsforlaget.

March, James (ed)(1970), *Handbook of Organizations*. Chicago.

James March & Johan P. Olsen (1989), *Rediscovering Institutions. The Organizational Basis of Politics*. New York. Free Press.

March, James & Simon, H.A. (1965), *Organizations*. USA. Wiley.

Meyer, Marshall W. (1979), *Change in Public Bureaucracies*. Cambridge University Press.

Mintzberg, Henry (1983a), *Power in and around Organizations*. Englewood Cliffs. N.J. Prenctice-Hall.

Mintzberg, Henry (1983b), *The Structure in fives. Designing Effective Organizations*. Englewood Cliffs. N.J. Prentice-Hall.

Mintzberg, Henry (1979), *The Structuring of Organizations. A Synthesis of the Research*. Englewood Cliffs. N.J. Prentice-Hall.

Morgan, Gareth (1986), *Images of Organization*. London. Sage Publications.

Nystrom, Paul C. (1981), "Designing jobs and Assigning Employees" in Nystrom & Starbuck (eds): *Handbook of Organizational Design*. Vol 2. Oxford University Press. p. 272-304

Nystrom, Paul C. & Starbuck (eds)(1981), *Handbook of Organizational Design*. Vol 1. & 2. Oxford University Press.

Perrow, Charles (m.fl.)(1986), *Complex Organizations. A Critical Essay*. New York. Random House.

Peters, T.J. & Waterman, R.H. (1984), *Hvad gør de bedste bedre?* (What do the best do that's better?). Copenhagen. Schultz Forlag.

Pugh, D.S. (ed) (1971), *Organizations Theory. Selected Readings*. Harmondsworth.

Pugh, D.S., Hickson, D.J. & Hinings, C.R (1964), *Writers on Organizations. An Introduction*. London. Hutchinson.

Quinn, Robert E. (1988), *Beyond Rational Management. Mastering the Paradoxes and Competing Demands of High Performance*. San Francisco. Jossey-Bass Publishers.

Ressner, Ulla (1985), *Den dolda hierarkin- om demokrati och jämställdhet*. (The hidden Hierarchy, about Democracy and Equality). Kristianstad. Raben og Sjögren.

Robbins, Stephen P.(1990), *Organization Theory. Structure, Design and Applications*. 3. udg. Prentice-Hall. Englewood Cliffs. N.J.

Røvik, Kjell Arne (1992), *Den "syke" stat. Myter og moter i omstillingsarbeidet*. (The 'sick' state. Myths and trends in the Work of changes). Oslo. Universitetsforlaget.

Schein, Edgar, H. (1986), *Organisationskultur og ledelse*. (Organizational Culture and Management). Forlaget Valmuen.

Scott, W. Richard (1981), *Organizations, Rational, Natural and Open Systems*. Englewood Cliffs. Prentice-Hall.

Schultz, Majken (1990), *Kultur i organisationer. Funktion eller symbol*. (Culture in Organizations. Function or Symbol). Copenhagen. Samfundslitteratur.

Sørensen, Curt (1976), *Marxismen og den sociale orden*. Bind 1. (Marxism and the Social Order). Århus. GMT.

Warner, Malcom (1981), "Organizational Experiments and Social Innovations". in Nystrom & Starbuck (eds): *Handbook of Organizational Design*. Vol 2. Oxford University Press. p. 167-186.

Weber, Max (1982), *Makt og byråkrati*. (Power and Bureaucracy). Oslo. Gyldendal. 4. oplag.

Weick, Karl (1969, 1979), *The Social Psychology of Organizing*. Addison-Wesley Publ. Reading, Mass, 2. udg.

Wolthers, Anette (1990), *Foredrag om ligestilling i DSB*. (Lecture on Equality in the Danish State Railways). Fra konference om Ligestilling på University of Copenhagen blandt TAP'erne den 20. januar.

2 Deinstitutionalizing the Gendered Structure of Labour: An organization change perspective

Deborah Hurst

Personnel Administration Office, Government of Alberta
Faculty of Arts, University of Alberta, Canada

John Usher

Faculty of Business, University of Alberta, Canada

Perhaps the most frustrating experience of any group attempting to bring about change is the perception that gate-keepers are listening, but not hearing; that there is action without any real movement; that the energy of the change movement is being deflected or dissipated without having any impact. Arguments are not refuted, nor positions challenged, but the net effect is that the system does not change. There is 'lip service' to the change agenda and attempts may be made to co-opt key proponents of the movement.

For many who are attempting to reduce gender inequalities in employment and pay within society and particularly within organizations, these are familiar experiences. Disillusionment with the pace and trajectory of change is growing (Cockburn 1989). Baron, Mittman, and Newman (1991) report several studies documenting extensive, continuing segregation of women into less privileged jobs, firms, and industries within occupations that *appear* to have become more integrated. Dex and Shaw (1986) and Martin and Roberts (1984) find substantial evidence of continuing vertical and horizontal segregation. Cockburn (1989: 213) attributes the problem to equal opportunity programs being "widely seen as a tool of management that has sanitised and contained the struggle for equality". Webb and Liff (1988) argue that such limited change is inherent in the dominant 'liberal' model of equal opportunity (Jewson and Mason 1986).

This paper arose out of a similar frustration on the part of one of the authors regarding the implementation of a flexible work schedule program. What appeared to be a very minor change in operating procedures (compressed work week) clearly required a profound shift in how organizational participants viewed the degree to which the organization should accommodate the social needs of members. The standard models of organizational development intervention provided standard answers about getting top-management buy-in and working to change attitudes and build commitment. We thought these remedies too focused on individuals for what seemed to be a structural problem. There was also something of the "cunning palliative" (Miller 1989: 91) in this approach. Change became something 'applied' to the organization by change agents on behalf of clients - top management - who were themselves exempt from the process.

This frustration with existing approaches prompted us to attempt to come to terms with the problem at a more conceptual level, particularly in relation to resistance grounded in institutionalized beliefs about the relationship between work and care-giving.

Williams (1989) argues convincingly that these beliefs arise because labour is premised on an ideal worker with no child care responsibilities. She invokes Gramsci's concept of cultural hegemony (Adamson 1980) to underscore how men and women face very different choices. For women to become ideal workers, they must choose not to fulfil their 'family responsibilities.' Men, of course, need not make such a choice. This conclusion is far from novel, but her next statement (Williams 1989: 831-2) raises an issue often overlooked; but one which we feel is vital to the pursuit of social equality:

> "...the underlying point is a deeper one: that society is structured so that everyone, regardless of sex, is limited to two unacceptable choices - men's traditional life patterns or economic marginality. Under the current structure of wage labour,

people are limited to being ideal workers, which leaves them inadequate time to devote to parenting, and being primary parents condemned to relative poverty (if they are single parents) or economic vulnerability (if they are currently married to an ideal worker)".

Such a construction of the issue permits all individuals disadvantaged by gender, i.e. those abandoning the ideal worker role to assume child-care responsibilities, to be addressed without regard for their sex. While this gendered structure of labour remains overwhelmingly a problem that women experience, there is a growing recognition by many men of their own disadvantage in this area. This is a recognition that should be exploited to clearly position the accommodation of organizations to employees as care-givers. This issue is not just about *mothers*; it is about *parents*.

We do not mean to suggest that all discrimination in organizations involving women relates to their actual or potential social roles as parents. That women are disadvantaged in organizations because of their different sex (Hearn and Parkin 1987) or that women are visibly different from entrenched elites (Kanter 1977) also constitute observed reasons for occupational segregation. We also do not intend to constrain the discussion of institutionalized gender roles only to the issue of child-care. Elder-care has also been institutionalized in Western culture as the responsibility of daughters, many of whom now find themselves "sandwiched" between duties owed to aging parents and growing children. Other issues tied up in the presumption that employees will be ideal workers include geographic mobility, hours of work and the delivery of benefits.

We seek to address two main questions in this paper. First, what can current organization change theories tell us about the feasibility of achieving gender equality in organizations ? Second, how might this knowledge and emerging theory in the area of deinstitutionalization (Oliver 1992) be combined to facilitate movement in that direction?

Before moving to that review, however, we would like to further position our interest in this area with a brief discussion of our current research site. (See Appendix 1 for additional information.) The data on the organization undergoing change and our evaluation of that data are at this time incomplete. However, we believe that some of the information currently available can usefully illustrate the need to extend existing organizational intervention models when evaluating and/or analyzing initiatives of this type.

We return again to the case following our review of the organization change literature to consider if these new perspectives enrich our understanding of the problem. Finally, we present some exploratory work on the boundary conditions for deinstitutionalization and speculate on its application to the gendered structure of labour.

Background Information

The Canadian Public Sector organization referred to in this paper developed a government-wide "Plan for Action for Women" predicated upon vaguely articulated social/economic / political pressures for change. No apparent crisis, social outcry, or other triggering event preceded the initiative. The Plan for Action was announced by the Minister responsible for its conception in August of 1989. It was structured to provide a framework for implementing and monitoring new change initiatives in important target areas for women each year on an on-going basis. The target areas of interest in this paper are those strategies that assist employees to balance and integrate their work and family lives. These strategies are intended to challenge the barriers preventing employees with family responsibilities from gaining access to employment opportunities. One approach has been to provide flexibility in the workplace. In this paper, we focus on one of a group of programs implemented to provide this kind of flexibility through alternative work arrangements.

Three variations on the traditional work arrangements were introduced for bargaining unit staff. Regular working hours were judged too restrictive and restrictive working hours were seen to exacerbate balancing work and family difficulties. Regular working hours prior to the alternative work schedule program were 36 1/4 hours weekly or 72 1/2 hours bi-weekly.

Daily hours were 8:15 a.m. to 4:30 p.m. with meal and rest periods as described in the master agreement. The alternative work schedule program included the availability of three program options: (1) flex-time, i.e., employee chosen start and finish times - with core periods daily between 9:00 a.m. to 11:30 a.m. and 1:00 p.m. to 3:00 p.m. for a total of 33 1/4 weekly or 72 1/2 hours bi-weekly. There was an added variation to accumulate time to allow employees the option of taking one day off per month. (2) The compressed work week program consisted of a bi-weekly combination of one 5 day work week and one 4 day work week. Employees work 9 days in a 2 week period for an equivalent total of 72 1/2 hours for a normal bi-weekly period. Daily hours could vary but, once chosen became fixed and structured. (3) Job sharing was a third option available which allowed employees to find a willing partner and equally share a job and pro-rated benefits. In this organization job-share partners could choose to work either 2 1/2 days each per week or three shortened days per week. In both cases total hours worked were 18 1/8 hours per week.

Selection of the change site was made by the Government's Management Policy Committee (M.P.C.). Several different departments were invited to submit proposals for alternative work schedule projects. The selected departments were then instructed to implement their projects on a pilot basis for evaluation by the central Personnel Administration Department representative. The function of the department change site discussed in this paper is to examine all documents submitted for registration which affect land in its district. When documents are accepted for registration, the office usually issues a new title or endorses an existing one with concise registration details. In addition the office provides title, document and survey plan searches to the public. The office is responsible for security of original titles and documents filed.

The staff of the case organization are expected to ensure that the examination and registration of documents, the issuance of titles, the provision of searches and statements and the maintenance of security land title records are performed with speed, accuracy and courtesy. The nature of work in this organization is very rigid and exacting. Employees must ensure correctness. This posture of perfection, permeates much of the organization's operations. The employees found in this group are largely lower-level administrative support and technical union positions. They are predominantly female, particularly at the lowest levels.

Of the three program options available, department management chose to offer only a variation of the compressed work week to their employees. Also, daily hours were not chosen by the employees, they were stipulated by management. According to the alternative schedule, daily hours would consist of 8 days of 8 hours each and one day of 8 1/2 hours for a total of 72 1/2 hours bi-weekly. The working day began at 7:00 a.m. and ended at 4:30 p.m. with a half hour lunch between 12 - 12:30 p.m. and scheduled staggered coffee breaks during the day. Employees were placed in two separate groups with each group receiving alternate Fridays off. Despite the appearance of flexibility, however, employees offered the following representative interpretations of the new program:

> Some of them (supervisors) are like drill sergeants, especially my supervisor. We have no freedom; the new program gives us little control over our lives.

I'm a single mom and on Wednesday, when we are expected to work the extra half hour, the traffic is so bad that I don't think I could get to the daycare by 5:00 to pick up Jessie even if I tried. This program isn't so great; you just trade in one set of rules for another set.

Although this new schedule was certainly lacking in its provision of flexibility from an individual perspective, employees were able to have one day off every other week. Our analysis of this initiative must, however, evaluate the success of this change in the context of the department's reluctance to implement the full spectrum of options as prescribed by the central department.

Feasibility of Change: Issues from Organization Theory

This section of the paper focuses on two related topics in the current literature on organizational theories of change and considers their application to the feasibility of deinstitutionalizing gender: First, what can an examination of types of change tell us ? Several writers (Cockburn 1989; Hall 1990; Williams 1989) posit an agenda which incorporates both first and second order changes. Second, what does our understanding of how fundamental change unfolds suggest ? Bartunek (1984), Ranson, Hinings and Greenwood (1980) address the process of organizational transformation with special consideration given to "interpretive schemes" as the locus for inertia and change.

To position this debate for our purposes; that is, to come to some conclusion on the ability of individual organizations to successfully deinstitutionalize gender, it is apparent that we must first be clear about what would constitute deinstitutionalization. What actually changes ? What would constitute evidence that the traditional, taken-for-granted relationship between work and care-giving was being eroded? Baron et al (1991) measure the progress of gender desegregation - the movement of women into jobs traditionally held by men. Williams (1989) suggests that at its simplest level, breaking free of traditional gender ideologies means being able to see how men nurture people and how women are competitive and powerful. Webb and Liff (1988) contend that encouraging the adoption of flexible work arrangements in all jobs will help to weaken the current equation linking part-time with low grade work. Encouraging men to seek flexible hours reminds employers and other employees that family responsibilities are not a woman's exclusive burden. In our own case study, the change is deliberately engineered so that its implementation will appear seamless when viewed by external clients. At one level, the accommodation of the organization to such changes in structural or procedural terms should be minimal, or even non-existent. In comparison to the issues that normally plague corporate planners, there is little here which appears to necessitate fundamental change. No strategic reorientation of mission or product-market scope is implicit in providing more flexible work arrangements; no new global competition or technological discontinuity confronts the organization if we substitute a woman for a man in any given job.

Yet at another level, the *recognition that these minimal changes are necessary at all* requires a profound change in the taken-for-granted character (Meyer and Scott 1983; Zucker 1983) of the gendered structure of labour in organizations. It is the nature of institutionalization processes that essentially arbitrary differences can become quite real in their consequences when they serve as bases for successful collective action, when powerful actors use them in defining rights and access to resources, and when members of the general population use them in organizing their social worlds. Once organizational activities are institutionalized, they may become relatively stable, enduring, reproducible, and sustainable over long periods of time without continuing justification (Zucker 1987). Williams (1989) suggests that it may have been the rigors of multiple childbirth and the domestic production of goods in the colonial era which forged the gendered structure of labour; a structure which endures today despite the removal of those formative instrumentalities.

We believe that organizations will be free of institutionalized gender bias when the performance expectations that are placed on employees are not based on William's (1989) "ideal worker", but on a holistic view of a person for whom his/her role as a member of a work organization is only one of several useful endeavours in a larger social context. As we argue below, gender desegregation will facilitate the achievement of that goal, but we expect the mechanism of change in organizations to be social fragmentation, not political action.

Types of Change

The types of change which an organization employs are often inextricably tied up with the agenda or phases of the change effort. Hall (1990) sees a three step process in the promotion of true work-family balance in the workplace. He begins with top executive "soul searching", but to his credit, Hall does not expect that many top managers (white males in their 50's and 60's) will understand or respect the choices being made by their middle mangers (male and female). He asks only (p. 12) that they "clarify and own up to their own values - not necessarily to change them, but to consider how they might support younger managers' career styles and lifestyles..." The recognition that *their* values are not necessarily *the* values is an important step.

Next, Hall recommends a corporate wide dialogue about work life, family life, and the meaning of success. The collection of hard data from organization members on work / family issues should be a part of this diagnosis phase. Finally, with the help of a top management appointed task force or committee, the organization should move to implement the necessary changes. Drawing upon recommendations developed by such companies as Du Pont, Hall (p. 14) suggests that "some companies need specific services (for example, dependent care, employee-assistance programs, childcare referral information, and flexible benefits). Others may need more flexible work arrangements, as well as more supportive, flexible supervision. Still others may need flexible human resources management policies (for example, relocation policies, spouse career assistance during relocation, recognition of family needs in relocation decisions, and policies about overtime work and travel)."

In overview, Hall (1990) envisions a two pronged attack on the inequities of the gendered structure of labour in organizations. Changes in hours of work and daycare referrals must be supplemented by "a restructuring of the work environment" and an examination of "the basic assumptions underlying the career culture of the organization" as part of "a holistic approach to management that makes the organization 'family friendly'". Williams (p.836) argues in a similar vein that "feminists should begin to work both toward cultural change and towards the kind of small, incremental steps that will gradually modify the wage-labour system to acknowledge the reality of society's reproductive needs." Similarly, Cockburn's (1989) short and long agendas for change see movement from the minimization of bias in recruitment and promotion (the liberal approach) to a "project of transformation" that re-evaluates the nature and purpose of institutions and is necessary to ensure equal opportunity in the long run. Organizations, she notes, are part of "a sex/gender system characterized by male supremacy that enables men as a sex to benefit economically, socially and sexually from the oppression of women."

One may be tempted to consider this a 'radical' approach in Jewson and Mason's (1986) terms. These authors make a useful distinction between the 'liberal' approach to equal opportunity which stresses fair selection and promotion procedures but does not intervene in outcomes, and the 'radical' approach which utilizes affirmative action to place employees directly into targeted positions. However, Cockburn (1989: 217) is quick to point out that affirmative action (positive discrimination), as advocated under that approach, gives "disadvantaged groups a boost up the ladder, while leaving the structure of that ladder and the disadvantages it entails just as before." We feel that the distinction between inclusionary usurpation and revolutionary usurpation defined in social closure theory (Parkin 1974; Murphy 1990: 560) captures more closely the distinction here: Inclusionary usurpation is "the struggle by the excluded group to become included as incumbents represented in the present structure of positions in proportion to their numbers in the population". Revolutionary usurpation aims for a modification of the system itself, rather than simply a more advantageous inclusion of members in the present distributive system. If, for example, performance expectations to achieve promotion, partnership or tenure are based on 60-80 hour weeks, then dual career couples with children need not apply. Where such results-based systems are based on 'ideal workers' (Williams 1989) and a clear separation of public and private spheres, relative performance criteria may erroneously assume that all individuals have equal time available in which to perform. Clearly, a 'life-style indexed' set of performance criteria (eg. a 'mummy- or daddy-track') to address such an issue would involve a major modification in how organizations evaluate and compensate performance.

This distinction is vividly illustrated by a recent article in Business Week (January 25, 1993: 102) in which Julia Stasch is lauded as a "revolutionary" with "a broader agenda" for employing women in 7% of the construction trades positions in her firm (industry averages are about 2%). Later in the same article, however, Stasch notes that she and her husband have chosen not to have any children and states: "I wouldn't be where I am today if I'd made the decision to have a family." Clearly, Stasch's "broader agenda" is more inclusionary than revolutionary.

One of the main ideas found in the study of organization change is that there are basically two types of change. Lindblom (1959: 79) differentiates between *branch change* which involves "successive limited comparisons that continually build out of the current situation, step-by-step and by small degrees" and *root change* which is "a rational comprehensive approach starting from fundamentals each time, building on the past only as experience embodied in a theory and always prepared to start from the ground up." Vickers (1965) speaks of *executive change* and *policy-making* change, where the conduct of executive change is limited to the execution of duties guided by the current policy, which may itself only be altered by the higher order change and revolutionary change.

Similarly, Greiner (1972:40) contrasts *evolutionary* and *revolutionary change*. He defines evolutionary change as the "modest adjustments necessary for maintaining growth under the same overall pattern of management." Revolutionary change consists of the "serious upheavals and abandonment of past management practices involving finding a new set of organizational practices that will become the basis for managing the next period of evolutionary growth."

The terminology for these two types of change which has come to be adopted by many organization change practitioners was introduced by Watzlawick, Weakland and Fisch (1974: 10-11). Thus *first-order change* "involves a variation that occurs within a given system which itself remains unchanged," while *second-order change* "involves a variation whose occurrence changes the system itself . . . it is a change of change." Clearly, this theme runs through much of the change advocacy on equal opportunity reviewed above. First order change is the short agenda, the liberal approach and inclusionary usurpation. Second order change is Cockburn's (1989) "project of transformation", as is cultural change and revolutionary usurpation.

Summarizing our concern with the feasibility of change to this point, we conclude from the empirical record that attempts at first order change are widespread and have been moderately successful in some limited cases (England 1981; Beller 1984). We agree with Kimberly (1988), however, in our appraisal of the likelihood of second order change in existing organizations. Kimberly (1988:167) cites governance, domain, core values (often embedded in expertise), and design as four elements that "strongly influence the future course of the organization by limiting the range of feasible alternatives, by shaping the internal culture, and by defining the organization's identity." He goes on to suggest that changing these elements is not impossible, but that the magnitude of the task implies that such changes will be infrequent and almost certainly accompanied by substantial external pressure. Moreover, institutionalized norms governing organizational behaviours and opportunity structures often operate at a "taken for granted" level (Zucker, 1983) rendering inequities opaque to many of those affected.

Process of Change

We have argued above that deinstitutionalizing gendered labour must involve change at a very fundamental level in the taken-for-granted nature of organizational structures. We have noted several authors who advocate continued incrementalism as an acceptable short-term goal, and who further recognize that significant, enduring improvement in employment equity must be predicated on profound changes in deeper, less clearly specified aspects of structure. To some extent, this lack of specificity may be a consequence of the process of institutionalization itself. What we take for granted, we may find difficult to describe. Our 'understanding' becomes preconscious. The justification for an activity becomes, "That's the way we do things around here." Ranson, Hinings, and Greenwood (1980: 4), however, provide an excellent means of re-establishing these lost linkages with the organization's deeper structures within their model of the process of structuring:

(1) Organizational members create *provinces of meaning* which incorporate interpretive schemes, intermittently articulated as values and interests, that form the basis of their orientation and strategic purposes within organizations.

(2) Since interpretive schemes can be the basis of cleavage as much as of consensus, it is often appropriate to consider an organization as composed of alternative interpretive schemes, value preferences, and sectional interests, the resolution of which is determined by *dependencies of power* and domination.

(3) Such constitutive structuring by organizational members has, in turn, always to accommodate *contextual constraints* inherent in characteristics of the organization and the environment, with organizational members differentially responding to and enacting their contextual conditions according to the opportunities provided by infrastructure and time.

Ranson et al. take the position that a strategic contingencies view of power (Hickson, Hinings, Schneck, Lee, and Pennings 1971) is the central dynamic in the flow-through from interpretive schemes to organizational structures and activities. DiMaggio (1988: 13) has observed that concerns about the relative power of actors is a necessary but often absent adjunct to institutionalization theory. He argues that the political perspective has been neglected because more recent interest in institutionalization as an outcome has dominated the classic inquiry into institutionalization as a process." Institutionalization as an *outcome* places organizational structures and practices beyond the reach of interest and politics. By contrast, institutionalization as a *process* is profoundly political and reflects the relative power of organized interests and the actors who mobilize around them."

Ranson, Hinings, and Greenwood (1980) go on to suggest, in one of several specific propositions about change derived from their discussion, that the political process within their model provides for at least the possibility of organizational revolution. Significantly, the pathway to revolution begins (p. 13) with "significant changes in resource availability and in other key sources of organizational uncertainty (which) can undermine the bases of dominant coalitions and permit the creation of new power dependencies. Changes in relations of power and domination may entail radical revisions in the interpretive schema that subsequently shape the production and recreation of organizational structures."

Hinings and Greenwood (1988a:18) develop these ideas further by including that objective structures and systems and subjective ideas, values and beliefs hang together to form coherent organization designs or archetypes. It becomes vital to uncover these coherent patterns if one's interest is to change them. Hinings and Greenwood argue that these patterns of organization design may be identified by isolating distinctive ideas, values and meanings that are reflected in and reproduced by clusters of structures and systems.

The central focus of this theory is the notion of radical strategic changes in the organizations design that signal a fundamental shift in the basic orientation of that organization. Radical change or re-organization of structures and systems occur when central ideas, values and beliefs are displaced.

The path of reorganization can be traced in a developmental form by looking at the past or present organization form "archetype A" and the desired new organization form "archetype B." The path of change between the two archetypes is referred to as a "track". The assumption is that organizations are on a change track from archetype to archetype in pursuit of "fit" with the organizations environment. The pursuit of "fitness" can lead to the desired changes but the change may also become derailed. Furthermore, tracks may be other than unidirectional and involve oscillations or incomplete excursions, or aborted, unresolved, schizoid and embryonic archetypes.

The objective and subjective conditions of change are given importance in this model. The archetype is said to contain objective structures and systems of the organization as well as a subjective interpretive scheme of ideas, beliefs and values. This holistic view of the organization allows for both prescribed and emergent changes to be incorporated. Prescribed change interacts with, but is subject to modification and replacement. The theory describes change results and also attempts to get at the process of the change itself, i.e. how organization strategists "accomplish their work, develop policy and allocate resources in an effort to take the organization from one track to another" (1988a:11).

Bartunek (1984) argues that the environment may trigger change, but that the effect of the environment in producing change in an organization is dependent on the organization's leadership. A leader may choose to enable or ignore different environmental forces for change or even the dialectical process of change itself. Second order transitions begin with a perceived crisis that is strong enough to "unfreeze" accepted interpretive schemes (Schein 1980). Examples of events powerful enough to do this are unsuccessful management practices, power shifts or a challenge to shared beliefs (Bartunek 1984: 364). The crisis acts as a challenge to the organization's interpretive scheme thesis. Other ways of understanding become the antithesis and what emerges from the interaction of the two is the synthesis. Conflict is a natural part of the unfolding of this process between those groups within the organization who hold opposing interpretive schemes.

Hinings and Greenwood (1988) and Bartunek (1984) thus argue that internally generated fundamental change - organizational reframing - is possible. However, Kimberly (1988: 168) in a critique of Bartunek's position argues for the necessity of external pressure: " Those who have become a part of the culture and the identity of the organization are those least able to precipitate major changes. For what Bartunek calls organizational reframing to occur... I would expect substantial external induction and involvement to be required."

There are some important conclusions which we believe may be drawn from this discussion of process. First, we might conclude from Ranson et al. (1980), Hinings and Greenwood (1988) and Bartunek (1984) that the short and long agendas for change must be parallel, not sequential. Since the pathway of change is from shifts in power to interpretive schemes to organizational structures and practices, we cannot hope to bring about fundamental change in the socially constructed provinces of meaning which underpin the gendered structure of labour by tinkering with structures and practices. This position would ask us to part company with those (eg.Williams 1989) who imply that small wins at the periphery will eventually overwhelm the centre. We believe that the centre will hold unless dependencies of power are altered or those in power act to alter existing interpretive schemes. We cannot build incrementally from first order change to second order change and revolutionary usurpation makes inclusionary usurpation obsolete and more than faintly collaborative. It is a common dilemma in social change: Work from within or tear down the walls ?

Case Illustration

The intervention which provoked this paper may be used to illustrate how Hinings and Greenwood (1988) and Bartunek (1984) might apply to a specific case. The organization is actively implementing strategy to attempt a shift from "traditional-inequitable" archetype A to a more "equitable" version archetype B. In this change, the pervasive ideas, values and meanings reflected in and reproduced by the structures and systems of archetype A are challenged. These structures and systems are those traditional practices and systems of operation that reproduce the gendered structure of labour which operates in favour of "white, able-bodied males" (Abella 1984).

The planned change thus represents an attempt to reorient the organization's interpretive scheme. A successful revamping would require a *radical* departure from the organization's historical operating philosophy, workplace culture and attitudes. It is also major due to the type of change it is. It does not lend itself easily to classification of events that "usually" require change. There is therefore some resistance simply due to its atypicality.

According to the model by Hinings et.al. (1989), the implementation of the change effort places the organization on a departure track from "archetype A" to "archetype B". The organization structures and systems still largely reflect and reinforce the previous traditional interpretive scheme but some important design elements have become discordant due to the introduction of the new interpretive scheme and the introduction of equity inducing programs. The alternative work schedule program referred to in this paper is an example of such a discordant element.

The final destination that this organization will achieve on its "change track" however, remains to be seen. It may turn out that due to inertia, decoupling with the existing 'traditional' interpretive scheme and recoupling with the new forms will fail. Proactive change is unlikely until the costs of not conforming are greater than the costs of conforming. In this organization, some departments argue that the equity programs are too costly in terms of the time and energy in implementing, retraining and replacing staff, and that they are costly in terms of the erosion caused to their pool of similar 'recruitable' others. With social closure, those in power often recruit similar others in terms of education, experience and social category membership. This is most likely to occur in a highly ambiguous environment such as an organization where it is important to be able to predict how one's subordinates will behave (Murphy 1988). Such recruitment practices, in combination with the subsequent socialization of new members by those with the greatest stake in the existing institutional order and decisions about firing, demotion, and promotion influenced by the extent of organizational participant's apparent allegiance to the institutional order are powerful tools for institutional reproduction (DiMaggio 1988).

Moreover, due to the sluggish economy, the effects of labour market dynamics as an external influence on management have been and promise to continue to be quite limited. One outcome of the failure to implement alternative work schedules might be difficulty finding employees who will work for the organization. This argument is weak at best, however, since it is founded on those relatively few applicants (often professionals) who can pick and choose among job offers. At the entry level, in recessionary times, it has no substance at all. Another potential source of pressure on management would be union demands on behalf of their membership. It is interesting that in this case the union asked that the issue of alternative work schedules not go to the bargaining table in deference to "more important matters". Union leadership was unconvinced that this was a problem in which the membership had a substantial interest. The union position on flexibility in the workplace may be related to the significance with which they view the problem. In most cases flexibility in the workplace is most critical for those holding the larger share of household responsibility, i.e., women. This department contains many lower level occupation, young women, probably the most passive of all labour market groups. With no pressure on the union leadership, there is no incentive for the union to approach management.

Bartunek (1984), like Hinings and Greenwood (1988), focuses on the interaction between the interpretive scheme and organization restructuring. However, her approach allows us to address the process of change between the old and new schemes at the group and individual levels. This allows us to look at how both schemes interact and move the organization toward a synthesis. This is Bartenuk's main contribution. Such interactions, or more appropriately, dialectical confrontations, between the old and new interpretive schemes (Bartunek, 1984) may be found in the comments of employees involved in the change initiative. Consider, for example, the young male employee who "did not wish to offend" one of the authors but stated that he thought that "as a rule it was more difficult to work with women." Clearly, the employee seemed aware of the emerging impropriety of such a comment under the new interpretive scheme, but still accorded sufficient influence to the old scheme to provide a defensible position. It may be that through an evolving understanding of the new interpretive scheme this employee and his organization will move to "archetype B" - the equitable version. But it is equally likely that the organization will remain locked into its inertial, almost "schizoid" state. But regardless of outcome, the presence of conflict indicates that the pressures for change are being noticed by organization participants. Bartunek argues that declining morale and perceived threat may be necessary to set the dialectic in motion. Thus, if the expected effect on the organization's systems and structures has not yet occurred, perhaps some threshold of discontent has not yet been reached.

Facilitating Deinstitutionalization

Much of the preceding discussion has employed a characterization of the process of deinstitutionalization whereby one relatively coherent package of interpretive schemes and associated structures is engaged in the supplanting of another, relatively more entrenched package of interpretive schemes and structures. Yet this 'collision of cultures' is only one way to conceptualize deinstitutionalization. In fact, the principle contribution of institutional theory is its ability to account for patterns of organization that are *not* attributable to interest or agency (DiMaggio 1988:6). Thus, while direct political action is one route to deinstitutionalizing the gendered structure of labour, its consequences are likely to be highly divisive and, given the entrenched nature of its defenders, unsuccessful. What our review of the literature on change suggests is that if the organizational vehicle can be turned at all, it must be turned from the driver's seat, and few women are sitting in it.

Other approaches to deinstitutionalization, because they focus on the *sources* of legitimation and institutional reproduction, may be less confrontational and potentially more effective. Oliver (1992) has identified a number of organizational and environmental factors that are hypothesized to determine the likelihood that institutionalized organizational behaviours will be vulnerable to erosion or rejection over time. She develops a list of empirical predictors of deinstitutionalization that bear close examination for our purposes.

Oliver (1992) argues that deinstitutionalization is determined by political, functional, and social mechanisms both internal and external to the organization. She further proposes that deinstitutionalization can occur through either dissipation - a gradual deterioration in the acceptance and use of a particular institutionalized practice, or through rejection - the discontinuation of a given practice. Given our arguments against direct political action, we focus on Oliver's (1992:578) discussion of social mechanisms:

> "...social pressures for change often deinstitutionalize established activities *in the absence of an organization's conscious recognition or control of these changes or in spite of contrary organizational intentions to sustain the status quo.* First, social fragmentation and historical discontinuities cause deinstitutionalization. These deinstitutionalizing predictors include high turnover, succession, increases in workforce diversity, weakening socialization mechanisms, and culturally disparate interorganizational relations (mergers, joint ventures, for example). Second, external social pressures, including changes in government laws and societal values or expectations, can cause organizations to abandon or relinquish institutional practices. Finally, structural disaggregation induces deinstitutionalization by reducing the proximity or opportunities for interaction among organizations or their members upon which the perpetuation and continuing reproduction of institutionalized values and behaviours depend. Predictors of disaggregation include diversification, geographic dispersion and structural differentiation". (emphasis added)

By combining these social pressures for change with the Hinings/Greenwood/ Bartunek description of how change takes place, we can develop a model of how a change in the prevailing interpretive schemes of an organization can evolve over time in a non-confrontational fashion. Figure 1 shows our preliminary model of this process. External social pressures are picked up by organizational boundary scanners charged with communicating relevant changes in the firm's environment to management. To the extent that such forces are viewed as intractable, they will be accepted as guiding assumptions antecedent to the formation of interpretive schemes. Social fragmentation and structural disaggregation both act to weaken the homogeneity and coherence necessary to support the interpretive schemes of the status quo by presenting alternative views. The "re-thinking" and "re-writing" of organization theory by feminist scholars (Calas and Smircich 1990) helps to fuel this process. Over time, these forces contribute to the erosion of institutionalized beliefs about organizational structure and processes (depicted here as a shift to flatter organizations). The application of this model to the problem of gender inequality is elaborated in the following section with empirical support from Baron et al (1991).

Figure 1

A Social Pressures Framework for Organization Change

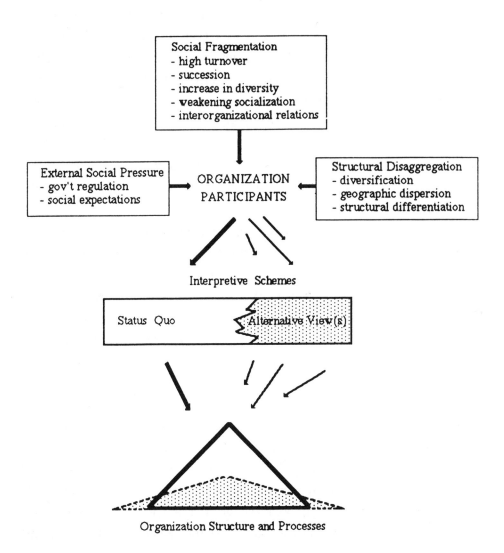

Organization Structure and Processes

The various factors in Oliver's category of social determinants help to bring into sharp relief the individual components of a powerful but sometimes amorphous force. Her social fragmentation thesis delineates how high turnover, leader succession, and increases in workplace diversity work against the continuity of organizational traditions and customs. Where socialization is ineffective in extinguishing this dissent, erosion of institutionalized norms and activities will naturally occur as they are questioned by those for whom such practices are not taken-for-granted. Baron et al. (1991) found that the percentages of women and non-whites employed were both positive influences on the rate at which agencies of the California civil service were moving toward gender integration between 1979 and 1985. Given the limits of racial solidarity, the positive influence of greater numbers of non-white employees may make more intuitive sense as a social force breaking down the cohesion and continuity of white norms and practices than in an alternate construction as part of a coalition of interest within a political model. Support for erosion may also be found in Baron et al's (1991) finding that the presence of a female director was positively related to gender integration.

The causal force of the state in obtaining compliance to the social agenda of equal employment opportunity has proven to be a useful, if somewhat recalcitrant, tool for deinstitutionalizing the myth of the able-bodied white male as the ideal worker. Here, Baron et al. (1991) found that the extent to which the activities of an agency could be scrutinized by legislative or other overseers was a more important factor in predicting rate of compliance than a measure of budgetary dependence used to evaluate the potential loss of instrumental rewards to agencies.

Oliver's last proposition - that structural disaggregation induces deinstitutionalization by reducing the mutual interaction that supports social reproduction - is not tested directly by Baron et al. Their consideration of the role of organization size, however, does provide some information on this relationship. Although they report that smaller organizations have made more rapid gains than larger organizations, they are puzzled (p. 1380) by the spectacular gains at the Department of Motor vehicles and the California

Highway Patrol "each employing more than 6,500 people *in more than 90 separate locations* (emphasis added)". Clearly, taking geographic dispersion into account might help to explain this apparent anomaly.

The reader may question our attention to gender desegregation as evidenced by the Baron et al (1991) study. After all, isn't increasing the proportion of women in an organization merely first order change; a way to include a disadvantaged group in an existing system ? At one level this is true if the newly included women (and men) do not question the institutionalized norms and behaviours of the organization. But because gender desegregation increases workplace diversity and facilitates social fragmentation, it also contains the seeds of second order change. In systems terms, gender desegregation is part of a positive feedback loop. The incidental hiring of people who question the prevailing norms about the relationship between work and care-giving will begin to erode those norms such that the next set of hires may find a moderated climate and weakened socialization in gender-hostile behaviours. A third set of newcomers may actually be attracted to the firm as its interpretive schemes continue to shift and are evidenced in 'family-friendly' organizational structures and processes.

Conclusions

We were drawn into this project out of a desire to better understand the phenomenon of deinstitutionalization as it relates to the gendered structure of labour. We have positioned our comments as being focused on how organizations can be brought to a better accommodation of the broader social obligations of employees. Our agenda has been to review the organization theory literature for insights into the feasibility and process of change at the level of institutionalized practices and procedures. Can the gendered structure of labour be deinstitutionalized ? We conclude from models of change in organizations such as Hinings and Greenwood (1988) and Bartunek (1984) that attempts to bring about the type of fundamental changes necessary for deinstitutionalization cannot be achieved by 'nibbling away' at the edges of the problem with incremental modifications of organizational structures and activities designed to better 'include' women. Underlying values and preconscious understandings as encoded in interpretive schemes must change first.

We further conclude based on Kimberly (1988), Baron et al. (1991) and our own case analysis, that the present managers of most organizations may be *able* to alter those dominant values, but are likely to do so only if they perceive such actions as necessary to maintain the organization's existing distribution of power and rewards in the face of intractable external forces. A process of deinstitutionalization which emphasizes political action on the part of internal constituents will thus provoke far more confrontation and resistance than real change.

It will be more fruitful in the long run, we argue, if activists recognize that a fuller understanding of the determinants of deinstitutionalization can provide their assault on the gendered structure of labour with tools not just to storm the walls, but perhaps undermine the foundations as well. At the least, our discussion of Oliver (1992) and Baron et al. (1991) should help internal change agents to better understand the role of external factors as well as organizational dynamics as they affect the relative success of policy initiatives in this area.

Finally, while this paper is dedicated to an exploration of the boundary conditions for deinstitutionalization *within* organizations, our efforts have also lead us to conclude that an equal, if not greater, potential for socially responsive structures of collective action lies in the gradual replacement of existing organizations with forms which are *founded* upon principles of equity. How such organizations might be structured and, more to the point, how such organizations might be assimilated into larger collectivities (industries, economies) are provocative questions for further study.

APPENDIX 1

Case Detail

A triangulated method was used to gather information about the change. This method was important as it was able to incorporate both male and female employee's views of all levels in aggregate form of overall trends and employees individual experiences of the changes occurring. This method of data collection was considered crucial due to the fact that the fundamental issue triggering change was to provide equity or provide females with equality of opportunity. For this reason the use of triangulation represents an important posture of discovery (Guba and Lincoln, 1983). This method allows us to establish convergent validation and capture a more complete, holistic portrayal of the organization in question (Jick, 1989). The evaluation of the work schedule program consisted of a collection of absentee data, an interview and observational stage and collection of data regarding service to the public.

Absentee Data

The absentee data indicated a savings in overall lost time. The savings were compared to lost time in the previous year, months before and after the program to look for other reasons for variation. In the final analysis, it was concluded that the change that occurred, i.e., the savings was a result of the alternative work schedule program.

Interviews

Person-to-person interviews were conducted with a small random sample of 20 respondents from the approximately 200 eligible employees to examine the organization change program and its effect on the overall interpretive scheme.

The new alternative work schedule (compressed work week) did not provide the full amount of flexibility anticipated. Rather, in one employee's words, it "traded in one rigid and fixed schedule for another one." A single mother opted out of the program due to the incompatibility of workplace and daycare hours of operation. A male employee added to this, "I would have to adjust my hours to accommodate driving my wife back and forth to work. It is not worth it to change everything for the short term of the pilot."

Customer Service

The third stage of the program evaluation consisted of information gathered concerned with the customer's perception of change in service provided. These data were collected from employees during their interviews and secondly from a sample of actual customers contacted by telephone. According to the organization's customers, the alternative work schedule program did not provoke a noticeable change in service, either positive or negative. Employees, on the other hand, thought that the increased access of clients to them, provided by additional daily hours, would improve service over time.

Observational Data Phase

These data were collected covertly and were intended to act as a supplement to the other data. They were collected during the two days of interviewing at the workplace location. I arranged to discretely collect data by asking to be taken on a tour of the workplace to get an idea of the paper flow for a better understanding of the organizations. In reality, I was doing more. I wanted to get a better idea of the organization's atmosphere and my own "feel" for the organization's interpretive scheme and how change might affect those who worked within it.

What the observational data provide is very real evidence of both management's resistance to the new interpretive scheme and female employees difficult experiences of that fact. From the women's comments, we learn a great deal about the formidable barriers preventing equity. But, we also pick up a great deal of the women's anger regarding those inequities and how favourably they view the recent program as an attempt at correction. These women are very sceptical and unhappy as highlighted by the following comments.

> D.M. "Yes there is. I don't see how compressed work week will change anything. Management treats us as children, you have no control over your life here, no memo's, no communication regarding changes, you can control your own work quality but, then they grade you by it."

> B.K. "some of them (supervisors) are like drill sergeants, especially my supervisor. We have no freedom, the new program gives us a little control over our lives. Maybe now I'll take fewer mental health days, but, maybe not. Your know, after a long weekend, I feel almost human again and ready to come back to work most of the time."

> M.L. "They time us when we go to the bathroom you know. We don't punch a time clock but we may as well have to. They force us to take afternoon coffee breaks too. Then they speak to us about democracy and trust and cooperation." J.F. "It's unbelievable, the stress around here. If they want change, they have to stop treating us like kindergarten children, we are responsible adults. They have to be consistent too and stop the favouritism."

In addition to these employee comments, my walk around the department supported the extreme control orientation of the management in a highly bureaucratic environment. The unhappy looking individuals were given very little space and were fully visible to management. There did not appear to be any attempt to make the working environment more pleasant or even recognize it to be linked to the inequity problem.

Further, the comments made provided a strong indication that the program was not altogether suitable for those individuals it was most intended to help. Those who opted out however, in many cases did not make their voices heard. It was their impression that it would not make any difference. Consider the following comment.

> M.G. "I don't have anyone to help me, I'm a single mom and on Wednesday when we are expected to work the extra half hour, the traffic is so bad, I don't think I could get to the daycare by 5:00 p.m. to pick up Jessie even if I tried. This program isn't so great, you just trade in one set of rules for another set."

This comment illustrates the importance of both the methodology used and the need to ask individuals about the changing interpretive scheme. Presumably, the manager of this department reported the successful implementation of flexible scheduling in his area and yet it is clear that the program's objectives were not achieved. The manager of this department was clearly resistant to the transfer of control implicit in the change and determinedly held onto the old interpretive scheme. He just "didn't get it." It is difficult to imagine how an organization such as this one will ever be able to shed its oppressive culture and philosophy and become a equitable workplace as long as management are permitted to observe the letter, but deny the spirit, of such changes.

References

Abella, Rosalie Silberman (1984), *Equality in Employment*, Ottawa. Royal Commission.

Adamson, W. (1980), *Hegemony and Revolution: A Study of Antonio Gramsci's Political and Cultural Theory*, Princeton NJ. Princeton University Press.

Baron, James N., Brian Mittman, and Andrew E. Newman (1991), 'Targets of Opportunity: Organizational and Environmental Determinants of Gender Integration within the California Civil Service, 1979-1985', *American Journal of Sociology*, 96/6: 1362-1401.

Bartunek, Jean (1984): 'Changing Interpretive Schemes and Organizational Restructuring, The example of a Religious Order', *Administrative Science Quarterly*, 29: 355-372.

Beller, Andrea H. (1984), 'Trends in Occupational Segregation by Sex and Race, 1960-1981', in Barbara F. Reskin (ed.) *Sex Segregation in the Workplace*, Washington D.C. National Academy.

Calas, Marta and Linda Smircich' (1990), Re-writing Gender into Organizational Theorizing: Directions From Feminist Perspectives', in Michael I. Reed and Michael D. Hughes (eds.) *Re-thinking Organization: New Directions in Organizational Research and Analysis*, London. Sage.

Cockburn, Cynthia (1989), 'Equal opportunities: the long and short agenda', *Industrial Relations Journal*, 20/3: 213-225.

Dex, Shirley and L. Shaw (1986), *British and American Women at Work: Do Equal Opportunity Policies Matter?*, London. Macmillan.

DiMaggio, Paul (1988), 'Interest and Agency in Institutional Theory', in Lynn Zucker (ed.) *Institutional Patterns and Organizations*, Cambridge MA. Ballinger.

England, Paula (1981), 'Assessing Trends in Occupational Sex Segregation: 1900-1976', in Ivar Berg (ed.) *Sociological Perspectives on Labour Markets*, New York. Academic Press.

Flynn, Julia (1993), 'Julia Stasch Raises the Roof for Feminism', *Business Week*, January 25: 102.

Galaskiewicz, Joseph and Stanley Wasserman (1989), 'Mimetic and normative processes within an organizational field: An empirical test', *Administrative Science Quarterly*, 34: 454-479.

Greiner, Larry (1972), 'Evolution and Revolution as Organization's Grow', *Harvard Business Review*. 50: 39-46.

Guba, Egon G and Yvonna S. Lincoln (1983), 'Advantages of Naturalistic Methods', *Effective Evaluation*, San Francisco Cal. Jossey Bass.

Hall, Douglas T. (1990), 'Promoting Work / Family Balance: An Organization-Change Approach', *Organizational Dynamics*, Winter: 5-18.

Hearn, J. and W. Parkin (1987), *Sex at Work: The Power and Paradox of Organizational Sexuality*, Brighton. Wheatsheaf.

Hickson, David J., Christopher R. Hinings, Rodney Schneck, Charles A. Lee, and
    Johannes Pennings (1971), 'A strategic contingencies theory of power',
    Administrative Science Quarterly, 16: 216-229.
Hinings, Christopher R. and Royston Greenwood (1988), *'The Dynamics of
    Strategic Change'*, Oxford. Blackwell.
Jewson, Nick and David Mason (1986), 'The theory and practice of equal
    opportunities policies: liberal and radical approaches', *The Sociological
    Review*, 34/2: 307-334.
Jick, Todd D. (1989), 'Mixing Qualitative and Quantitative Methods: Triangulation
    in Action' in John Van Maanen (ed.), *Qualitative Methodology*, Beverly
    Hills, Cal. Sage.
Kanter, Rosabeth Moss (1977), *Men and Women of the Corporation*, New York.
    Basic Books.
Kimberly, John R. (1988), 'Reframing and the Problem of Organizational Change',
    in Robert E. Quinn and Kim S. Cameron (eds.) *Paradox and Transformation*,
    Cambridge MA. Ballinger.
Lindblom, Charles (1959), 'The Science of Muddling Through', *Public Administrati-
    on Review*, 21: 78-88.
Martin, Joanne and Carlene Roberts (1984), *Women and Employment: A Lifetime
    Perspective*, Department of Energy. OPCS.
Meyer, John W. and W. Richard Scott (1983), 'Centralization and the legitimacy
    problems of local government', in J.W. Meyer and W.R. Scott (eds.)
    Organizational environments: Ritual and rationality, Beverly Hills. Sage.
Miller, Eric J. (1989), 'Organizational Development and Industrial Democracy', in
    Roy McLennan (ed.) *Managing Organizational Change*, Englewood Cliffs,
    NJ. Prentice Hall.
Murphy, Raymond (1988), *Social Closure*, Oxford. Clarendon Press.
Murphy, Raymond (1990), 'The Structure of Closure, A critique and development
    of the theories of Weber, Collins and Parkin', *British Journal of Sociology*,
    XXV: 4.
Oliver, Christine (1992), 'The Antecedents of Deinstitutionalization', *Organization
    Studies*, 13/4: 563-588.
Parkin, Frank (1974), *The Social Analysis of Class Structure*, London. Tavistock
    Publications.
Peitchinis, Stephen G. (1989), *Women at Work: Discrimination and Response*,
    Toronto. McClelland and Stewart.
Ranson, Stuart, Christopher Hinings and Royston Greenwood (1980), 'The
    Structuring of Organizational Structures', *Administrative Science Quarterly*,
    25: 1-17.
Vickers, G. (1965), *The Art of Judgement*, New York. Basic Books.
Watzlawick, P., J. Weakland and R. Fisch (1974), *Change*, New York. W.W.
    Norton.

Webb, Janette and Sonia Liff (1988), 'Play the white man: the social construction of fairness and competition in equal opportunity policies', *The Sociological Review*, 36/3: 532-551.

Williams, Joan C. (1989), 'Deconstructing Gender', *Michigan Law Review*, 87: 797-845.

Zucker, Lynn G. (1983), 'Organizations as Institutions', in S.B. Bacharach (ed.) *Research in the Sociology of Organizations*, Greenwich CT. JAI Press.

Zucker, Lynn G. (1987), 'Institutional Theories of Organizations', *Annual Review of Sociology*, 13, 443-464.

PART II

Changing Organization - Does Gender make a difference?

3 Women at the Top - more than just a passing fad? The 'New Management Culture' and Sexual Politics

Eva Brumlop

Institute for Social Research Johan Wolfgang Goethe
University Frankfurt, Germany

Translated from the German by Tobe Levin

In the past few years, a new species of being has begun to haunt the pages of women's magazines and executive reading matter, provoking heated discussion within the women's movement about its seeming challenge to traditional assumptions of business education and organizational training: I'm referring to the career woman, the woman in management, the ambitious climber to executive heights previously reserved for men only. In Germany women in upper management positions are still as hard to find as men in part-time work or serving as househusbands - in all major German companies taken together, the percentage of women in upper management positions remains, as it has always been, about 3 % or slightly higher, and in middle management the picture doesn't look very much better. Despite this, however, entire bookstore shelves are loaded down with popular scientific studies of women's entry into management, describing feminine styles of management and female leadership potential. Handbooks of advice for the new "business Amazons" top publishers' charts. The backgrounds, interests, life styles and consumer habits of women "who have made it" are examined, as though the collective invasion of women into boardrooms of major corporations were imminent (see Antal 1988 b; Bischoff 1990; Demmer 1988; Helgesen 1991; Stechert 1988; Schenkel 1986). Has the 'Age of women' already dawned? Or are we at the very least standing on the threshold on the era? Something appears to have taken place on the road to equal rights.

If we are to believe the new management forecasters, the feminine era is at hand: "Feminine is in - masculine is out.". Men stand for the tyranny of mediocrity, while women bear the hope of a new age (Bauer 1988). Whereas before the route to the top was barred to women because of their ascribed specifically 'feminine' attributes, supposedly marking the female personality as devoid of 'leadership potential', suddenly the situation appears to have been reversed: here I'm referring above all to high-flown, trendy headlines like "the new corporate culture" or "participatory management" used to describe a new style of management heralded by American business consultants in the early eighties (see Peters/Waterman 1984; Ouchi 1981; Pascale/Athos 1982).

Thus it would appear that future leaders of the business community are expected to demonstrate precisely those characteristics which the West is accustomed to regarding as 'feminine': intuition, awareness of context, thought and action based on holistic assessments, social competence, communication talents and a people orientation - all so-called "soft touches" scorned by managers of the old school.

Have we women realized our goals, or attained at least certain grounds for optimism? The fact is that prognoses of a change in leadership style and a growing need for socially competent executives can be found not only in the business press mainly directed toward women, but have also raised expectations among qualified, ambitious women hoping for increased opportunities to climb the corporate ladder. Could these forecasts really mean that in the future not only the most robust but also those women with so-called 'feminine' characteristics will be promoted? Indeed, theories of particularly 'feminine innovatory leadership potential' have found a positive echo in executive circles (see Der Bundesminster für Jugend, Familie, Frauen und Gesundheit 1988; Pathe 1988; Stödter 1989). As a result of economic and technological change in organizations, a perspective seems to be opening up which - in contrast to the standard pronouncements of

Western organizational and management theorists - sees the successful transferral to the business environment of communicative and co-operative forms supposedly effective only within the family. Wouldn't such a development be of intrinsic interests to women?

Reflecting on the current 'Managerial culture' debate and its reception by researchers concerned about female managers, I would like to examine the extent to which changes in management theory have actually increased women's access to power. Have avant garde concepts of a humanised work force promoted reform of traditional management theories that disadvantaged women? Have they opened new arenas in which women can participate, without forcing them, as in the past, to pour themselves into career molds shaped by male needs? Or, instead, do the seemingly new philosophies cover up the age-old exclusion of women under their aegis of cultural homogeneity? Can we not discern a tendency to create new stereotypes capable of preventing any form of border hopping?

To anticipate any possible misunderstanding: as a critic of ideology, I am concerned with challenging a certain type of women-oriented management literature which, first in the US and more recently here, has created quite a stir, and whose theses have strongly influenced any discussion of 'Women and Management'. I'm referring to women's fantasies of a 'Cultural Revolution from above,' inspired by the Japanese model of a communication-oriented company culture. Critical contributions to this discussion have been scarce, with the exception of an inspiring essay by Claudia Weber (1986) on Japanese organization and management style.

New Age in Business Studies: 'Participatory Management' and the 'Feminisation of Leadership Styles'

In the wake of the so-called 'Japan Shock' at the end of the seventies, a stiffening of competition for market share in the global marketplace brought with it a clearly felt need for broader technological and organizational adaptations and restructuring processes. Occurring first in the USA and later in other Western countries, the vision of a 'new managerial type' followed suit, suggesting a change in theme for management theory. It began questioning the universally accepted traditional hierarchical and bureaucratic organizational company model. To deal with the growing rate of economic insecurity and opacity of the market, as well as its requirement that firms adapt quickly to an ever-changing landscape of markets and production, a newer, more flexible concept for personnel management was propagated (Streeck 1986; Staehle 1987; Osterloh 1989), mirroring the increased accent modern management consultants place on employees as an important source of productivity and creativity. And for good reason: if the advantages of rationalisation and growing flexibility proceeding from new technologies are to be enjoyed, increasingly dedicated and qualified personnel are needed. But traditional bureaucratic hierarchical management styles have proven incapable of directing this potential. If the success of today's global industries is to be assured, they must produce and distribute more differentiated and expensive products. This in turn demands a flexible, technical organizational chart, intelligent and humane, which allows a large measure of self-regulation to individual working groups and assign tasks in a horizontal rather than vertical way. To realize the full potential of human productivity and creative resources - including the ability to tap individual capacities - hierarchies and specialties must be dismantled and the former impersonal compulsory management style form above replaced by 'high-trust-relations' (mutual trust on the basis on controlled autonomy) by means of delegating responsibility downward and securing socio-moral consensus on the basis of shared values and norm. In short: Management by Commitment (Walton 1985).

Inspired by the Japanese organizational model of the 'clan' or 'company family,' management is redefining its traditional functions and organizational forms. And in many cases where cooperation simply cannot be compelled , there's no getting around management's need to take the helm in encouraging cooperative communication. Increasingly, managers are becoming integrators, motivators, 'organizers of communication,' who, more and more often, will be tasked with researching opportunities for steering the social side of company communication (Deutschmann 1989, 382). In theorising this new 'communicative company culture,' therefore, a higher estimate is being placed on values, feelings, intuition, and intimacy - the previously exclusive trademarks of family and the private life. With growing frequency, executives are being required to exhibit those qualities and skills which the West has traditionally ascribed more readily to women than to men, so that the question Claudia Weber asks, complementing Pascale and Athos (1982) becomes unavoidable, whether 'managing people in modern, innovative firms, coordinating their tasks, maintaining motivation, and easing conflicts isn't much closer to the work of reproduction than has generally been thought' (Weber 1986, 135).

From Walton, spokesperson for this innovative management concept, we learn that, at present, very few middle managers possess the qualifications needed to realize such a communicative, consensual management style. Indeed, the best-selling authors of Secrets and Art of Japanese Management (1982), Pascale and Athos, admit that 'attempts to introduce teamwork on the Japanese model in Western organizations fail because the managers are incapable of motivating their personnel by stroking, care, and nurturance, even though the 'birth of a team' resembles in many ways the 'birth of a child' (quoted in Weber 1986, 134). "A vague consciousness that team nurturance is needed exists, but the words used in the West capture the inherent scorn which the male world brings to this sort of care-taking activity. Western executives talk about 'holding hands', hugging' or 'stroking'. As men, they are embarrassed at the expectation that they should perform traditional women's work, as though nurturing were exclusively a mother's, and not a father's, affair" (Pascal/Athos 202, quoted in Weber, ibid. Reverse translation).

It thus comes as no surprise that so much of the management literature in the USA and Germany hails the New Age influence on management theory: it should be opening executive suites to women. Indeed, we can discern such a potential, given the changing economic and technological environment in many companies, in contrast to the standard expression of Western organizational sociology. Forms of communication and cooperation have traditionally been thought of as restricted to the primary kin group, as functional only in the family, but now they are coming into play in (larger) firms: "Wouldn' that be of interest to women," Claudia Weber asks, "but also a major irony?" (ibid 125).

Historical Exposé: The Male Domain of Management

Such theories present an extreme contrast to women-identified management research and critical feminist studies of traditional value systems and cultural patterns in Western companies. In particular, during the seventies, American researchers repeatedly underscored just how far the theme of 'leadership' and the qualities deemed essential to it have been treated as 'masculine' in traditional management theory and practice.

In the pioneering book Men and Women of the Corporation (1977), Rosabeth Moss Kanter, American sociologist of organizations and management consultant, speaks of a 'male ethics' as the salient characteristic of American management philosophy and praxis. The ideology positing an 'objective', goal-oriented and rationally acting person, seen as the executive's raison d'être and the precondition for the functioning of a bureaucratic system, coincides with normative characteristics our Western society ascribes mainly to males. This so-called 'masculine' management ethic has functioned to a large extent as a gate-keeper excluding women. A similar conclusion was reached by Hennig/Jardim at the end of the seventies in The Managerial Women (1977) and by Harragan in Games Mother Never Taught You (1977). Harragan and Hennig/Jardim paint a picture of American corporate culture built primarily on the classical hierarchical-authoritarian pattern of the military, in which employees' interactions resemble those on a football field. The only goal of this game is to dispose of money and power, in short: to leave the field as victor. Western enterprises are, according to Harragan, a 'male cloning production', a 'no-women's land', a 'foreign culture' which elicits from women entering its domain classic symptoms of culture shock because, in Harragan's view, they

92

have been raised on a diet of 'sentimental and touching fictions' (Harragan, pp. 42-45; Hennig/Jardim p. 40 ff.). If women want to succeed in such a corporation governed by military culture and masculine gamesmanship, they must study the rules and adapt themselves to novel communication and relational patterns (Harragan, pp. 79-89; Hennig/Jardim, p. 176 f.).

Similarly, critical feminist studies in Germany based their conceptualization of 'women's labour-market potential' on a view of bureaucratic, sex-segregated enterprise organized hierarchically, which discriminated against and excluded women whose ethics, stressing the 'inner world' values of relationship, empathy and nurturing, was thought incompatible with successful profit-making (Beck-Gernsheim/Ostner 1978; Beck-Gernsheim 1981). Although they criticized the market based on a sex-segregated division of labour and called for change, they shared with the quoted American studies the impression that 'feminine' ways of thinking and acting would have in the foreseeable future, little chance of influencing modern management and held that women - should they want business success - would find themselves forced to adapt to male norms and career patterns.

From Deficiency to Difference

In contrast, since the late eighties concepts have been developed that depart from the traditional models of an efficient management culture, and, moving toward a new 'communication-oriented management ethic'. These concepts nourish the hope that egalitarian reform within enterprises is both possible and capable of fulfilling the needs of both women and business, bringing their interests closer together. In the avant garde of such considerations is a new type of women-focused management literature which at first triggered considerable controversy in the U.S. but has since witnessed increasing sales in Germany. Whereas in the older literature, 'feminine' qualities were more likely to be considered deficits, or at least as incapable of actually promoting a career, the situation has now been reversed, with such qualities thought essential to productivity and the assessment of creative potential. 'Human touch' is a feminine thing, and consideration, awareness of context, intuition, and people-orientation are now 'in'. Does this make women the 'change masters' in a technological and social restructuring process gone out of control? Instead of women conforming to male behavioral norms and career patterns as predicted by Hennig/Jardim and Harragan, this type of business literature emphasizes gender difference, that is, it urges a broader acceptance of feminine personality traits by companies as a mark of their innovative and integrative business acumen. Aspects of the 'new managerial culture' claimed to be 'positive' are highlighted and wedded to feminist visions of a revalued 'new femininity'. The fiction promoted by the new 'communication-oriented management-culture', in favour of allowing feeling and intimacy to enter even into economic relationships, is viewed not only as increasing women's access to business careers in a purely quantitative way but it also seduces us into supposing that in the future, professional success for women will no longer be bought at the price of conformity. Instead, without relinquishing their 'feminine identities', women will be able to influence the rules of the game in the business world.

One good example of such a position is the study by Sally Helgesen (1991). New knowledge derived from recent psychoanalytic studies of gender difference (see Gilligan 1984) suggests that increased opportunities for women to enter, and to rise, in management should be welcomed because women, beneficiaries of a more complex existence shaped by reproductive and familial duties, have been trained in 'nurturing', relationship-orientation and communication skills which are considered essential for management in the nineties. Women - so we are told - place value on interpersonal relationships, prefer doing without complicated rules and authoritarian structures, and judge process to be more important than product. Business run by women develop 'Networks of Influence' - working groups that share information and by-pass the rules of hierarchy. Western women managers as the new Japanese? At least Helgesen and her like-minded colleagues consider women in management positions to be essential in the future not only on the grounds of innovation and efficiency. They urge the incorporation in the public sphere of values traditionally ascribed to women which, it is hoped, will 'humanize' the workplace and transcend the traditional organizational dichotomy between efficiency and humaneness.

In contrast to this naively optimistic view of innovation characteristic of numerous new American publications, German management researchers focusing on women are slightly more critical and hesitant (see Antal 1988 a/b; Bischoff 1990; Henes-Karnahl 1988). In addition to the American arguments, the Germans, when looking positively toward the future, primarily follow the prognoses of business associations and mass media who note a lack of managers in the nineties. Still one of the strongest arguments in favour of increased career and promotion opportunities for women is, that the absence of females in executive positions in combination with the anticipated need new managerial qualities means a 'waste of valuable human capital' which could be used to promote both productivity and humane values in the business world.

'New Management culture': Opportunities for an increased share of power for women or a subtle variation in the masculine theme?

In conclusion I want to ask an audacious question, whether the so-called transformation of values in management, the alleged advance of male leadership culture toward the 'feminine environment' really brings with it improved chances for promotion for women. If it is true that women really fit management's description of 'new managerial qualities', do we see business offering women real opportunities? Can this thematic transformation in management and organizational theory really be interpreted as a quasi natural confluence of interests between 'innovative' enterprises and ambitious women? Does it mean that women per se can expect to be more easily promoted without their being forced, as in the past, to adapt to male career patterns? Don't we find hidden behind all of this a patriarchal society's philosophy which, readily exploited by women, is attempting to turn those values traditionally ascribed to women into capital?

The answers of these questions are necessarily speculative, as long as we are dealing with visions of the future, prognoses of a trend characterized by transformed corporate cultures and leadership styles. Therefore, to avoid misunderstanding, we have to be cautions in reading this type of management literature and avoid taking its prognoses and pronouncements as literal truth, its descriptions and images as reflections of reality. Many of the pronouncements and projected trends are models, deliberately launched as guides to behaviour, suggesting that politics is here more important than verisimilitude. Without doubt ideologies drafted by women for women concerning a new 'feminine managerial culture' have their attractive side: how else are we to interpret the high sales figures of female-related management literature? The danger, however, lies in the new theory's failure to give the whole truth and thus to arouse false hopes.

Still, I would like to mention several considerations that are leading me in a rather more sceptical direction than the alleged transformation of values associated with improved promotional and career chances might encourage. For one thing, facts suggest that the new theories demand a qualitatively different management potential but not necessarily more of such qualified persons. This stands in sharp contrast to the often expressed expectation that there will be a greater number of positions than of candidates to fill them.

American protagonists in the 'new corporate culture debate' point out that one effect of the planned de-bureaucratization and reduction of hierarchical levels will be a reduction in the number of managers themselves, especially in middle management ranks. For this reason we should reckon with significant 'silent opposition' to the proposed re-organization of management structures from precisely this level in the hierarchy (Walton 1985). It's precisely middle management that has most to fear from women's promotion to executive posts. In the face of this threat, what is more logical than for male managers - as is the custom in large enterprises - to attend expensive courses designed to train them in 'feminine' leadership skills, instead of urging an increase in female personnel, thereby opening the door to their own competition (see Demmer 1988, p. 131).

This corresponds to the situation in Germany where male decision-makers in modern corporations consider women for executive positions only if either the company's targeted consumer is female or if women compose the majority of employees. This negative assertion can be backed up by results from numerous international studies which prove that the percentage of women in executive positions has risen only slightly in the last decade and that, even where women have made it, wage and other discriminatory practices continue, such as slotting women into the less influential sectors like personnel, advertising, or public relations (see Adler 1986/87; Kanter 1987; Bischoff 1990).

American feminist critics of the 'new management culture' therefore warn against a false 'politics of optimism' and the illusions underlying a view of organizational reform 'from the top down' that neglects the material and economic context (see Blum/Smith 1988). Such a perspective overestimates the potential and possibilities for organizational reform within a market-oriented, competitive society (Ibid, p. 8). Most problematic in this view is the hope that women will rise to positions traditionally closed to them without generating conflict, a painless transformation made possible by the convergence of business and women's interests. Such a position not only overlooks the dilemma caused by a limited number of managerial positions available, but also fails to note that in a profit-oriented market economy business will tend to promote the most qualified and valuable personnel, in whom the company has invested a great deal. Relevant promotional opportunities for women will exist, in the opinion of these critics, only in cases where a business is expanding rapidly, when a location suffers from lack of workers, and the enterprise therefore finds itself forced to increase its pool of employees.

But even if modern, innovative firms offer females more opportunities for advancement than before, we still cannot conclude that women in such companies can realise their own visions of femininity and difference, that they can place radically different demands on their work, put work and leisure in another relation to each other, or redefine the public and private. The optimism propagated by a part of women-related management literature in this regards seems misleading. Nonetheless, this trend toward 'new communication styles in company culture' takes values from the traditional private sphere in order to turn a profit on them. The integration of norms, values and intimacy is an instrument designed to draw the 'whole person' into economic activity. Deutschmann called this management's new 'cultural imperialism'. On such a basis, how in the world are women to criticize male-oriented professional standards? How are they to redeem their demand for increased humanity in the workplace if a new ethos of 'caring' and 'community' is already being propagated in order that the employee's private life be co-opted in 'another, more pervasive way' than before? Deutschmann 1989, 376). The fiction propagated by the new concept of corporate culture, presaging imminent transcendence of the abyss between workplace and home, does not shelter domestic values or protect the private individual, but instead co-opts these for economic aims. Deutschmann draws out attention to the fact that in Japan the team-oriented new management type renounces nearly all claim to a life outside the firm, an aspect which, particularly where women are concerned should give reason to pause. Even American management sociologist Rosabeth Moss Kanter, otherwise a proponent of the 'new innovative manager', felt compelled to admit that the new management concept she espoused demanded 'a surplus of time' - certainly more than the old bureaucratic, hierarchical model, and that this circumstance would make it even more difficult for women envisioning their lives as mothers to reach executive positions (Kanter 1987).

But there is still another reason why upper management has integrated so few women. Apparently those at the top place great importance on cultural homogeneity as a criterion for promotion which automatically works to men's advantage. Precisely this mixing of the sexes is thought to prevent generation of a 'we-feeling', or team spirit that feeds on homogeneity, intimacy, and all those other factors held by modern management theory to be indispensable to the smoothly-running business (see Deutschmann 1987, p. 14; Weber 1986, p. 126).

How else can we explain the fact that American women managers given specific opportunities for promotion to middle management are still denied access to the upper echelons in spite of equal opportunity programs, excellent qualifications, and partial compatibility of life-style and career patterns? One answer: the 'corporate culture', entrance to which is still, as before, blocked by the gatekeeper of cultural homogeneity. American top management, like German, is white, male and of middle class origin (Ouchi 1981, p. 77). Thus, the cultural interpretation seems the most likely to explain the low representation of women. A striking example of continuing cultural divergence between men and women is a trend that has been visible to American researchers for quite some time: many highly qualified women managers are leaving their corporations to strike out on their own. What could be motivating them to take such risks with their lives and careers - women who, after all, were supposed to be the pioneers, the models for the coming generation? Answer: the struggle has taken its toll; they've had problems with the value systems and traditional modes of behaviour in their companies. Could this mean that descriptions of American business stemming from the seventies are truer to reality than contemporary images of a new 'feminine' corporate culture would suggest? Or is this 'new corporate culture' really only a subtle variation on a old masculine theme?

Conclusion

Although I think the question of whether women are more qualified than men to embody these 'new managerial qualifications' merits discussion. I also feel that recourse to the peculiar 'feminine' patterns of behaviour, management styles, and self-descriptions of a revalued femininity, raises a number of problems. I consider misleading the use of the difference thesis, as it occurs in this case, to include a concept of efficiency. It suggest a misunderstanding of what feminist researchers have actually intended the thesis to mean. They were concerned with the culturally learned otherness of women, with revealing the specificity of female life experience in order to show how distorted it was when confronted by male theory and practice. At the same time, they wanted to reverse the devaluation of the 'feminine' and replace it with a more positive attitude. Female management philosophers' incorporating the difference thesis - in the sense of an affirmative identification with feminine-motherly potential, or the reductive description of woman, what she isn't, or not only, or only under certain circumstances wants to be - risks propagating a universalist vision of 'women' that nails her to 'feminine' characteristics and thus reproduces the old sex role stereotypes (see Knapp 1988). Not only do we find 'femininity', feeling and trust degraded to factors of production, but also that increasingly women are expected to bring to the 'new management cultures' their old 'female potential' if they are to be successful, and such expectations foster the prejudice which holds that women's disadvantage in the business world flows from their own subjective characteristics or, reversed, that once they have the required subjectivity and qualifications, promotions will follow. Entirely ignored are relations of power, hierarchies of interest and exclusionary mechanisms, decisive in limiting women's chances and not influenced by formal qualifications.

The objections, both empirical and analytical, that I have presented give little cause for sharing modern management philosophers' optimism vis-à-vis improved opportunities for 'women, the innovative potential of the future'. To date there is little evidence that companies plan, of their own free will, to increase their complement of female employees and smooth their climb up the ladder. On the contrary, it appears that this whole business can be reduced to a modernising of patriarchal structures by means of 'feminizing' traditional Management.

What is it then that inspires the defenders of a new, revalued 'femininity' and a growing number of business representatives to sing the praises of a 'clever, intuitive woman', women as the 'potential for innovation' of the future? In addition to the fact that there are surely well-meaning people among those in the upper echelons who earnestly urge equality, I see two reasons: for one thing, the woman-friendly rhetoric of many large firms - in the absence of empirical data assuring that the company in question actually has hired women insignificant numbers for executive positions - arouses no small measure of hope for a management career in many qualified and ambitious women with intensified aspirations, higher performance goals and fantasies of female power (see Schulz 1989). The company's advantage lies in the resulting reservoir of potential candidates for promotion, important in an era of growing economic insecurity and complexity combined with the constant need to adapt to a rapidly changing market and production landscape. Managers can then draw on these reserve troops of qualified women to cover gaps in their personnel needs.

However, it appears that this tactic will work only if the company does not have to accept any binding rules or agreements such as might be required by the Damocles' sword of government regulation (affirmative action laws, state sanctions or quotas). Here we can almost predict a situation in which companies, forced by the increase in young qualified women with corresponding demands for representation at all levels of the hierarchy, will respond with 'voluntary' job offers to prevent passage of any stricter measures bound to interfere with flexibility. Thus, women-friendly rhetoric concerning a 'new femininity in the executive suite' can be interpreted as symbolic acceptance of themes and demands launched by the women's movement and feminist spokespersons in political parties and associations, with the purpose of pre-empting legal measures to assure equal opportunity for women. Given this relationship, we can better understand why a company which on the one hand prides itself on its own programs to promote women and ensure equal opportunity will on the other exhibit quite an allergic reaction to demands for institutionalized rules assuring equal treatment, such as quotas or antidiscriminatory legislation.

International experience has shown that women have always made the most significant gains where discrimination has been countered by legal sanctions and fines, in such countries and companies (for instance the USA, Sweden or Canada) in which the hiring and promotion of women and minorities has been helped along by affirmative action programs (Zauner 1990). But it is precisely the American example, as we have also seen in the former Federal Republic, that such legal prescriptions can be too easily ignored.

References

Adler, Nancy (1986/87), Women in Management Worldwide, in: *ISMO*, Vo. 16, No.3/4

Antal, Ariane Berthoin (1988a), Managementkarrieren für Ingenieurinnen: Zu neuen Leitbildern, veränderten Kulturen und starken Verbündeten. In: Janshen, Doris/Rudolph, Hedwig (Hg.), Frauen gestalten Technik, Pfaffenweiler, Centaurus.

Antal, Ariane Berthoin (1988b), Mehr Frauen ins Management, in: Demmer, Christine (Hg.), *Frauen ins Management. Von der Reservearmee zur Begabungsreserve*, Verlag Th. Gabler, Wiesbaden.

Bauer, Winfried (1988), Die Tyrannei des Mittelmaßes - Oder: Haben Männer Angst vor den Frauen? Referat auf dem Berliner Kongreß "Frauen und Wirtschaft in den 90er Jahren", Der Senator für Jugend und Familie, Berlin.

Beck-Gernsheim, Elisabeth (1981), Der geschlechtsspezifische Arbeitsmarkt. Zur Ideologie und Realität von Frauenberufen, Frankfurt, Aspekte.

Beck-Gernsheim, Elisabeth/Ostner, Ilona (1978), Frauen verändern - Berufe nicht? in: *Soziale Welt*, 29.Jg., Heft 3, Göttingen, Otto Schwarz Verlag.

Bischoff, Sonja (1990), Frauen zwischen Macht und Mann. Männer in der Defensive. Führungskräfte in Zeiten des Umbruchs, Hamburg, Rowolt.

Blum, Linda/Smith, Vicki (1988), Women's Mobility in the Corporation: A Critique of the Politics of Optimism, in: *Signs, Journal of Women in Culture and Society*, Vol. 13, No. 3.

Demmer, Christine (Hg.) (1988), *Frauen ins Management. Von der Reservearmee zur Begabungsreserve*, Wiesbaden, Verlag Th. Gabler.

Der Bundesminister für Jugend, Familie, Frauen und Gesundheit (Hg.) (1988), Frauenförderung in Unternehmen der Bundesrepublik Deutschland. Die Durchsetzung der Gleichberechtigung als Chance für die Personalpolitik. Bericht zur Konferenz vom 23. November 1987 in Bonn.

Deutschmann, Christoph (1987), Der Betriebsclan, in: *Soziale Welt*, Heft 2, Göttingen, Otto Schwarz Verlag.

Deutschmann, Christoph (1989), Reflexive Verwissenschaftlichung und kultureller "Imperialismus" des Management, in: *Soziale Welt*, Heft 3, Göttingen, Otto Schwarz Verlag.

Gilligan, Carol (1984), *Die andere Stimme*. Lebenskonflikte und Moral der Frau, München/Zürich, Piper Verlag.

Harragan, Betty Lehan (1977), *Games Mother Never Taught You*, New York, Warner Brooks.

Helgesen, Sally (1991), *Frauen führen anders*. Vorteile eines neuen Führungsstils, Frankfurt/New York, Campus Verlag.

Henes-Karnahl, Beate (1988), Wertewandel im Management: Die Schwachen werden die Starken sein. In: Demmer, Christine (Hg.), *Frauen ins Management. Von der Reservearmee zur Begabungsreserve*, Wiesbaden, Verlag Th. Gabler.

Hennig, Margaret/Jardim, Anne (1977), *The Managerial Woman*, New York, Anchor Press/Doubleday.

Kanter, Rosabeth Moss (1977), *Men and women of the Corporation*, New York, Basic Books.

Kanter, Rosabeth Moss (1987), Men and Women of the Corporation Revisited, in: *Management Review*, March 1987.

Knapp, Grudrun-Axeli (1988), Das Konzept "weibliches Arbeitsvermögen" - theoriegeleitete Zugänge, Irrwege, Perspektiven, in: *ifg frauenforschung, Institut Frau und Gesellschaft*, 6. Jg., Heft 4, Bielefeld, Kleine Verlag.

Osterloh, Margit (1989), Die neue Unternehmensorganisation im Spannungsfeld von Unternehmensstrategie, Unternehmenskultur und Unternehmensethik, in: Dabrowski, Hartmut/Jacobi, Otto/Schudlich, Edwin/Teschner, Eckart (Hg.), Tarifpolitische Interessen der Arbeitgeber und neue Managementstrategien. Referate und Diskussionen einer Arbeitstagung vom 22./23. November 1988, Düsseldorf.

Ouchi, William G. (1981), *Theory Z: How American Business Can Meet the Japanese Challenge*, Reading, Mass., Addison-Wesley Publishing Company.

Pascale, Richard T./Athos, Anthony G. (1982), *The Art of Japanese Management*, Applications for American Executives, New York, Warner Books.

Pathe, Helmut (Hg.) (1988), Frauen in Wirtschaft und Gesellschaft, Symposium des Instituts der deutschen Wirtschaft, Köln, Deutscher Instituts-Verlag.

Peters, Thomas/Waterman, Robert H. (1984), *Auf der Suche nach Spitzenleistungen*, 10. Aufl., Landsberg a. Lech, Verlag Moderne Industrie.

Schenkel, Susan (1986), *Mut zum Erfolg*, Warum Frauen blockiert sind und was sie dagegen tun können, Frankfurt/New York, Campus Verlag.

Staehle, Wolfgang (1987), *Management*, Eine verhaltenswissenschaftliche Einführung. 3. verbesserte und erweiterte Aufl., München, Vahlen.

Stechert, Kathryn (1988), *Frauen setzen sich durch*. Leitfaden für den Berufsalltag mit Männern, Frankfurt/New York, Campus Verlag.

Stödter, Helga (1989), *Neue Führungsstrukturen in der europäischen Wirtschaft der 90er Jahre*, Hamburg, Helga-Stödter-Stiftung.

Streeck, Wolfgang (1986), The Uncertainties of Management in the Management of Uncertainty: Employers, Labor Relations and Industrial Adjustment in the 1980s, discussion paper des Wissenschaftszentrum Berlin, IIM/LMP 86-26.

Walton, Richard E. (1985), *From Control to Commitment in the Workplace*, Harvard Business Review, March-April

Weber, Claudia (1986), Die Zukunft des Clans. Überlegungen zum japanischen Organisationstyp und Managementstil. In: Feministische Studien, 3. Jg., Heft 1, Deutscher Studien Verlag, Weinheim.

Zauner, Margrit (1990), Förderung für Chancengleichheit. Frauenförderpläne als Mittel zur Erschließung weiblicher Führungskräfteressourcen, München und Mering.

4   Women: a force for democracy

Su Maddock

Corporate, Policy and Management Services
University of Manchester, Great Britain

Many women I know who work as local government officers in Britain are desperate for a greater openness and democracy within management. However their voice is frequently unnoticed and ignored. Research too often focuses on women's career development (White, Cox & Cooper 1992) and categorises women in ways that do not reflect the complex dimensions by which women decide how to manage not just their work but gender relations at work. Isolated women are frequently forced to adopt conforming strategies to cope and survive in management (Harragan 1977, Kanter 1977) and consequently do not have the space or the inclination to articulate their views on management practice or their thoughts on organizational practice. Visible women are vulnerable women (Kanter 1977). Yet, it is my experience that the majority of women do have a deep seated belief that organizations would run more efficiently if staff were able to be open with each other because then they could plan and negotiate their work. Women in my experience are frustrated not just by the personal oppression of gender cultures at work but also by its stifling effect on working practices. Their male colleagues prefer to ignore gender as an issue in organisations and in organizational theory. But by ignoring the power of traditional gender relations they in effect stifle and silence women and other employees at work, who in many instances could bring a more open style of practice which could be beneficial to both public and private sector organization. Organizations are suffering because they are not utilising women who are a valuable force for change. A force which would carry companies and organizations towards a greater democracy. Women experience stress and frustration in hierarchical bureaucratic organizations (Marshall forthcoming 1994) and when the opportunity arises seek out more flexible work-environments either in independent organisations or as consultants. Organizations are not only not recruiting or promoting women they are also losing those few talented women who have struggled to survive as managers.

I started to interview women managers in northern UK local authorities in 1990 in order to investigate how far women believed in democracy at work was connected to gender relations and what held them and other women back from expressing themselves and effecting change.

A recent study of the European Equal opportunities Unit showed many women to be change agents (Page/Grazzioni 1993). Page and Grazzioni reported that it was often difficult to evaluate women's contribution to organisation effectiveness because the balance of gender-relations on which women based their strategies at work were constantly changing, but they reported that many chief executives in the UK were coming to believe in the significance of women's contribution to the management of change and were head hunting women for senior posts.

This is also my belief that womens' potential contribution to organizational life and development is stifled and under-developed because they are so few role models or women secure enough to direct changes. I think some of the women in this study show that women managers when free to develop new ways of working often develop more open forms of management and facilitate greater internal democracy.

Methodology

The women interviewed for this research were aged between 35 and 50 years, almost all were graduates, white and experienced in their work as public sector managers. They all held management positions in northern English local authorities and had worked for local government for over 10 years. 75% of middle managers had children as did 50% of the senior managers. They were interviewed between 1989 and 1992. As the author has had experience of local government management she was fully aware of the pressures on women managers and of their concern for public services. All the women were involved in some way in the management of change and the majority were committed to improving local services as well as their own careers. There were 50 women in all, 50% in senior positions and 50% in middle management. These managers were all aware of the fact that their gender influenced others and their working relationships,and referred to having to manage 'gender relations' as well as work itself. This was true of both feminists and those antagonistic to the women's movement.

The Influence of Gender Culture

Gender culture is very powerful in it's influence on how men and women treat each other (Mills 1988), and it's influence over women and how they consider themselves and how they behave (Maddock & Parkin 1993). The power of organisational cultures over employees is well documented by E.H. Schein (1984) and others. Virginia Schein showed how the work culture affected women managers' ideas on how to behave and what characteristics to develop to succeed (1975). Her results replicated in 1988 demonstrated that women in the USA and Europe continue to think that the 'masculine' traits of competitiveness, decisiveness and non-involvement are crucial for ambitious managers. Those that can not or do not conform to the prevailing sub-culture within organisations are under a strong pressure to adapt or to leave (Schein 1984).

Prior to Judy Rosener's article in 1991 few American management writers would acknowledge womens' diverse skills and instead focused totally on how similar men and women are ; they were afraid least any hint of a difference in style between men and women would render women devalued and less than competent in male eyes. In the past women managers have advised other women to conform if they wanted to succeed (Hennig & Jardim 1978).

The European context appears to be slightly different from that in the USA.

Those women who have succeeded in the public arena in the UK were usually typecasted as 'nannies', 'school-mams' or 'iron maidens'. In the past a successful woman in Britain was a single spinster and called a 'blue-stocking'. Women like Mrs Thatcher could either flirt or boss their way to the top or both. In any highly sex-segregated culture, women are left with two options either rebel or conform to the roles allocated to them. Women in the public arena could either be a 'man' and desexualized, a bullying 'school mam' or pander sexually to male interests. In the UK the latter strategy continues to be dangerous and few professional women would consider flaunting their sexuality at work because they recognise they would be outcast and demeaned by being sexually active.

Gender cultures not only render women segregated in lower status jobs they also determine how men and women behave within those positions. For instance the culture of the 'Gentleman's Club' is friendly but fatherly to women who conform to the traditional roles of daughter, mother and wife; whereas the sexual banter of the 'Locker Room' culture can be very offensive and oppressive for younger women in particular because it is highly sexual culture where women are primarily viewed as sexual objects not intelligent beings (Maddock and Parkin 1993).

Those with no experience or confidence in change cling to traditional practice and respond and conform to traditional roles . As women have only recently entered the management sector of the labour market much in traditional practice at work has been developed by men. As women are less comfortable in work cultures and with working practices they are advised to mirror men's style if they want to succeed. There appears to be a general recognition by women that they are struggling with how to behave as women as well as their work.

Women's own voice in such a traditional gender culture frequently goes unheard, and is ignored because of cultural stereotyping. As equal opportunities becomes more acceptable as 'just' and 'fair' as new culture of the 'gender-blind' has emerged where men and women are assumed to be the same and so the power of gender-relations and gender-culture is ignored. The culture of 'Lip Service' is in evidence in the commercial and public sectors (Maddock & Parkin 1993). Lip service is paid to both democracy or openness in organisations and to equality. In such a culture women can succeed but they must not affirm or suggest that women have peculiar circumstance or a special voice, the effect of this culture is to silence women further; they have been accepted into organisations and now must conform and adhere to the status quo. To demand special treatment or consideration is becoming less acceptable in the UK and ambitious women reject a common voice with other women, because to do so might threaten their careers.

In the context of increased privatisation a new 'efficient macho' version of this gender-blind culture is emerging. Women are assumed to be as competent and as able as the men - but they can only be successful if they present themselves as having similar lives to that of their male colleagues. These women are usually educated, white, single and ambitious. These are managers who are extremely performance and target orientated - they work hard for very long hours, they do not expect favours and do not give any. Such a culture is still gendered - 'masculine' even if many women have adapted to it and succeed within it.

It is parents not single people who suffer most from such a competitive work culture, they cannot work until 7 p.m. at night because they have domestic commitments.

Women worldwide continue to carry the burden of caring, either for children, relatives or partners. Women manage both gender-culture and their work, and act strategically to be personally effective (Cockburn 1991). I think that this research indicates that the many women in the UK public sector, want to make the working environment more humane and want a balance between good service delivery and working conditions. This is also reinforced by work by Alimo Metcalfe, (1990) and Cox and Cooper (1992), it appears that many women managers in the UK public sector are still more interested in generating improved services and working conditions than they are in promotion.

Kakabadse (1986) also noted that women in the main were not traditionalist managers but were more likely visionaries and innovators. Cox and Cooper (1992) suggest that women measure their success by their strengthening an organisation and not necessarily by promotion - they tend to value development.

What UK women managers say

Although the women interviewed held diverse political views all unanimously agreed that 'gender relations' at work had influenced their careers and working lives.
It was the strategies to cope that they adopted that differentiated them.
Almost all the women interviewed although often politically experienced felt that women's development was secondary to service development, and that their own careers came second to their client's interests.

Middle managers

The most common frustrations expressed by the women middle managers can be summarised as:
* being patronised by managers
* the detail of their work being ignored
* their comments on work details and problems being trivialised
* there being no forward planning or discussion of work
* crisis management being the norm.

The trouble is they do not have any confidence in anything other than the old ways, a lot of the time managers play at work. When I sorted out a potential disaster the other day it went

unnoticed, a rather macho male manager instead of listening to
some of his staff went into an industrial dispute - and he was
acclaimed for being 'tough' and ready to make difficult decision
by the directors. It was ridiculous the whole thing was so easy
to resolve - the trouble is he was interested in proving his
virility at work not in solving the problem at hand.

Leeds

There was very little variation in these complaints between organizations or departments, apart from a few fortunate women managers who felt able to control their work programmes these frustrations were at the time, the norm in the UK. The most significant of these complaints shows that the management within these authorities was clearly ineffective. These managers were earning £25,000 per annum but no-one was listening to them. Whilst in some authorities it was understandable given central government's actions that some crisis management would prevail, most of the women interviewed said that this had been the norm long before the attack on finance by central government.

The overwhelming majority (86%) said that they felt women had a more conciliatory style of negotiation and that women wanted to plan outcomes and consider strategies, and that often their male colleagues didn't think enough about work at all.

I'm sure it isn't true of all men, but there is tendency here to
think that it is rather beneath managers to consider detail -
sometimes its difficult to believe they work in the same
organisation. Women over plan and worry- men don't seem
to worry enough - they do not challenge each other and if I
suggest something they look to each other first before reacting
it is a very gendered-culture here. I'm not sure they're really
got used to women working in management.

Manchester

I think men get a buzz from paperwork, they like firefighting whereas women like to plan - Officers often has little confidence in their own decisions - the present climate has made it worse, now the insecurity has created a culture of 'blame'- middle managers are afraid not to stick rigidly to the rules and senior managers avoid systems altogether.

Leeds

They are obsessed with systems and never delegate, they treat people like machines. The director is a processes man, he likes everything to be pre-ordained,they are scared and don't ever take risks.

Rochdale

Senior managers

Those women who were senior managers did not complain of a lack of respect. However, 40% of senior women had applied more than once for their current post, two women had to apply and be interviewed three times before being appointed.

They were looking around the country to see if they could find a man who was better than me - as they couldn't they gave up in the end and appointed me.

Director of Education

Senior women in directorship positions were much more likely to suffer from
*   other senior managers withholding information from them
*   being excluded from meetings
*   frustration at the slow rate of change.

All the senior managers interviewed expressed their commitment to a more 'open style' of management but more importantly most had changed structures in order to facilitate a greater openness at work. For instance; many visited local offices, kept their office doors open, brought in junior staff into strategic meetings, had arranged open staff meetings and restructured to fast-track able men and women.

The majority of the women interviewed were attempting to introduce a more open style of debate and management in their departments, even those women managers with little power were attempting to insist on greater collaboration often at their own expense.

Whilst only two women referred to this process as one which encouraged a greater sense of democracy within the department and with the public; they sensed that the future of public services depended on both more democratic relations with the community and between staff.These women were trying to flatten management structures, introduce team working and a greater responsiveness to customers.

> *It took me a year to get the corporate team to accept my*
> *department's restructuring plan - but in the end we won because*
> *the rest of the department were behind me - they knew it would*
> *be good for education and for them - They tried to criticise my*
> *style of openness and said I'd lose respect, then they said the*
> *planning group was too big - it's complicated you have to be*
> *firm and tough but open and flexible - in the end I negotiated*
> *over the size of the team on the condition two junior members*
> *could discuss but not vote.*
>
> Director for Education

So why is the voice of women managers so muted in this debate and why are women so quiet about their views at work and within the political arena.

The most significant finding from senior managers was that the majority of them had experienced rumour and innuendo about their personal lives, (especially if single with no children). Those that experienced the worst type of malicious gossip tended to work for authorities unused to women in senior positions, where there was an assumption that it was natural for women to be deferential to men but certainly not to women. Equality audits in various authorities (CMPS 1992-93) reinforce this view. Women in traditional gendered cultures are either seen first and foremost as women not as managers,they experienced gossip about their relationships, their clothes, behaviour, and childcare arrangements. They were frequently attacked for not fulfilling traditional female role models of passive assistant or good wife and mother. These attacks came from men and women staff.

Even those women who did not feel close to women's dilemmas and who were somewhat antagonistic to feminism said that they knew that they had to find a way of becoming presentable or invisible at work.

> *I adopted a beggared cloak approach, no-one would know that*
> *I was there women who are visible get attacked.*
> Liverpool

This may be very specific to Britain, but it was also found to be in the case by Rosabeth Kanter in the USA. In the 'Men and Women of the Corporation' she described how powerful organisational culture was in perpetuating sexually stereotypes of both men and women. Many women do not want to adopt a male management style, it makes them feel uneasy with themselves.

> *I did not like myself, I felt disagreeable inside of myself, I was*
> *always arguing, always sad, always heavy, always boring*
> *having no pleasure - I decided to be myself.*
> Leeds

Coping strategies

Women appeared to have long and short term strategies this was also observed by Cynthia Cockburn (1992). Their short term agenda may be in gaining power within the organisation or in supporting clients at their own expense and appearing to conform- while their longer term agenda may in transforming the organisation they work in quite a radical way. Some women may also wait until it is clear to them that they have supportive colleagues on a similar grade before taking any risks.

Women in some authorities such as Leeds and Newcastle are still very suspicious of women who have reached senior management, but the gap between middle and senior women is closing in other authorities where women are networking and supporting each other across grades. Many of the senior women interviewed in this study were aware of the fact that women junior to themselves needed role models and were ready to mentor junior women. A black woman manager said:

I know I have to stay in management, just because they are hardy any black women in management in the UK.
Manchester

Most of the women in this study said they would not work for an organisation that didn't enshrine public sector values and were not persuaded by Conservative measures to promote women into senior positions as they doubted many women could work in the current competitive environment.

Lip service or real change

It is becoming more and more acceptable for people in the commercial world as well as the public sector to talk of the need for greater openness within organisations, between managers and employees and between organisations.

Democracy is inevitable - because it is the only system that can successfully cope with the changing demands of contemporary civilization, in business as well as in government.

Philip Slater and Warren Bennis (HBR 1990)

Although cynics would point accurately to the fact that many businesses and public institutions are finding it hard to achieve change in this direction, none the less many are persuaded that there are business as well as ethical arguments for a greater levelling of power between employees if performance is to be improved through a task orientated culture.

What Bennis and Slater are referring to when they talk about democracy is not greater permissiveness or a culture of 'laissez-faire' attitudes but a new system of values, where people are compelled or reinforced for their work rather than for their status. The values that are enshrined in an open culture of communication, consensus rather than coercion, influence based on competence rather than whim, an encouragement of creativity and expression, and the general valuing of people. They sum up this perspective with a wave good -bye to the 'Great Man'. The qualities that IBM are now looking for in their executives are creativity, strategic thinking and customer orientation and an ability to make change happen and inspire the workforce (Financial Times 1993).

The problem for all organisations is how to achieve change, not just at an organisational level but at a personal level. In Britain the term 'democracy' is avoided, but the 'open company' is encouraged. Smythe, Dorward and Lambert (1991) surveyed chief executives working for major companies in Britain. All said that they recognised the need for their companies to become more 'open'.

What they meant by this was that they should:

a) encourage employee involvement and participation

b) support personal initiative

c) promote internal communication.

Many of these Chief Executives (Smythe,Dorward & Lambert 1991) believed that by adopting a more 'open' style of management that would increase efficiency. They have been prompted in this thinking by international and global changes, the most significant being that their markets are changing so rapidly, sometimes overnight, that competition is so fierce, they need flexible,committed and effective staff to survive. Yet, even this market pressure has not pushed cultural change fast enough, there is still a huge gulf between rhetoric and reality.

In British public sector, the pressure from central government to cut costs and restructure into smaller trading units is causing despair and confusion amongst many managers, But, some chief executives in local government now understand the need for their mangers to be more open and responsible. However the process of cultural change in local government only really started in 1990 and is confused because the agenda is not being set by local government and it's chief executives but by central government who are taking away responsibility from managers by determining their priorities and budgets.

Without this change towards a greater openness the commercial world will not survive. Senior managers realise this and are driving the change. My own research suggests that the motor for change in local government is more complex and coming from a number of directions where each is suspicious of the other. One such force is women managers. My research in local government suggests that many women are frustrated by the slowness of the rate of change, are desperate for a more task driven culture and thwarted by bureaucratic structures and the behaviour of officers in the authorities in which they work.

Choosing Change and Social Values

Women because they have been managing options and alternatives throughout their lives do appear to understand better the connection and coherence between internal democracy and quality service delivery.

I think women in general are closer to clients and the community than are men- they have kids at school - they visit schools more often, they care about the services that's why they want to talk about the detail and plan what to do - they think about what can go wrong and do not assume everything will sort itself out. I think men go unchallenged so much here that they are lazy, they think less, they are less pressured to think in terms of options and strategies.

Principal officer and mother of three

Many of the women interviewed recognised that the women's movement had led some women to avoid management positions - because they assumed that if they became managers they would automatically become tainted. This is still a common belief, at a recent conference of Women in Medicine the workshop on women managers was entitled, *'Going over to the enemy'*. But this is changing, many of the middle managers said that in the past they would have been very suspicious of women in senior positions and now the realise their value.

I've learnt how to watch Christine in meetings, she waits for her chance, in the past I thought her weak but now I realise its as hard for her as it is for us lower down, she has to be strategic - the difference is that she explains to us what she is doing, I think in the past women in management have felt so isolated that they have rejected women lower down and said things like - 'if I made than why can't they?' I don't always agree with Christine but I know she wants the same sort of change as I do.

Leeds

The majority of senior managers agreed that they were probably different from the generation of women managers before them. Many had children which had previously been unusual for a senior woman professional positions.

My door is always open, I think the fact I have two young children and sometimes I have to go home early to see them make some more acceptable to all other women here. Women need support and I need the support of both men and women in my department I need to trust them and they need to trust me. I know I operate differently from the other senior managers.

Financial Director with two children

As the tension for women between being themselves and adapting to a male work culture appears to exist for the majority of women, it is not surprising that when given the opportunity women seek to transform existing practices and remodel organisational culture into something more women-friendly. The problem for women is that the more closed the system the harder it is for women to change it, and the more they are forced into strategies of: remodelling, invisibility and flirtation.

The level of gender-awareness in the UK is much higher now than it was for the previous generations of women managers. One of the reasons one woman stated that women were more aware of the need for flexibility was that they had to learn to juggle with decisions early in life - either in their domestic lives, because they had changed jobs or careers or in the mere management of gender-relations.

I worked in a collective for a number of years and although it was hard and we argued a lot it taught me how to negotiate, how to persuade, how to take criticism and how to plan. I'm sure most managers local government have not had enough experience of working outside of an institution and do not realise that it is possible to be open and informal and yet effective at the same time. They have no confidence in openness or in development.

Adviser in Bradford

None of the women interviewed here was comfortable with internal management practices.

I am convinced that there is a woman's way of doing things - this is to be firm but to be tender too - we pay attention to detail and fit things together, men are not trained in this way. Women tried being like men and now we must be women.
Education service director

It is of course true that many men were also unhappy about the same practices and many men interviewed suffered the same frustrations, but in the main most of the male officers felt easier and more at home in the way decisions were made and departments organised. One of the reason why women said that they were frustrated was not just because they had to manage gender and sexism but because they *did have* confidence in the possibility of new ways of working (unlike many men who do not). This view was particularly stress by the six women middle managers who had experience in non-government organisations.

I think women are freer in a way to develop, we never had jobs for long, women tend to move sideways rather than up in organisations and they have to be flexible o survive - they have to know how to persuade, manipulate and negotiate, they have no choice.
Burnley

Because women consciously or unconsciously have recognised the fact that they need to be alert, aware of new possibilities and open to new ideas they are keen to train, to learn and to develop themselves

I think women learn from training, men are less interested in training. Men continue to bang their fists on the table whereas women listen, learn and try to open-up conflicts.
Sheffield

120

This propensity of women to want to learn is also found by Cox and Cooper (1992). Women are also very confident of the need for an open-approach and their reticence or reluctance to push for revolutionary changes at work reflects the fact that they know they will go unheeded. Whilst the women in this study articulated some difference in how they as individuals could promote open-management not one dissented from the view that it was a better way to manage and improve services. The real problem as a director of education reported was:

> *that women are unheard, for two reasons:*
> *one because they are women and not listened to because of their gender, and two because the listener does not understand what they mean when they say it. Men do not understand what women mean when they talk of collaborating, the need for planning and a discussion of detail - they cannot see what the issue is.*

Conclusion

Many women managers in Britain now appear to be more conscious of their own strategies at work and are less dominated by divisions between other women. This study endorses the view that many women managers who have reached senior positions in the public sector clearly believe in the possibility of change need for a greater openness at work. The women interviewed here believe in flatter management structures, decentralisation, team working and in the need for better communication between staff and with clients or customers. Women will make mistakes but they also have the capacity to develop new visions in organisations particularly in the public sector where the majority of women work - it is societies and the commercial's worlds loss if they remain frustrated outside of decision making by a very gendered culture. Women have a life long experience of managing conflictual situations, negotiating between antagonists and planning or avoiding making difficult decisions. The oppression of gender-cultures has given women their training, they now have the skills to develop a democracy in the community and at work, but unfortunately most women remain unnoticed at the bottom of organisations. The 'cream' in many UK public sector organisations is at the bottom not the top. It is not only destructive for women to remould themselves as managers in a male image it is also damaging for organisations who are in desperate need of a democratising force which many women can provide if only they are encouraged and given the opportunity.

References

Alimo-Metcalfe, B. (1990), *Gender, Leadership and Assessment*, paper for 3rd European Congress on Assessment Method, Belgium.

Bennis, J. & P. Slater, (1990), *Democracy is Inevitable*, Harvard Business Review. Sep.-Oct. pp. 164-176.

Cockburn, C. (1991), *In the Way of Women: Men's resistance to Sex Equality in Organisations*, MacMillan: London.

Dorward, Smytthe and Lambert (1991), *The Power of the Open Company A survey of chief executives views on corporate change, 40-42 Newman St London W1P 3PA*.

Financial Times (March 29 1993), *It takes a lot to be a Superstar*, Martin Dickson.

Harragan (1977), *The Games Mother Never Taught You*, New York, Warner Books.

Hennig, M & Jardim, A. (1978), *The Managerial Woman*, London, Marion Boyars.

Kabadase, A.K. (1986), *The Politics of Management*, London, Gower.

Kanter, R.M. (1977), *Men and Women of the Corporation*, New York, Basic Books.

Maddock, S. & Parkin, D. (1992-1993), *Equality Audits for Corporate*, Management and Policy Services.

Maddock S. & Parkin, D. (1993), *Gender Cultures: Women's Choices and Strategies at Work*, Women in Management Review, Vol. 8 no. 2, p. 3.

Marshall, J. (1994), *Why Women leave Senior Management Jobs*, in: Women in Management: The Second Wave. (eds) Tantum, M., London, Routledge.

Mills, A.J. (1988), *Culture, Gender and Organizations*, Org. Studies 9/3 pp. 351-369.

Page, M. (1993), *Women Change Decisions*, A final report to EC Equal Opportunities Unit, Brussels, Women, decision making and local strategies: some comparisons between Italy and the UK.

Rosener, J.B. (1990), *The Ways Women Lead*, Harvard Business Review, Nov-Dec pp. 119-125.

Schein, E.H. (1985), *Organisational Culture and Leadership*, San Fransisco, Jossey-Bass

Schein, V.E. (1977), *Think Manager, Think Male*, Atlantic Economic Review, pp. 95 March-April.

Schein, V.E. & Mueller, R.E.(1992), *Sex role stereotyping and requisite management characteristics: A cross cultural look*, Journal of Organisational Behaviour Vol 13, pp 439-447.

White, B. Cox, C. & Cooper, C. (1992), *Women's Career Development: A Study of High Flyers*, Oxford, Basil Blackwell.

5 Management, Masculinity and Manipulation: from paternalism to corporate strategy in financial services in Britain[1]

Deborah Kerfoot and David Knights[2]

Financial Services Research Centre, Manchester School
of Management, Great Britain

Strategic management as an organisational imperative began to enter
financial services around the 1970's in response to a change in the competitive climate resulting partly from a redefinition of their relationship with the
state. In its concern to ensure that London remained a world financial centre
and that the financial services expand their foreign trade, the Thatcher
regime in Britain sought both to regulate and deregulate the financial
services. In doing so it continually propagandised competition and
entrepreneurialism, and the industry has tended to respond by modifying if
not discarding its previously risk-avertive and conservative traditions. In
their place financial services have adopted what may be seen as a policy of
corporate growth through horizontal integration and the expansion of
consumer markets.

In pursuit of success, or at least the size and power thought to
guarantee its potential, financial services companies adopted plans for
strategic growth involving takeovers, foreign ventures, lending to lowly
developed countries, credit expansion and an extension of distribution
outlets. Fearing to be left behind in the rush to diversify into associated
financial services or to take advantage of markets that had a potential well
beyond current levels of development, banks, building societies and
insurance companies sought to abandon previously conservative and
paternalistic modes of management. Attempts were made to displace these

by strategic approaches to management which were thought to advance corporate control of internal and external business practices and enhance a company's competitive position in the market place[3]. Our concerns in this chapter however, are not with transformations in financial services per se, but with these modes of management in relation to the historically specific manifestations of masculinity they sustain, as management seeks to manipulate both internal and external social relations for purposes of organisational control and competition.

Common-sense assumptions about men and masculinity in everyday conversation for example, in pubs, workplaces, on street corners and in the home, frequently become generalised into implicit notions of how men behave or to what extent individual men are more or less masculine than others. Several studies have noted the prevalence of sexualised 'banter' in either all or largely male work environments (Collinson, 1988: Reimer, 1979) or within mixed-sex workplaces (Filby, 1991; Pollert, 1981:140) where talk of men, either about them or by them, concerns men's strength, physical presence and sexual prowess (also Willis, 1977) and where the potential for conquest and bodily force is emblematic of what it means to be a man (Connell, 1983:17-20). Masculinity then, from a common-sense perspective is unproblematically what men do and what men are; consequently, men need no more theorise masculinity "than a fish need theorise water" (Hearn and Morgan, 1991). In an attempt to analyse masculinity critically, this chapter looks at the dynamic interconnections between masculinity and work, or more particularly as our title suggests, between forms of management, masculinity and manipulation. Our purpose is twofold: to explore what sustains the privileging of a highly specific version of what masculinity can be at any one time, observing the work of its construction in certain sites and practices; and to highlight the linkages between modes of management and historically distinct forms of masculinity. In so doing, we aim to render masculinity problematic, to make visible the predominant 'discourse of masculinism', and to render this analysable as a topic of social inquiry (Coleman, 1991). Through questioning the facade of masculine invulnerability, we see the contribution of this chapter as opening

126

up space for a discussion of how management practices can silence or displace the expression of weaknesses, fears and uncertainties of men and women in organisations.

Drawing on our experience of extensive fieldwork in the financial services[4], the chapter examines the way in which gender becomes an 'organising principle' in the managerial workplace. By this we mean the continual reinterpretation and redefinition of the boundaries between masculinity and femininity, the social division of men from women, the separation of some men from other men, and how gender comes to structure the operation of particular forms of management and organisation. Our discussion of masculinity is informed by an understanding of power as a social process that classifies, distinguishes and divides individuals from one another (Foucault, 1982), and reconstitutes masculine subjects through their attachment to a particular manner of rendering the world controllable and ordered.

Accepting Brittan's (1989) conception of 'multiple masculinities' (also Hearn, 1987), the paper argues that particular forms of masculinity are sustained, reproduced and privileged in work and within management practice. Through our discussion, we identify and describe two of these forms - 'paternalistic masculinity' and 'competitive masculinity'. While acknowledging a vast and complex literature on gender at work, we focus principally on those texts which provide an insight into the construction and reproduction of masculinity.

The paper is organised as follows: the first section offers an outline of some of the literatures on masculinity; the second gives a brief summary of the genesis of strategic imperatives within financial services in Britain. This analysis provides a backdrop for the third section in which we examine paternalistic managerial culture prior to the intervention of strategic imperatives. In common with strategic management, we identify this culture as one that describes a way of managing organisations grounded in a masculinist discourse which reflects and reinforces a 'man'- agerial prerogative that serves to order human productive capacities and rank individuals in accordance with their competitive competencies. Pointing to some of the tensions and contradictions that subjects experience in sustaining "the burdensome persona of masculinity" (Cockburn: 1983) from which there is little or no retreat, we hope to stimulate some debate on masculinist management practices, and the construction of masculinity in the workplace.

The following section elaborates on what is meant by the 'discourse of masculinism' and provides some introduction to the literatures on masculinity. It is to these that we now turn.

On masculinity and the discourse of masculinism

Before any discussion of the discourse of masculinism, some general comments are apposite by way of introduction to the topic of masculinity. Brittan (1989) draws a distinction between what he regards as three commonly confused terminologies in academic literatures and in general debate seeing these as analytically separable: masculinity, masculinism and patriarchy. Briefly, masculinity refers to the features of male behaviour that can change over time; masculinism denotes the ideology that naturalises and justifies men's domination over women; and patriarchy is the structure of unequal power relations sustained by this ideology (ibid:3-5). It is masculinity and masculinism we are concerned with here, rather than with patriarchy as their 'result' (see Walby, 1986, for example). For the moment, Brittan's distinction is a useful starting position in that it enables some basic points about masculinity to be made.

The first point is that where 'man' is a biological category, describing the genetically determined formation of flesh linked to certain reproductive capacities, 'masculinity' is not: together with a multitude of accompanying behavioural associations, it is rather an 'outcome' of socially generated ideas, behaviours and practices surrounding the group named men. And in turn, masculinity comes to inform those ideas, behaviours and practices in reciprocal relation. Some studies have attempted to identify and measure psychological traits of masculinity and femininity (e.g. Bem, 1974) where the explicit terms of reference are sex-roles linked to the make-up of men and women as biological categories. From this perspective, masculinity can be made quantifiable and individuals then ranked in accordance with the 'amount' of masculinity they possess. Our approach differs in seeking to study masculinity as a social construct, or how masculinity comes to be 'made', so to speak, as a continuing process within the social context. We are thus concerned with exploring how and in what way masculinity is constituted in certain settings at certain times, as part of a wider discussion of the dynamic process of gender relations, and where gender history is itself "lumpy" (Connell, 1987:149).

A second point is that masculinity is as such not 'fixed' but continually shifting, calling forth distinct behaviours in different chronological periods, and within the lifetime of individuals themselves. The lifespan of one person will encompass a number of experiences, disruptions and challenges in connection with certain facets of masculinity, for example in relation to youth, old age and parenthood. Masculinity then, is produced within history and culture: in terms of childcare for example, the media image of the "real man" in the 1990s is far more likely to be at least partially involved in rearing children than was his mid-Victorian or post-war counterpart. Therefore, masculinity is not some trans-historical 'essence'. The definition of what a "real man" is affects and is affected by prevailing political, economic and social conditions at any given time, and by the emergence of 'expert' disciplines or forms of knowledge (Foucault, 1970) about masculinity and men[5]. Weeks (1977, 1985) for example, charts the rise of homosexuality as a 'deviant sub-group' of masculinity, the emergence of which served not only to criminalise the behaviours described as homosexual but to denigrate and stigmatise those individuals thus categorised. In so doing, this historically specific discourse on sexuality, here in relation to homosexuality and homophobia, served to redefine and sustain the category of the normal man[6], explicitly delineate what 'proper men' did, and outline how "real men" should live their lives in the second half of the nineteenth century and beyond. Clearly then, if homosexuality is merely one variety or version of masculinity co-existing, albeit uneasily, with others we must accept the existence of a 'plurality of masculinities'.

Acknowledging this multiplicity, a third point is that forms of masculinity sustain themselves in contrast not only to one another, the gay in contrast to the 'straight' for example, but to femininity over which they are elevated (Moi, 1985). Although the possibilities vary greatly since masculinities find numerous permutations in history and at any one time, these are always in opposition to 'femininity', and the threat to masculinities which femininity suggests. In the common parlance of shop-floors, bar rooms and sports grounds, the language of public degradation, humiliation and routine put-down is at once explicitly heterosexual and misogynistic, where 'lesser men' become defined as "big-girls" and "pansies" (also Willis, op. cit.). Yet femininity is itself sustained in reciprocal relation to masculinity: it would be equally possible to re-work the above points with reference to femininity, to explore the cultural construction of predominant images and stereotypes of femininity (Vicinus, 1973) and the "real woman"[7], or to chart a history of the policing of women's lives and sexuality through the regulatory mechanisms of medicine, psychiatry and the law (see for example Webb-Johnson, 1925; Stopes, 1937). Suffice to note that varieties of masculinity are constructed in response to, and in relation with, prevailing forms and definitions of femininity.

Following from this and given its diversity, we cannot therefore speak of masculinity per se (also Hearn and Morgan, 1991) but only of 'multiple masculinities' (Brittan, op cit). This does not preclude any discussion of masculinity nor necessarily result in a collapse into relativism where there are as many masculinities as there are men. Rather, we suggest that masculinity may be examined on two levels: on one level, acknowledging its multiplicity, the term 'masculinity' may be deployed as a theoretical construct of academic study and debate, but one which imputes no trans- or a historical consistency to the experience and behaviours of all males. At another level, that of individual men, masculinity has significance and finds resonance for those whose experience of masculinity and of being a man is a very real source of anxiety (also Easthope, 1986; Seidler, 1989). Consequently, following Coleman (op cit:191) a fourth point is that from the standpoint of individual men, masculinity has to be achieved, worked at and accomplished moment by moment in the drive to attain a secure masculine identity and as part of what it means to be a "real man". Thus we make a distinction on the one hand between masculinity as an object of theory, and on the other, as the embodied experience of gendered identity.

Turning to Brittan's concept of masculinism, while masculinity may change over time, masculinism by contrast "remains in tact" (1989:6), bound up in the substance of male domination and the ideology that sustains it "giving primacy to the belief that gender is not negotiable" (op cit:4). Modifying his use of the term 'ideology', he notes that it is impossible to think of all men in general as conspiring to form a collective or 'class' in order to dominate or suppress women, and that men themselves are routinely dominated and exploited by other men. Yet as Brittan suggests, this does not of itself negate male domination. Although masculinity may be fluid and shifting, what remains constant is a set of gender relations underpinning social life in which 'the power of men' is assumed. It is therefore still possible to speak of masculinism as the continuous presence of male domination, itself bound up in the complex workings of sexual power relations (also Connell, 1987).

In talking of the 'discourse of masculinism', we add a number of qualifications to Brittan's conception. First, where masculinism justifies and naturalises male domination, we regard this domination occurring as **an effect** of the interplay of sexual power relations within and between particular practices, rather than as existing **a priori** to those relations and practices in which it is continually reconstituted. This is not to deny the very real material inequalities between men and women, or the vastly different life-chances of individuals within distinct structures of race and class. On the other hand, we do not see male domination as in every instant a social, political, economic or institutional inevitability, existing outside of the human practices and behaviours which continually maintain that domination.

Second, while it has remained historically constant, in the sense that as far as one may speculate there has always been some form of male domination, the discourses that constitute and sustain it continue to change. This change coincides with transformations around particular masculinities.

For example, images of the 'New Man' in the media and advertising suggest men can be caring and sensitive with respect to their partners and children, without threatening or 'losing' their masculinity. But far from reversing institutionalised male domination in marriage and the household, these 'new' ideas can be seen as facilitating the conditions within which individual men can come to acquire a few more masculinist 'brownie points' in the struggle to differentiate themselves from other men, and from women. Rather than overturning the unequal power relations between the sexes in relation to domestic work or childcare, the New Man image arguably opens up legitimate space for the colonisation and appropriation of those aspects of childcare which are the most rewarding and which offer immediate creative expression, couched in the language of enhancing men's masculinity and social prowess.

Third, relationships between individual men and women are obviously more complex than discussions of domination at an abstract level would suggest. Accepting the material and symbolic domination enshrined in for example, the institutions of marriage, the employment contract (Pateman, 1988) and the law (O'Donovan, 1985), we make a distinction between institutionalised domination of women by men, and the complex interplay of power relations occurring in examples of particular relationships (e.g. Pringle, 1989).

Acknowledging these caveats then, although forms of masculinity may change, masculinist practices have continued to sustain male domination throughout a long and diverse range of historical contexts. This is not to suggest that masculinity exhausts the social practices in which it is embedded - that everything is always and in every instance masculinist. Social relations are clearly more than their masculinist features. However, this paper focuses both on a shorter historical period and a narrower range of social relations than in the Marxist and radical feminist literatures on sexual divisions of labour (e.g., Barrett, 1984; Brenner and Ramas, 1984). But a restricted historical focus is pertinent to a discussion of gender and masculinity. Since the late 19th century, gender relations have become increasingly sexualised in the sense that there has been a proliferation of ways of thinking of, speaking about and classifying sexualities (Foucault, 1990). Indeed sexuality has come to define our very sense of what we are, our very identities, and how we are to understand ourselves. The thematic focus on management is also interesting because it is a sphere where the sexual, personal, erotic and intimate features of social relations are expected to be absent, or are denied (also Burrell, 1984). Yet while formally denied or displaced, intimate sexual and erotic interest is a continuous feature of everyday work relations (Hearn and Parkin, 1987).

For our purposes here, we focus on management as a set of practices reflecting and reinforcing masculinist modes of being which in turn create and sustain particular forms of masculinity. Having provided some analysis of masculinity and the discourse of masculinism, the paper now turns to an examination of the transition from paternalistic to strategic management. Rather than chart an exhaustive history of the development of the financial services, we highlight those aspects that are relevant to the organisations that have informed our research (see note 2).

From paternalism to strategic management

Paternalism in management can be seen to have arisen from the close links between philanthropy, religion and the early industrialists at the end of the last century (Weber, 1958). More concrete evidence is available concerning the tendency of the new mill owners in the 19th century and the bourgeois entrepreneurs of the 20th century to have non-conformist and quaker religious convictions in their concern for the physical, moral and spiritual well-being of their employees (e.g. Smiles, 1887). This involved a principle of 'industrial betterment' where workers were to be seen not merely as a factor of production but human beings whose social and moral welfare was to be promoted both in the workplace and in the community beyond (also Rose, 1990). Without necessarily questioning the virtues of industrial philanthropy, we are more concerned here with the specific content of paternalistic management that has come to be associated with it. In our view, paternalistic management is a way of controlling employees through the pretence of family imagery, thus providing space for the manager to act as 'caring' and 'protective' head of the industrial 'household'.

But whatever its early development, paternalism seems to have survived long beyond any potential pastoral roots both in industry and within state institutions. As we will argue, this may be partly at least because, as a form of management it helps to ease some of the difficulties that derive from hierarchical and sexual inequality as well as those troubles of a more existential character for individual masculine subjects (e.g., doubt, anxiety, guilt and uncertainty).

Very prevalent throughout much of the 20th century in both state institutions and work organisations, paternalism facilitates a reduction of the tension surrounding management and individual masculinities by simulating typically patriarchal, family-like relations where power is exercised for the 'good' of the recipient. Not unlike the father in the family, management is seen as the fount of all corporate wisdom and is believed to exercise its power always within the constraint of protecting and improving the lives of its employees. But the relief of tension is not only available to those who are subjected to paternalism. There is the obvious fact that the reduction of tension renders employees more compliant and predictable and therefore, the lives of those exercising the power more comfortable. However, equally important is the sense in which adopting a paternal role helps legitimise managerial prerogative both in the eyes of those who are 'protected' from the harsh reality of decision-making, and the decision-makers themselves.

Although perhaps particularly pervasive in small owner-managed companies within the industrial sector, a paternalistic style of management in financial services may be traced back historically to the friendly society and savings banks movements of the nineteenth century. Savings Banks and mutual insurance societies were distinct from proprietary or joint stock companies in the financial sector in sofar as they were managed and controlled by a small elite of 'the great and the good' who acted as guardians of their members' interests. This self-selected elite perceived its responsibility in terms of facilitating systems of 'self-help' where less privileged

134

citizens could establish for themselves a measure of security and stability through mechanisms of thrift and saving.

Since such organisations were unconstrained by the voting rights of shareholders, this elite group felt the need to develop some system of internal self-regulation and control. Consequently, membership of this elite tended to be based upon certain 'gentlemanly characteristics' (sic) derived from notions of social class acceptability supposedly indicative of high standards of personal conduct. The impact of this 'ethic of guardianship' with respect to the financial well being of customers, was one of projecting highly specific and narrowly defined duties upon employees, on the grounds that staff of a lower status and 'respectability' could not be trusted with the levels of social responsibility presumed to reside in high office.

Although the legacy of paternalism continues today in financial services, attempts to displace it by a more strategic mode of management are increasingly prevalent. As we see it, a reason for this displacement is the growing pre-eminence of problems of sales and marketing in a market where, broadly, the supply of products and services has come to exceed demand. In short, paternalistic management and its preoccupation with finding less coercive ways of managing the 'internal' problems of labour and production has begun to give way to a 'harsher' form of strategic manage-ment, where the problem to be managed is also 'external' to the organisation in the competitive sphere of distribution and consumption.

It has been argued that the genesis of strategic management can be traced back to mid-19th century American business (Hoskin, 1990), but it was not until after the second world war that the discourse and practice of strategy spread throughout a majority of industries and the larger business and non-business enterprises (Chandler, 1962; 1977; Bracker, 1980; Knights and Morgan, 1991).
However, the development of strategic management has been variable with respect to particular countries, industries, organisations and even specific specialisms within corporations (Knights et al., 1991). This uneven development is particularly significant with respect to UK financial services for strategic developments are comparatively recent in this sector by contrast

with manufacturing industry. Partly this is because the financial services have until recently enjoyed comparatively comfortable markets as a result either of cartel-like conditions in the case of banks, or fiscal privileges provided by successive governments in the example of life insurance companies and building societies. In addition post-war affluence, the comparative security of cashless paper or card transactions and the dramatic boom in domestic home ownership and house prices have all facilitated the growth and diversification of financial services.

For the banks these cosy conditions came to an abrupt end during the 1960s when the government's competition policy questioned the cartel-like arrangements operating in banking. This forced the banks to abandon the restrictive practices that had kept the cost of their services high and comparatively standardised between the 'big five'. As a result, inter-bank rivalries stimulated a competitive environment which has been further reinforced by more recent regulations and deregulations (e.g. the Building Societies Act, 1986; the Financial Services Act, 1986) affecting insurance, building societies and the City. Not only have banks faced competition with each other but the absolute size of the customer base has been subjected to some erosion as a result of competition for personal bank accounts from the building societies who are in a strong position to offer a wider range of services. The overall effect, however, has been to intensify competition in the market for personal financial services such as insurance, mortgages and other lines of credit[8]. Strategic management was quickly embraced as constituting the problems of the market and the environment in such a way as to then be able to offer itself as a solution.

Within the life insurance industry where we have also conducted research, the adoption of strategy has been even later and more limited. The comparatively late development of strategic management here was not so much the result of a cartel situation and oligopolistic markets. Rather, the market has been comfortable because of a number of conditions which are more or less unique to the life insurance sector. It has enjoyed a steady growth due partly to the increasing levels of excess income of large sections of the population, and the tax incentives to save through the insurance or pensions medium provided by the UK government. Also the industry's markets have experienced a degree of 'protection' by virtue of the fact that they were constructed by personal selling to a far greater degree than other markets[9]. In addition, the mutual structure of many UK life insurance companies has provided a degree of protection in that they are free both from the pressures of shareholders and those of aggressive predators stalking the capital markets for takeover opportunities. Finally the industry operated a commission agreement until quite recently which given the distribution system through privately owned broker outlets, has protected insurance companies from the full impact of competition (Knights et al., 1991).

Again, as with the banks, the complacency concerning the market has begun to erode as both existing general insurance companies, new more dynamic direct sales companies and foreign competitors have begun to enter what is seen as a comparatively profitable market. While the old established life companies have continued to enjoy steady growth, the rapid construction of a 'new' market in unit-linked contracts through aggressive selling and marketing and the greater competition following from a considerable expansion in the number of suppliers has shaken the industry. The market then has become 'a problem' and many companies have searched beyond their boundaries for ways of responding to the new competitive conditions.

But what is distinctive about strategic management as opposed to for example, paternalistic or bureaucratic systems which have preceded it? First, it has to be said that although a strategic approach may seek to displace earlier systems of management, rarely are they obliterated and indeed in the case of bureaucracy, they overlap such that there is a degree of mutual reinforcement. For as Hoskin (1990) argues, the genesis of the modern concept of strategy was coterminous with the development and transformation of the internal discourses and practices of organisations into a written recorded and calculable form. From this point of view, strategic management is grounded in the knowledge and power that makes it possible to control labour and the organisation of production. It could be accomplished when "everything and everyone was turned into writing, examined and rendered calculable" (ibid:23). In this sense, strategic management is bureaucratic in character. It involves quantifying, examining and grading both people and events whereupon they are brought readily within the disciplinary gaze and the techniques of surveillance of those exercising power and constituting knowledge in organisations.

Strategic management differs from conventional bureaucratic systems insofar as it involves extending the application of the techniques of recording and quantifying objectives and achievements to manage 'external' as well as 'internal' problems of the organisation. In post-war Britain at least, strategic management proliferated as problems in the 'environment' or 'the market' began to displace problems of internal production and administration. The impact of strategic management on financial services companies is resulting in numerous changes particularly in connection with the management of staff and relations with customers both existing and prospective. Although these implications vary within and between banks and insurance companies, there is a common link in that strategic management of the market usually involves a greater degree of intervention and planning around attempts to extend business to a broader range of financial services.

Section 2 has examined the character and conditions of the transition from paternalism to strategic management in financial services. Our concerns in this paper however, are less in the conventional implications of strategic management for business and competitive performance but in how it reflects, reinforces and constructs certain forms of masculinity and the gender relations in which they are embedded. Drawing on our experience of research in financial services (see Note 2), section 3 seeks to trace the ways in which these forms of management represent distinct manifestations of a masculinist discourse, and in turn, sustain predominant forms of masculinity.

Management, masculinity and manipulation

In general, paternalism can be seen as a way of managing that involves the exercise of power by senior staff who 'shield' subordinates from any decision-making responsibility. By contrast, once having designed a set of corporate and business plans, strategic management aims to 'cascade' decision-making responsibility down the hierarchy so as to engage staff at various levels in the business. Whereas staff in paternalist companies are simply expected to execute the decisions handed down to them from 'on high', the adoption of strategic management imposes demands upon all members of the organisation to be more directly concerned with the immediate success of particular business initiatives, and the longer term survival and strength of the overall enterprise. But it is our purpose here to suggest that paternalistic and strategic management are of much broader significance than as mere 'devices' by which business objectives can be achieved. The implications of this approach lead us into the field of masculinity, gender and power, since both paternalism and strategic management involve highly particular ways of managing social relations. More specifically, they have the effect of rendering these relations less problematic - by displacing or dissimulating intimacy, sexuality and hierarchy. The following paragraphs develop this theme first with respect to paternalism, and then in relation to strategic management.

With regard to intimacy, in part by feigning family imagery (Bradley, 1986:65), paternalism attempts to delineate the extent and type of intimacy, and the space in which it is permitted[10]. Conducted within what, on the surface, appear pleasant and 'gentlemanly' (sic) relations, this behaviour not only renders authority less blatant and severe, but provides those exercising it with an opportunity to conceal their own foibles and weaknesses behind the formal requirements of the 'informal' paternal role. In distancing the individual from the superior/subordinate role which he or she occupies, it can therefore 'protect' individuals from potential personal intimacy, especially that of a sexual character to which all relations are subject. Interactions can thereby be managed as occurring between depersonalised layers in an organisational hierarchy, rather than as interactions amongst embodied human subjects.

With respect to sexuality, paternalism exists in relation of complex mutual interdependence and elaboration. As has been suggested above, paternalism can act as a mechanism for shielding the paternalist from explicit or covert sexual intimacy. But at the same time, paternalism actively constructs sexuality and can invite sexual intimacy whilst simultaneously, giving the appearance of denying or preventing it. Here we follow Hearn et al (1989: 13) in broadening the definition of sexuality to see it as an ordinary and frequent public process rather than an extraordinary feature of private life, and also to see sexuality as one aspect of an all-pervasive 'politics of the body' rather than a separate, discrete set of practices. In so doing, we define sexuality as being a range of behaviours and practices "from feelings to flirtations to sexual acts, accomplished willingly, unwillingly or forcibly by those involved" (Hearn et al 1989:13)[11]. Thus, the separateness and distance sought between the paternalist and the subordinate can, in itself, be sexual[12].

Subordinates may voluntarily submit to paternalistic managers for, as some writers have suggested (e.g. Pringle, 1989; Benjamin, 1980), at one level, submission is itself intimately related to pleasure and desire. From this perspective, paternalism can be seen to result in, or indeed be articulated through, the themes of control and submission, mastery and domination. In turn these are enmeshed in fantasy, desire and erotic pleasure, and thus, are themselves sexual (Benjamin, 1980, 1983). Paternalism at once acts to sustain and reconstitute the sexual positioning (sic) of both parties, the sexually charged nature of the interaction, and the sexuality of the workplace more generally (cf Burrell, 1984). In so doing, paternalism constitutes sexuality in such a way as to reinforce and provide confirmation for the behaviour that can be characterised as paternalistic.

In relation to hierarchy, paternalism seeks to generate a relation of trust through the pretence of equality for the purpose of securing instrumental gain. Such trust is more readily sustained given that the 'gentlemanly relations' alluded to earlier in part involves a tacit agreement to provide lifetime employment in exchange for moral rectitude by the employee. In itself an exercise of power, paternalism gives the illusion ultimately of displacing power. It is an "economy of power" (Foucault, 1980) in that the dignity of the subordinate appears to remain in tact at the same time as he or she is manipulated, enabling hierarchical interactions to occur as if they were personal, and so softening their coercive impact without damaging the effectiveness of their control.

As in the case of paternalism we find that strategic management displaces or dissimulates intimacy, sexuality and hierarchy. Within strategic management, work becomes defined as a rational and depersonalised enterprise where there is minimal space for interpersonal contact beyond the 'purposive intimacy' geared towards realising corporate objectives. In the organisations we have studied for example, varieties of 'Team Building' aim to "energise" workforces and determine a specific set of social relations between and within work groups which attempts to re-engage individuals in terms of company loyalty and commonality of purpose (Kerfoot and Knights, 1990). In this way, Team Building and similar human resource management programmes elsewhere can be summarised as an attempt to elicit commitment to corporate objectives of profitability under the rubric of success and efficiency by means of 'synthetic sociability'. In these instances management in effect, seeks to manipulate intimacy within social relations and channel it in the direction of achieving corporate goals. Intimacy thus becomes reconstituted and transformed into purposive-rational action.

With reference to sexuality, strategic management can be seen as an attempt to 'desexualise' organisations since overtly or explicitly sexual behaviours would detract from the achievement of business goals. This is not too distinct from the way in which bureaucratic management functions for the "suppression of sexuality is one of the first tasks the bureaucracy sets itself" (Bede, 1907 quoted in Burrell, 1984:98). A difference is that in contrast to bureaucracy where sexual relations contradict the demands of an impersonal, rule-based order, strategic management seeks to channel energies that might be 'dissipated' in sexual encounters into activities designed to accomplish organisational objectives. But while bureaucracy segregates sex, emotion and the 'personal' from the functionary displacing it onto the 'private' sphere, strategic management could be said to utilise sexuality in its operation: where the strategic goals of the organisation become objects of conquest, and where the act of conquering, in and of itself, becomes its own validation.

In relation to hierarchy, strategic management both emphasises and de-emphasises differential power and status, simultaneously individualising and collectivising the workforce. On the one hand, by removing layers of managerial authority from the chain of command, strategic management generates the appearance of 'flattening' hierarchical structures. Yet on the other, it elevates and reinforces hierarchical distinctions through encouraging career and corporate success by means of individual competition. In attempting to involve staff in collective commitment to the enterprise, this flattening of the hierarchy in effect relocates managerial control 'at the heart' of the workgroup, for responsibility and accountability are shifted down to lower hierarchy employees (Kerfoot, 1990). This has the effect of individualising staff since each member of the workgroup is personally responsible for a given task or stage of production, and is thereby thrown back on their own resources in the quest for its achievement. At the same time, strategic management seeks to transform organisational culture so as to generate a collective loyalty and a corporate identity. We have suggested that both paternalism and strategic management constitute intimacy, sexuality and hierarchy in distinctive ways; it is now important to link these modes of management to the predominant forms of masculinity sustained by them.

As a mode of management, paternalistic practices can be seen as both producing and informed by a 19th century middle-class conception of masculinity in which men were expected to behave with quiet detachment in accordance with 'gentlemanly' principles. Because managerial positions were largely ascribed on the basis of seniority, social privilege and a 'natural right to govern', paternalists need not engage themselves in the rough and tumble of everyday struggles for power; indeed, these were to be avoided as unseemly and undignified. In so far as paternalists are never under threat of their position, this form of masculinity reflects and reproduces a self-satisfied complacency that remains secure as long as external competition is absent. In terms of gender relations, this 'paternalistic masculinity' elevates its womenfolk to the status of frail and rarefied beings to be protected from the corruptive influence and base desires of humanity[13]. Accordingly, the notion of "respectable womanhood" (Nead, 1988) is sustained by placing women

women on a pedestal of 'other-worldliness' that seeks to ensure their sexual and moral purity. In effect, paternalistic masculinity protects women from the harsh world of business and politics (Nead, ibid; Jeffreys, 1985) not for reasons of perceiving them to be incompetent, but because they are seen as too angelic or 'precious' to be exposed to the indignities and unpleasantries of the 'real world'.

By contrast, we identify strategic management with a variety of masculinity corresponding to Seidler's (1989) semi-autobiographical account of contemporary masculinity - a way of relating to the world wherein everything becomes an object of and for control. He describes this form of control as one that equates with reason, logic and rational process; generates and sustains a hierarchy imbued with instrumentalism, careerism and the language of 'success'; stimulates competition linked to decisive action, 'productivism' and risk-taking; and renders sexual and bodily presence manifest through physicality, posture, movement and speech (Seidler, ibid: also Bologh, 1990). It is these features we identify with the 'competitive masculinity' produced and sustained by strategic management. In the organisational sites where our research has taken place, competitive masculinity serves to rank individuals in terms of their capacity to display attributes of control over the definition of the reality of events, and to secure the compliance of others with regard to that definition. Whereas the masculinity sustained through and by paternalism is self-assured and thereby unconcerned with the struggle for achievement, competitive masculinity is caught in ceaseless striving for material and symbolic success, and where conquest and domination become exalted as ways of relating to the world.

Since competitive masculinity is neither self-contained nor self-assured, the successful validation of individual competencies also requires continuous confirmation from others. But the perceptions of others can never be firmly predicted or controlled. Consequently, this form of masculinity is always precarious and insecure, constantly preoccupied with purposive action in the drive to be 'in control'. Yet control is always tantalisingly out of reach, throwing competitive masculinity back on itself in ever more intensified and spiralling efforts to secure that control.

In turn this demands a degree of self-discipline, self-repression and self-control in the continuous pursuit of success, where the world presents itself as a never-ending series of challenges and conquests (Seidler, 1989: 44-71).

Accordingly, competitive masculinity transforms individuals into subjects who not only dominate others, but also ultimately, themselves[14]. At the level of embodied experience then, competitive masculinity can result in the position whereby individuals feel 'driven' for no discernable reason, other than as a part of what it means, and how it feels, to subscribe to an ideal of competence, and where the display of vulnerability is to threaten the image of that competence. This may translate into the denial or suppression of emotionality, fear and uncertainty; the denial of human intimacy or suppression of embodied experiences of pleasure and desire; and the denial of 'contented passivity' as an alternative mode of engaging with the world (Burrell, 1990). By providing continuous rationalisations (e.g. breadwinner responsibilities, financial security, career promotion, status and success) which account for this "bias for action" (Burrell, 1990:4), individuals thus create and sustain the conditions under which they struggle "to live up to this ideal of themselves" (Seidler, op cit:147).

This self-validation produces the conditions of subordination of other masculinities, and where women and 'lesser men' feature as objects of psychological, intellectual, emotional and sexual conquest. Since competitive masculinity secures ultimate validation through conquest of the 'other' outside of itself, it provides no retreat or 'safe haven'. Rather, individuals are caught in a circle of securing themselves through presenting a successful image to others. But the cost of maintaining this facade can run high; a price is anxiety and fear, of their own sexuality, of 'real' intimacy and of those masculinities and femininities which can be a threat in representing an open manifestation of sexuality and intimacy.

Alongside the connection with dominance and control, arguably the most significant feature of competitive masculinity is its explicit heterosexualism, serving to close off alternative sexualities. Here we subscribe to Carrigan et al's description of "hegemonic masculinity not as 'the male role', but a particular variety of masculinity to which others -

144

among them young and effeminate as well as gay men - are subordinated" (Carrigan et al, 1985:587). Moreover while the "hegemonic model" is privileged within and by competitive masculinity, clearly not all men exhibit to the same degree or with the same intensity, the behavioural characteristics sustained by it. In terms of masculinity at the level of individuals therefore, this can exclude some men as much as it includes others. In turn, exclusion can have the effect of generating considerable tension and insecurity, since the symbolic significance of being excluded for example from teams in sport, employment or promotion at work, or 'normal' sexuality, is threatening to this masculine identity, further intensifying its precariousness.

Summary and Conclusion

This paper has analysed two modes of management practice in terms of the particular yet predominant forms of masculinity sustained by them. We see different management practices as sustaining and recreating varying forms of masculinity in dynamic process, where management is but one site of its reproduction. In turn, those masculinities reproduce the modes of management in which they are embedded. As a historically contingent feature of social life, masculinity is visible in distinct manifestations under different modes of management: we have identified two such manifestations, describing these as 'paternalistic' and 'competitive' masculinity.

Section one introduced the topics of masculinity and the 'discourse of masculinism'. We see this discourse as justifying and naturalising male domination and hierarchy, where domination and hierarchy occur here as an effect of the interplay of sexual power relations in management. Section two described the transition from paternalistic to strategic management in financial services, and how this shift in management 'styles' created the conditions under which competitive masculinity could flourish and challenge alternative forms of masculinity. Although clearly not exhaustive of systems of management, the choice of our examples of paternalistic and strategic management was shaped by the prevalence of these within our research sites.

Our purpose was not to suggest that paternalism and strategic management exist as discrete entities at any one time, rather, the two overlap and co-exist. Similarly, a general shift in the predominance of a particular form of masculinity does not signal its overall demise: as we have suggested, masculinities exist in a multiplicity of guises in different historical periods.

Section three explored 'paternalistic' and 'competitive' masculinity in relation to intimacy, sexuality and hierarchy, both in terms of managing organisations, and as ways of managing social relations on the part of individuals. The form of masculinity that sustains and is produced by paternalistic management gives the appearance of displacing the emotional and sexual aspects of social relations by 'treating' others as in need of care and protection. Yet in so doing, it reconstructs the emotional and sexual aspects of those relations in a particular way, reproducing these in hierarchical form. By contrast, the competitive masculinity generated within strategic management involves an attachment to a disembodied and emotionally estranged conception of reason, where power, strength, and self-validation equate with the successful demonstration of individual competencies in subordinating and conquering a multiplicity of tasks in the real world. At the same time, competitive masculinity can generate tension in relations with others since the 'other' becomes either an object of conquest or a subject of competition in the struggle to secure the self.

Although at one level paternalistic and competitive masculinities are a manifestation of predominant forms of management, they are at another level, devices for managing some of the tensions that are an effect of masculinity. These tensions include, for example, those of sexuality, sexual conquest and the indignity that stems from the embodied experience of subordination and dependence in a culture that emphasises male dominance and individual autonomy (Reimer, op cit; Willis, 1977). Yet as 'positive' techniques for managing lives, both paternalistic and competitive masculinity have the effect of constituting subjects with minimal resources for expressing feelings and emotions, and offer little vocabulary to acknowledge or describe weakness and failure. In pointing to some of the tensions and contradictions that subjects experience in relating to masculinity at work, we want to

146

encourage a challenge to forms of management whose self-defeating practices are further concealed by masculinist rationalisations.

Notes

1.   Published in *Journal of Management Studies*, Vol. 30, No. 4. 1993.

2.   We acknowledge the TSB funded Financial Services Research Centre at UMIST for the financial support provided during the preparation of this paper. We also acknowledge our colleagues Fergus Murray and Theo Vurdubakis, and the anonymous reviewers of JMS for their comments on an earlier draft of this paper.

3.   The very constitution of banking, credit and insurance markets as personal financial services was both a condition and consequence of the new entrepreneurialism that was stimulating more strategic approaches to management within the industry at this time. In this paper we do not wish to discuss the complexities of these changes (see Knights et al 1991) so much as merely to note them.

4.   Our research has taken the form of a sectoral analysis of financial services comprising a series of diverse studies of, for example, strategic management, state and self-regulation, management control, information technology, and gender and the labour process. It has also involved two detailed case studies of a bank and an insurance company that developed out of a 19th century middle-class philanthropic practices. Over a period of four years our research methods have included in-depth interviews, participant observation, documentary research, and observation of several decision-making meetings. The quality of research access enabled the authors to interview managers, supervisory and clerical staff (many on more than one occasion), to attend departmental and senior management meetings, and to observe the progress of special projects as well as the cycles of operational activity.

5.   See also Nead (1988) on the construction and reconstruction of femininity and 'womanhood' in artistic representation around the Victorian period in Britain.

6.   See Krafft-Ebbing (1866) on homosexuality, for example.

7.   See for example Russell Hochschild (1983:162-184) on the "nurturing proto-mother" and the "sex queen" figures of femininity in a study of airline cabin staff, and Dally (1982) on the regulatory effects of the ideal of motherhood during the nineteenth and twentieth centuries.

8.   There are a number of other conditions which have stimulated this move towards the consumer of personal financial services not least of which, in the case of the banks, has been the disastrous experiences of lending to less

developed countries (LDC's) and, more recently, poor returns on corporate lending.

9.   All markets are, of course, constructed but none rely for business so heavily on the personal sales interview as life insurance. So, for example, banks have traditionally traded primarily on the 'security' and convenience of holding bank accounts although they have clearly benefited substantially from large corporations preferring to transfer salary payments to employees' bank accounts. Insofar as they have sought to intervene more actively to construct a market, banks have resorted to mass advertising. Life insurance companies have themselves begun to use mass advertising but this has been relatively late in the day and has rarely acted as a substitute as opposed to a support for personal selling.

10.   Clearly, we would acknowledge that paternalism operates outside of organizations in a more generalised way as an option for the management or control of any social interaction. In this text however, having noted the distinction between paternalism and paternalistic management, we choose to focus on the workplace as a site in which paternalism finds concrete expression in management practices.

11.   See also Hearn and Parkin (1987) on the relations of mutual interconstitution of sexuality and organisations, and the ways in which organisations 'direct' and construct sexualities more generally.

12.   See also Pringle (1989) on the boss/secretary relationship.

13.   For example, Cohn (1986) in his discussion of the process of occupational sex-typing in the British General Post Office (GPO), describes the physical segregation of women clerical workers, and the procedure whereby orders to remain office-bound were issued to male workers at times when "the ladies" were likely to pass through areas of mens gaze. On the 'social purity' of women see for example, Jeffreys (1985) and Nead (1988).

14.   See also Frank (1991: 69-79) on the construction of the 'dominating body' and masculinity.

References

Barrett, M. (1980), *Womens Oppression Today: Problems in Marxist Feminist Analysis*, London, Verso.

Bede, (1907), *Bede's Ecclesiastical History of England*, Ed. J. A. Giles, London, Bell.

Bem, S. (1974), 'The Measurement of Psychological Androgyny', *Journal of Clinical Psychology*, Vol. 42, No. 2, pp.155-162.

Benjamin, J. (1980), 'The Bonds of Love: Rational Violence and Erotic Domination', *Feminist Studies*, Vol. 6, No. 1, pp. 144-174.

Benjamin, J. (1983), 'Master and Slave: The Fantasy of Erotic Domination' in: A. Snitow, C. Stansell, and S. Thompson, (eds.), *Powers of Desire: The Politics of Sexuality*, New York, Monthly Review Press.

Bologh, R. W. (1990), *Love or Greatness: Max Weber and Masculine Thinking - A Femininst Inquiry*, London, Unwin Hyman.

Bracker, Jay (1980), 'The Historical Development of the Strategic Management Concept', *Academy of Management Review*, 5/2: 219-224.

Bradley, H. (1986), 'Technological Change, Management Strategies and the Development of Gender-Based Job Segregation' in: D. Knights, and H. Willmott, (eds.) *Gender and the Labour Process*, Aldershot, Gower.

Brenner, J. and M. Ramas, (1984), 'Rethinking Women's Oppression', *New Left Review*, No. 144, pp. 33-71.

Brittan, A. (1989), *Masculinity and Power*, Oxford, Blackwell.

Burrell, G (1984), 'Sex and Organizational Analysis', *Organization Studies*. 5/2:97-118.

Burrell, G (1990), 'The Organisation of Pleasure' unpublished working paper, University of Warwick, November, 1990.

Carrigan, T., R.W. Connell, and J. Lee, (1985), 'Toward a New Sociology of Masculinity', *Theory and Society*, Vol. 14, No. 5, pp. 551-604.

Chandler, A. D. (1962), *Strategy and Structure*, Cambridge, Mass., MIT Press.

Chandler, A. D. (1977), *The Visible Hand: the Managerial Revolution in American Business*, London, Harvard University Press.

Cockburn, C. (1983), 'Masculinity, the Left and Feminism' in: R. Chapman, and J. Rutherford, (eds.) *Male Order: Unwrapping Masculinity*, pp. 309-329. London, Lawrence Wishart.

Cohn, S. (1986), *The Proces of Occupational Sex-Typing*, Philadelphia, Temple.

Connell, R. W. (1983), *Which way is Up?: Essays on Sex, Class and Culture*. Sydney, Allen and Unwin.

Connell, R. W. (1987), *Gender and Power: Society, the Person and Sexual Politics*. Oxford, Polity/Blackwell Books.

Coleman, W. (1991), 'Doing Masculinity/ Doing Theory' in: J. Hearn, and D. Morgan, *Men, Masculinities and Social Theory*, London, Unwin Hyman.

Collinson, D.L. (1988), 'Engineering Humour: Masculinity, Joking and Conflict in Shopfloor Relations', *Organization Studies*, Vol. 9, No. 2., pp. 181-199.

Dally, A. (1982), *Inventing Motherhood: the Consequences of an Ideal*, London, Burnett Books.

Easthope, A. (1986), *What a Man's Gotta Do: the Masculine Myth in Popular Culture*, Paladin, London.

Filby, M. (1991), '"The figures, the personality and the bums": gender, sexuality and service work in the retail betting industry'. Unpublished paper given at the 9th *UMIST/Aston conference on the Organisation and Control of the Labour Process*.

Foucault, M (1970), *The Order of Things*, London, Tavistock.

Foucault, M. (1980), *Power/Knowledge*, Ed. Gordon, C., Brighton, Harvester.

Foucault, M. (1982), 'The Subject and Power' in: Dreyfus, H. L. and Rabinow, P. *Michel Foucault: From Structuralism to Hermeneutics*, Brighton, Harvester.

Foucault, M. (1990), *The History of Sexualty: Volume One*, Harmondsworth, Penguin.

Frank, A. (1991), 'For a Sociology of the Body: An Analytical Review' in: *The Body: Social Process and Cultural Theory*, London, Sage.

Hearn, J. (1987), *The Gender of Oppression: Men, Masculinity and the Critique of Marxism*, Brighton, Wheatsheaf.

Hearn, J. and W. Parkin, (1987), *Sex at Work: the Power and Paradox of Organisation Sexuality*, Brighton, Wheatsheaf.

Hearn, J., D.L. Sheppard, P. Tancred-Sheriff, and G. Burrell, (1989), *The Sexuality of Organisation*, London, Sage.

Hearn, J. and D. Morgan, (eds.) (1991), *Men, Masculinities and Social Theory*, London, Unwin Hyman.

Hoskin K. (1990), 'Using History to understand Theory: A Re-Consideration of the Historical Genesis of "Strategy"' paper delivered at the *EIASM Workshop on Strategy, Accounting and Control*, Venice, October.

Jeffreys, S. (1985), *The Spinster and Her Enemies: Feminism and Sexuality 1880-1930*, London, Pandora.

Kerfoot, D. (1990), '"Getting the Right Attitude": Employee Participation, Teamworking and Control at Seraglio', *Unpublished working paper*, Manchester School of Management, UMIST.

Kerfoot, D. and D. Knights, (1991), 'Human Resource Management and the Gendered Terrains of Paternalism' paper presented at the *Group for Anthropology in Policy and Practice Conference*, Swansea University, January.

Knights, D. and G. Morgan, (1991), 'Corporate Strategy, Organizations and Subjectivity: A Critique', *Organization Studies*, 12/2: 251-273.

Knights, D., G. Morgan, and F. Murray, (1991), 'Corporate Strategy, Financial Services and Information Technology' Paper delivered at the *ESRC PICT Conference Wakefield*, Yorkshire, 20-22nd March.

Krafft-Ebing, R. von (1866/1965), *Psychopathia Sexualis*, New York, Paperback Library.

Moi, T. (1985), *Sexual/Textual Politics: Feminist Literary Theory*, London, Routledge.

Nead, L. (1988), *Myths of Sexuality: Representatioons of Women in Victorian Britain*, Oxford, Blackwell.

O'Donovan, K. (1985), *Sexual Divisions in Law*, London, Weidenfeld and Nicholson.

Pateman, C. (1988), *The Sexual Contract*, Oxford, Polity/Blackwell.

Pollert, A. (1981), *Girls, Wives and Factory Lives*, London, Macmillan.

Pringle, R. (1989), 'Bureaucracy, Rationality and Sexuality: The Case of Secretaries' in: Hearn, J. et al (eds.) *The Sexuality of Organisation*, London, Sage.

Pringle, R. (1990), *Secretaries Talk: Sexuality, Power and Work*, London, Verso.

Riemer, J.W., (1979), *Hard Hats: The Work World of Construction Workers*, London, Sage.

Rose, N. (1990), *Governing the Soul: The Social Shaping of the Private Self*, London, Routledge.

Russell Hochschild, A. (1983), *The Managed Heart: Commercialization of Human Feeling*, California, University of California Press.

Seidler, V.J. (1989), *Rediscovering Masculinity: Reason, Language and Sexuality.* London, Routledge.

Smiles, Samuel (1887), *Life and Labour: Or Characteristics of Men of Industry, Culture and Genious*, London, John Murray.

Stopes, M.C. (1937), *Married Love*, London, Putnam Press.

Vicinus, M. (ed.) (1973), *Suffer and be Still: Women in the Victorian Age.* Bloomimgton, USA, Indiana University Press.

Walby, S. (1986), *Patriarchy at Work.* Cambridge: Polity.

Webb-Johnson, C. (1925), *Woman's Health and Happiness*, London, Methuen.

Weber, M (1958), *The Protestant Ethic and the Spirit of Capitalism.* New York: Wiley.

Weeks, J. (1977), *Coming Out.* London, Quartet Books.

Weeks, J. (1985), *Sexuality and its Discontents*, London, Routledge and Kegan Paul.

Willis, P. (1977), *Learning to Labour: How Working Class Kids Get Working Class Jobs*, Farnborough, Saxon House.

6   Gendered Structures in Organizations

Kea G. Tijdens

Department of Comparative Population and Gender Economics
Faculty of Economics and Econometrics
University of Amsterdam, the Netherlands

Women's work and men's work is highly segregated. Three forms of sex segregation can be distinguished in the labour force: industrial, occupational and hierarchical. Industrial segregation refers to the phenomena whereby men outnumber women for instance in the manufacturing industry, while the opposite holds true for the service sector. Occupational segregation means the unequal distribution of women and men over occupations compared to women's share in the labour force. Hierarchical segregation is the unequal distribution of women and men over job levels. Sex segregation is explained by several theories (see e.g. Rosenfeld 1984; Reskin 1984;, Reskin & Hartmann 1986). In human capital theories, in status attainment theories, and in socialization theories, women's labour supply is seen as the main cause of segregation. Employers' demand behaviour is considered the main cause of segregation in economic theories of discrimination, in statistical discrimination theories, and in feminist theories on patriarchism. Most theories focus on occupational segregation, some on hierarchical segregation and only a few on industrial segregation. Hardly any theories exist on interwoven mechanisms between the three forms of sex segregation.

Segregation ratios tend to be higher at disaggregated levels of labour force analysis. This applies especially for occupational segregation which has been investigated for the US (Bielby & Baron 1984), for Sweden (Jonung 1985), and for The Netherlands (Tijdens 1990). To analyze the interweave of segregational forms organizations - a low disaggregated level - are a proper locus for analysis. This chapter focuses on the three forms of sex segregation in organizations, comparable to the three forms in the labour force as a whole, i.e. departmental, job and hierarchical segregation. The intertwining of these three forms is referred to as the gendered structure in an organization. The main proposition is: how are job segregation, hierarchical segregation, and departmental segregation related to each other? The next section summarizes previous empirical findings and section three provides a theoretical framework. Hypotheses, research method and data are provided in the following four. An overview of female office workers in manufacturing industry -the group under study- is given in section five. Results are presented in sections six and seven. The last section contains the conclusions.

Gendered structures in organizations

Gendered practices in organizations include organizational culture, power assignment, decision-making, etc.. Here, the study of gendered practices is limited to the three forms of sex segregation in organizations, called collectively gendered structures in organizations. This section contains an overview of the empirical findings on gendered structures in organizations. The relationship between the three forms of segregation has only been studied in a few cases, most research focuses on explanations for segregation or on its impact.

Job segregation in the work place is much higher than could be concluded from the overall figures on occupational segregation. In Great Britain, 63% of women work in jobs performed by women exclusively, and 80% of men work in exclusively 'male' jobs (Martin & Roberts 1984). In Canada, the percentage of women in female-dominated jobs is also less than the percentage of men in male-dominated jobs (Chaykowski & Currie 1992). These figures also indicate that women are less likely to enter male jobs than vice versa. Processes of social exclusion are gender biased. Research showed

154

that women's integration in male-dominated police forces caused more problems than men's integration in female-dominated nursing teams in hospitals (Ott 1985).

Much attention has been paid to the proportion of minorities within groups and the structuring of mutual social relationships within groups (Kanter 1977). Kanter did not acknowledge sex biases in the social relationships, whereas Yoder (1991) states that the minority's behaviour depends very much on the status category he or she belongs to in relation to the majority's status category. However, this applies to special groups, because the majority of workers have colleagues of the same sex only. In Finland, 66% of women and 73% of men work in groups which are composed of one sex (Kauppinen et al. 1988). In the US, the corresponding figure for women is 54% and 70% for men (Treiman & Hartmann 1981).

Some research has been done on the relationship between occupational and departmental segregation. Barker & Downing (1980) argue that women in unskilled or semi-skilled clerical jobs work more often in female-dominated departments, whereas skilled secretaries are likely to work in isolation in male-dominated departments where they have few contacts with their colleagues. Relationships between women's share in organizations and departmental or job segregation have also been studied. If women's share in organizations increases, the chance that they will occupy integrated jobs and/or be employed in integrated departments also increases, but if women's share increases, it is also likely that female-dominated departments emerge (Bielby & Baron 1984).

The impact of occupational segregation on wages has been studied at length. Women in female-dominated jobs earn 6-15% less than women with the same characteristics in other occupations (Sorensen 1989). In the competition-segregation debate on the relationship between labour force composition and wages in occupational groups, a discussion arose on whether the entrance of subordinate groups into occupations would depress the relative income level of the majority, or whether minority groups would not enter due to exclusionary practices, resulting in perfect wage competition within groups (Semyonov & Lewin-Epstein 1989). Effects of marital and parental history on women's wages are weakest in female-dominated occupations, stronger in integrated occupations, and strongest in male-dominated occupations (Peterson 1989). The wage implications of departmental segregation have been investigated by Chaykowski & Currie (1992). Their findings show that workers in predominantly female bargaining units have more generous leave provisions, but are less likely to have pension coverage than workers in similar predominantly male bargaining units. Finally, industrial segregation explains the magnitude of the gender gap in health insurance coverage in the US (Perman & Stevens 1989).

To summarize, empirical findings show that in organizations women and men are highly segregated along occupational lines as well as along departmental or group lines. Due to exclusionary practices, men work more often in male-only groups than women. Occupational segregation is related to sex-related wage differences; on average women earn less than men, on average women in female-dominated occupations earn less than women in other occupations, and female-dominated departments have more generous leave provisions but less pension coverage than male-dominated departments. Though the mutual relationship between the three forms has not been studied as such, the effects of segregation have been studied to a large extent.

Theorizing segregation in organizations

In organizations three types of sex segregation have been distinguished; departmental or group segregation, job or occupational segregation, and hierarchical or grade segregation. The actors involved in the segregation processes are employers, predominantly male, male employees and their organizations, either trade unions or professional bodies, and female employees and their organizations. There are conflicting interests in the segregation processes among and between the actors. Let us look at these actors.

Employers' behaviour is characterized by conflicting rationalisms. Women's wages are lower than men's, thus employers prefer women due to lower wage cost. This would imply gender-based wage and employment competition. However, occupational boundaries impede general competition. If for wage policy reasons employers intend to substitute men's labour with women's labour, these occupational boundaries need to be broken down. However, male workers can organize themselves against substitution by strengthening occupational lines. On the other hand, female workers can organize themselves and demand equal pay for equal work by breaking down occupational boundaries. Moreover, occupational boundaries have to be reinforced if the clients of the organization in question prefer stereotyped jobs according to gender. Thus, by reinforcing segregation, employers avoid vulnerability to labour unrest among male workers or client dissatisfaction, but at the same time this limits their possibilities of replacement and they would not meet female workers' demands.

Traditionally, male employees' interests in segregation also have been dual. On the one hand, women's low wages could lead to gender-related wage and employment competition that would benefit women. Male employees could react in two ways, either by demanding higher wages for women agreeing to equal pay for equal work, or they could try to keep women out of their jobs to prevent downward wage pulls. While most unions support equal pay and equal allowances, male employees' strategies in the work place concentrate mainly on exclusion practices. Male employees' strategies also concentrate on subordinating women at work, thus establishing home and social hierarchical segregation also in the work place. That is why women are not likely to supervise men (Nieva & Gutek 1981). These strategies also include sexual harassment as women in male-dominated occupations report sexual harassment much often than women in female-dominated occupations (Gutek & Cohen 1987).

Female employees' strategies for desegregation have been twofold. Breaking through the glass ceiling and forcing one's way into male-only occupations in higher grades has been a dominant strategy for many years. Upgrading female-dominated occupations by means of comparable worth has been a strategy developed more recently.

Hypotheses, research method and data

How do the three forms of sex segregation interlock in organizations? Job segregation does not necessarily imply hierarchical segregation because women might have different jobs than men, but in the same grades. There are also no obvious reasons why job segregation should be related to departmental segregation. Due to employers' strategies on division of labour female-dominated jobs could be concentrated in female-dominated departments, and the same could apply for men. In that case, women working in male-dominated departments would be likely to work in male-dominated jobs. But the opposite hypothesis can also be stated; women in male-dominated departments are likely to work in female-dominated jobs, due to segregation processes in departments. And what about the relationship between job segregation and hierarchical segregation? Is hierarchical segregation related to either occupations or departments? In this chapter the interlocking of departmental, job and hierarchical segregation in organizations is investigated. The following hypotheses underpin this focus:

1)   For the relationship between departmental and hierarchical segregation, it is first hypothesized that departments are supervised by their own sex. Thus, male-dominated departments are supervised by men and female-dominated departments by women. The second hypothesis states that female supervisors are supervised by men, thus introducing hierarchical segregation one level above work floor departments.

2)   For the relationship between departmental and occupational segregation, it is first hypothesized that male-dominated jobs are concentrated in male-dominated departments and female-dominated occupations are concentrated in female-dominated departments. If job segregation does not coincide fully with departmental segregation, two hypothesis can be made. First, women in male-dominated departments work in female-dominated occupations. Second, less skilled occupations are concentrated in female-dominated departments and skilled occupations are concentrated in male-dominated departments.

158

3) For the relationship between job segregation and hierarchical segregation, it is hypothesized that male-dominated jobs are supervised by men, and female-dominated occupations by women.

The analysis is based on a questionnaire among female office workers in Dutch manufacturing industry and carried out in 1991 under the auspices of the Industrial Workers Union FNV (Tijdens & Goudswaard 1992). Traditionally, the union is oriented towards blue-collar workers, but they are also expected to represent white-collar workers in manufacturing offices. The survey aimed to fill a lack of knowledge about this group. A few thousand questionnaires were sent to union members throughout the country who had agreed to distribute the questionnaire among female office workers at their firm or plant. Because some respondents had non-office jobs, 1,264 questionnaires could be used in statistical analysis. According to the official Labour Force Statistics 1991, about 60,000 women were employed in offices in manufacturing industry. Thus, the survey covered 2.11% of the population. When comparing the sample with labour force statistics, the sample's distribution is very close to that of the total population of female office workers in manufacturing in so far as the variables age, weekly working hours, nationality, marital status and number of children are concerned. Education level was a few percentage-points higher than expected, and 15% of the respondents were unionized, whereas only 10% was expected.

In the questionnaire, a large number of questions applied to the three forms of sex segregation. Departmental segregation is defined as departmental sex-typing, that is the percentage of women in the respondent's department. Job segregation is defined as occupational sex-typing, that is the percentage of women in the job category (see also section 6 for the job titles). This percentage is based on whether the respondent's colleagues performing the same job as the respondent are mainly women, both men and women in equal numbers, or mainly men. Respondents who had no colleagues performing the same job are assigned the average value of their occupational category. Hierarchical segregation is defined as sex-typing of the respondent's supervisor. In order to classify departmental and job segregation, male-dominated departments and jobs are defined as those

159

where men comprise more than two-thirds of the work force; female-dominated departments and jobs are those where the reverse applies. Integrated departments and jobs are in between. For the statistical analyses two more groups of variables were used. The individual variables take into account respondents' education level, age, tenure, re-entrance, working hours, and hourly wage. The organization variables used in the analysis are size of the department, whether respondents have colleagues performing the same job, promotion prospects, and previous career steps.

Female office workers in manufacturing industry

Before analyzing the data, the most important characteristics of female office workers in manufacturing industry are sketched. According to the respondents, 47% of the female office workers are married and a further 22% live with a partner. Nearly all women in these two groups are dual-earners. Another 12% of the women live with their parents, and 19% are single or divorced. More than three-quarters (76%) of the women have no children. One-quarter have children, and the majority of these children are over 12. More than 16% of the women are returners to the labour market. The mean age of female office workers is 32.1, and they have been with their present employer for 7.5 years, working 35.5 hours per week. On average, they earn Dfl. 12.76 nett per hour (standard deviation 3.30).

In 1991, about 1,176,000 people were employed in the Dutch manufacturing industry, of which 20% is female (Labour Force Statistics 1991). The percentage of clerical workers is much higher among female workers than among male workers in manufacturing: 32% as opposed to 7 %. Thus, 77,000 women and 68,000 men are employed in a broad range of clerical occupations in manufacturing offices. In the survey, the respondents mentioned around 200 job titles. Quite a number of women appeared to have a combined job, for example as secretary and file clerk. For the analysis related job titles have been grouped together into five occupational categories. The miscellaneous clerical workers, mostly clerical assistants, are the largest category, forming more than one third (36%) of the sample. 29% are secretaries, including executive secretaries, and 11% are telephonists/receptionists. About 21% work in staff departments, and the remaining 4% are supervisor. Three female-dominated job categories were found, together representing 75% of the respondents, and 25% are employed in the integrated occupational categories, i.e. the women in staff departments and the supervisors. No male-dominated job categories were found.

Considering departmental segregation, 40% of the respondents work in male-dominated departments, 35% work in integrated departments and 25% work in female-dominated departments. Male-dominated departments have an average of 29 employees, whereas integrated departments are smaller; on average 11 employees. Again, these are larger than female-dominated departments, which on average have less than 5 employees. Departmental sex-typing appears to be related to departmental size, correlation is significant and rather high (R=-.32). The organizational variables show that within female-dominated departments, respondents have colleagues performing the same job relatively more often than in integrated and male-dominated departments, and promotion prospects and previous career steps are lowest. Individual factors show that in female-dominated departments, educational levels, tenure, and hours per week are lowest, whereas the re-entrants percentage and age are highest. Hourly wages are lowest in male-dominated departments and highest in integrated departments.

Focusing on hierarchical segregation, nine out of ten respondents had a male supervisor, one out of ten had a female supervisor, and a very small minority had no supervisor at all. Compared to female supervised respondents, male supervised respondents are employed in larger departments, have fewer colleagues performing the same job, have average promotion prospects, but have made more career steps. The relationship with supervisors' sex-typing and colleagues performing same job is positive and significant though low (R=.13). Education and tenure is lower and working hours per week are shorter for female supervised respondents, whereas the percentage of re-entrants is higher. Tenure and working hours having significant, though not high negative correlation coefficients.

Office women's occupations

In this section the five occupational categories are discussed brief, to get more insight in the way job segregation is related to departmental and hierarchical segregation.

The *secretaries* are the most female sex-typed category. These women work in the largest, most male-dominated departments and have almost the highest percentage of male supervisors. They have made average previous career steps and they have average prospects on the internal labour market. They have a higher than average education women, and are of average age and tenure. Secretaries work more than average hours per week, whereas their hourly wages are below average. The percentage of re-entrants is average.

Though the *telephonists/receptionists* are almost as female sex-typed, this category differs greatly from the secretaries. These respondents work in the smallest, most female-dominated departments and they have the highest percentages of female supervisors and colleagues performing the same job. They have no position whatsoever on the internal labour market. They are the least well educated, the oldest women in the survey, and they comprise the highest percentage of re-entrants. Their tenure has an average score. They are the most likely to work on a part-time basis, and they earn almost the lowest hourly wages.

The *miscellaneous clerical workers* are classified as a female sex-typed job category, working in average-sized, integrated departments. They have an average percentage of male supervisors, and of colleagues performing the same job. Their position on the internal labour market also has an average score. Considering the individual factors, they are relatively young, not very well educated women, who earn the lowest hourly wages.

The *supervisors* belong to the integrated job categories, and are very likely to supervise small, female-dominated departments. They themselves are supervised by men. They consider their position on the internal market the best. They also are the best educated women in the survey, they are of average age, but they have both the lowest years of tenure and percentage of re-entrants. They work the most hours per week and they have the highest hourly wages.

Finally, the *clerical workers in staff departments* also belong to the integrated job categories. They work in integrated, relatively small departments, where they are very likely to have a male supervisor. Their position on the internal labour market is above average. So are their educational levels, age, tenure, working hours per week, and hourly wages.

Statistical analysis shows that there is no clear relationship between occupational sex-typing and organizational and individual factors. The two most female sex-typed job categories show very different patterns, and so do the two integrated job categories. Organizational variables are hardly related to occupational sex-typing, except previous career steps (R=-.16). A few individual factors show negative, significant correlations with the job categories' sex-typing, i.e. hourly wages (R=-.17) and working hours per week (R=-.13).

The interlocking of sex segregation at work

To analyze the relationship between the three forms of segregation, regression analyses are made to explain the variance in departmental sex-typing, i.e. the percentage women in the department, and in occupational sex-typing, i.e. the percentage women in the occupation. A logistic regression has been made to explain hierarchical sex-typing, i.e. female (=1) or male (=0) supervisor. In addition, the above mentioned four organizational and six individual variables have been used as independent variables to explain departmental, occupational and hierarchical sex-typing.

First, we analyze departmental sex-typing. Correlations show that departmental sex-typing is related positively to hierarchical sex-typing (R=.30). This relationship is awry, because integrated sex-typed departments are much more likely to be supervised by men. Departmental sex-typing is also related positively and significantly to occupational sex-typing, though correlation is not very high (R=.19). This is due to the fact that female sex-typed occupations are either found in most female-sex-typed departments (telephonists/receptionists) or in the least female-sex-typed departments (secretaries). Regression analysis shows that departmental sex-typing is explained significantly by number of employees ($\beta = -.31$), followed by sex-typing of the supervisor ($\beta = .26$), occupational sex-typing ($\beta = .15$), and hourly wages ($\beta = -.07$). Therefore, the relationship between departmental sex-typing and hierarchical and occupational sex-typing remains, other variables taken into account.

Secondly, occupational segregation is studied. Relationship between occupational sex-typing and hierarchical sex-typing is not high, though positive and significant ($R = .15$). For occupational and departmental sex-typing $R = .19$. Regression analysis shows that the relationship between occupational sex-typing and hierarchical as well as departmental sex-typing remains, though departmental sex-typing makes a much stronger contribution to the explanation than hierarchical sex-typing ($\beta = .17$ compared to $\beta = .7$). Occupational sex-typing is explained significantly by hourly wages ($\beta = -.23$), followed by departmental sex-typing ($\beta = .17$), number of employees in the department ($\beta = .16$), working hours per week ($\beta = -.12$), age ($\beta = .11$), previous career steps ($\beta = -.10$), and hierarchical sex-typing ($\beta = .7$). Non-standardized regression coefficients show that if the percentage of women in a department increases one percentage point, women's hourly wages decrease by Dfl 0,02.

Thirdly, hierarchical segregation is analyzed. Logistic regression shows that both the sex-typing of the department and the sex-typing of the job significantly contribute to the explanation of the supervisor's sex-typing. Only one more variable explains the supervisor's sex-typing significantly, i.e. tenure (B=-.07). If a female office worker has a female supervisor, the sex-typing of her department is 3.1 times more female than if she had had a male supervisor. If a female office worker has a female supervisor, the sex-typing of her job is 1.1 times more female than if she had had a male supervisor. The percentage correct predicted is 90%.

Now it is time to bring in the hypotheses that have been formulated for the interweaving of sex segregation. For the relationship between

164

departmental and hierarchical segregation two hypotheses were developed. The first considered supervision along gendered lines in departments. Indeed, if female office workers work in female-dominated departments, they are very likely to have a female supervisor. This relationship is rather strong and it holds when other variables are taken into account. In the second hypothesis it was stated that the pattern of supervision according to sex would be broken one level above work floor departments. This appears to be the case, because 90% of the female supervisors themselves have male supervisors.

For the relationship between departmental and occupational segregation, it was hypothesized that job segregation was realized along departmental lines. This hypothesis holds, although the relationship is rather weak, but it remains when other variables are taken into account. This is the case when departmental segregation is predicted from occupational segregation as well as vice versa. Two other hypotheses have been formulated in case where job segregation did not fully coincide with departmental segregation. At first, it was hypothesized that women in male-dominated departments work in female-dominated occupations. This hypothesis also holds. It appears that women in the most female-dominated occupations either work in the most female-dominated or in the most male-dominated departments. Women in integrated occupations are likely to be found in integrated departments. Secondly, less skilled occupations are concentrated in female-dominated departments and skilled occupations are concentrated in male-dominated departments. This hypothesis also holds ($X^2 = 115.2$, $p < .001$). To describe the results; 55% of women in the most skilled occupation is found in male-dominated departments compared to 20% of the women in the least skilled occupation.

For the relationship between job and hierarchical segregation, it was hypothesized that female-dominated occupations are supervised by women. Occupational sex-typing is positive though not strongly related to supervisors' sex-typing, but this relationship holds when other variables are taken into account. Thus, the more female-dominated the occupation, the more likely these women will be supervised by a woman. However, this relationship is far more weaker than the relationship between departmental and hierarchical segregation.

Conclusions

In this chapter, gendered structures in organizations have been defined as the interweaving of departmental, hierarchical and job segregation. The survey results show that some important conclusions can be drawn about these gendered structures in organizations.

First, the descriptive statistics show that female office workers are more or less equally divided over male-, integrated and female-dominated departments. Three out of four women work in a female-dominated occupation, and one out of four in an integrated occupation. There were no women in male-dominated occupations. Nine out of ten women have a male supervisor. This is a first glimpse of gendered organizational structures and it highlights the dominance of hierarchical segregation.

The second conclusion is that departmental and hierarchical segregation are strongly intertwined. In general, supervisors at departmental levels are male. This appears to be the case far more often in male-dominated and in integrated departments than in female-dominated departments, though this latter percentage still does not exceed 25. Female supervisors themselves are supervised by males. Moreover, male-dominated departments tend to have far more employees than integrated departments and these outdo female-dominated departments. This suggest that the gendered structures in organizations also include a status hierarchy between departments, female-dominated departments being marginalized.

The third conclusion is that occupational segregation is far less intertwined with departmental segregation than with hierarchical segregation. Irrespective of the type of department, most women work in female-dominated occupations, though this is lowest in integrated departments. Female office workers who work in female-dominated departments are very likely to have a female-dominated occupation. Female office workers in male-dominated departments are also very likely to work in a female-dominated occupation. In male-dominated departments, women tend to perform solo work, i.e. they do not have colleagues performing the same job, with the opposite obtaining for female-dominated departments. One must conclude that if gendered organizational structures are not realized along departmental lines (women working in male-dominated departments), then they are realized along occupational lines.

The fourth conclusion is that job segregation is strongly related to hourly wages and to working hours, as well as to previous career steps and to promotion prospects. The characteristics of women in integrated jobs probably look more like men's characteristics, whereas women in female-dominated jobs are a fringe group as far as wages and career prospects are concerned. Wage inequality and other forms of inequality between women obviously run along occupational lines. This indicates a gendered pattern as far as the division of benefits in organizations is concerned.

To conclude, gendered organizational structures have been studied in so far as the intertwining of three forms of sex segregation were concerned. These three phenomena are mutually interlocked, the positive relationship between departmental sex-typing and hierarchical sex-typing being strongest. However, relationships between sex segregation, and power and authority in organizations, and how these relate to women's subordinate positions, have not been studied. Further research is necessary on how gendered organizational structures coincide with unequal attribution of power, including for example the allocation of budgets, internal career opportunities, managerial commitment, authority, and contacts within and outside the organization.

References

Barker, J. & Hazel Downing, (1980), 'Word processing and the transformation of the patriarchal relations of control in the office', *Capital & Class*, nr. 10: 64-99.

Bielby, William T. & James N. Baron, (1984), 'A Woman's Place Is With Other Women: Sex Segregation Within Organizations', in: Barbara F. Reskin (editor), *Sex segregation in the Workplace*, Washington D.C., National Academy Press: 27-55.

Chaykowski, R. & J. Currie, (1992), Sex segregation on the job and the structure of fringe benefits, Paper presented at the Universities Research Conference, The Labor Market in International Perspective, National Bureau of Economic Research, Cambridge, Massachusetts, USA, April 10 and 11.

Gutek, Barbara A. & Aron G. Cohen, (1987), Sex ratios, sex role spillover and sex at work: A comparison of men's and women's experiences, *Human Relations*, 40/2: 97-115.

Jonung, Christina, (1985), 'Patterns of occupational segregation by sex in the labor market' in: G. Schmidt, and R. Weitzel (eds.). 1984, *The labour market and employment policy*, Berlin, WZB Publications.

Kanter, Rosabeth Moss, (1977), *Men and Women of the corporation*, New York, Basic Books.

Kauppinen-Toropainen, Kaisa, Irja Kandolin & Elina Haaivo-Mannila (1988), 'Sex segregation of work in Finland and the quality of women's work', *Journal of Occupational Behaviour*, 9/1: 15-27.

Martin, J. & C. Roberts, (1984), 'Women's employment in the 1980's', *Employment Gazette*, Vol. 92 (May), pp. 199-209.

Nieva, V.F. & Barbara A. Gutek, (1981), *Women and work: a psychological perspective*, New York, Praeger Publishing Co.

Ott, Marlies (1985), *Assepoesters en kroonprinsen*, Een onderzoek naar de minderheidspositie van agentes en verplegers [Cinderella's and princess royal, Research on the minority position of policewomen and nurses] Amsterdam, SUA.

Perman, Louise & Beth Stevens, (1989), 'Industrial Segregation and the Gender Distribution of Fringe Benefits', *Gender & Society*, Vol. 3/3: 388-404.

Peterson, Richard R., (1989), 'Firm Size, Occupational Segregation, and the Effects of Family Status on Women's Wages', *Social Forces*, 68/2: 397-414

Reskin, Barbara F. & Heidi I. Hartmann (editors), (1986), *Women's Work, Men's Work. Sex Segregation on the Job*, Washington D.C., National Academy Press.

Reskin, F. Barbara, (editor), (1984), *Sex Segregation in the Workplace*, Washington DC, National Academy Press.

Rosenfeld, Rachel A., (1984), 'Job Changing and Occupational Sex Segregation: Sex and Race Comparisons', in: Barbara F. Reskin (editor), *Sex Segregation in the Workplace*, Washington DC, National Academy Press, pp. 56-86.

Semyonov, Moshe & Lewin-Epstein, Noah, (1989), 'Segregation and Competition in Occupational Labor Markets', *Social Forces*, Vol. 68/2: 379-396.

Sorensen, Elaine, (1989), 'Measuring the pay disparity between typically female occupations and other jobs: a bivariate selectivity approach', *Industrial and Labour Relations Review*, 42/4: 624-639.

Tijdens, Kea & Anneke Goudswaard, (1992), *Kwaliteit van de arbeid van kantoorvrouwen in de industrie* [Quality of working life, office women in manufacturing] Amsterdam, Industrial Workers Union FNV.

Tijdens, Kea, (1990), Beroepssegregatie en werkgelegenheid. [Occupational segregation and employment], *Tijdschrift voor Arbeidsvraagstukken*, 6/4: 13-23.

Treiman, Donald J. & Heidi Hartmann, (1981), *Women, work and wages: Equal pay for Jobs of Equal Value*, Washington DC, National Academy Press.

Yoder, J.D., (1991), 'Rethinking tokenism: looking beyond numbers', *Gender & Society*, 5/2: 178-192.

7   Equal Opportunity of Men and Women and Organizational Change

Jacqueline Laufer

HEC School of Management
Jouy-en-Josas, France

Gender relationships have long been a "hidden dimension" of organisations. The traditional structure of jobs and roles could not be questioned as long as the familial status of women and their interrupted working lives appeared as a consequence of a "natural" division of labour between the sexes, and as long as the family and the firm appeared as separate institutions. The rise of equality between men and women has revealed the essential role of gender relationships in the structuring of organisations, but also and reciprocally, the contribution of organisations to the production and the reproduction of unequal gender relationships as sexual discrimination is embedded within the very structure and the culture of organisations.

More specifically, the development of equal opportunity legislation and the implementation of equality in the workplace has led to a development in the institutional role of the firm. Organisations have become a privileged locus for social and cultural change. While traditionally, organisations could legitimately assign women to low qualified jobs and disregard their career development in the name of family commitments and constraints, equal opportunity legislation and equal opportunity schemes make organisations accountable for the unequal treatment of men and women, and require the establishment of new organisational strategies and practices to implement equal treatment. Through this evolution, work organisations are explicitly designated as a privileged locus for the production of new social norms in the area of gender relationships.

During the seventies through the mid-eighties, the focus was on the introduction of equality between men and women in the work place. Now a new debate has arisen which focuses on the issue of a combination of work and family roles as crucial to establishing equal opportunity among men and women, both in the work-place and in the society at large.

As more women work outside their homes while raising a family, employers have to accommodate this new situation by defining new patterns of work and time organisation. The emergence of this issue can be related to a deep transformation in the nature of organisational boundaries. As the question of a clear separation between the "inside" of an organisation and the rest of society becomes more acute, organisational boundaries become less and less clearly defined.

It is these two steps in organisational change influenced by gender relationships that we want to analyse here. Although the focus here is on the French situation, we will also introduce some comparisons with other national contexts.

The implementation of the principle of equality between men and women in the work-place: toward a growing institutional role of the firm

Four stages can be distinguished in describing evolution in the implementation of the equality principle:
- the traditional model of inequality
- the claim for legal equality
- the recognition of the enduring nature of unequal social processes, in spite of the introduction of formal and legal equality
- the implementation of equality through affirmative actions.

The traditional model of inequality

Traditionally, the firm and the family have been functionally separate - separate but articulated thanks to the primary assignment of men to the productive sphere and of women to the reproductive sphere. Through the nineteenth century and up to the beginning of the twentieth century, the legal and economic inequality of men and women, women's unequal access to jobs and their subordination within the family and within the firm have represented the cornerstones of an economic and social system structured through the division of labour between the sexes.

During that period, the institutional role of the firm strengthened these gender relationships, either through specific protection of the female labour force - limitation of working hours or of night-work - or through paternalistic policies which contributed to marginalizing women and keeping them on the fringes of the labour force.

The claim for equality

In the work sphere, equality between the sexes was first approached through the principle of equal pay. At European level, the principle of equal pay - equal pay for work of equal value - was the subject of the first EEC Directives, which applied the principle incapsulated in article 119 of the Treaty of Rome, and which was subsequently incorporated into all EC national legislation[1].

The paradoxical nature of the 1972 French law on equal pay is that while it recognises the gendered structure of organisation, it is posed as a neutral rule: the objective may be to establish equality through the application of a general formal rule, but it fails to take into account the "true" origin of the unequal value of jobs, i.e. the lower value of traditionally female jobs and the gender-based division of jobs.

In this sense, the introduction of a formal principle of equal pay does not modify the institutional status of the firm in terms of equality. While the firm is formally expected to comply with and to submit to a formal legal rule

- equal pay for equal jobs or jobs of equal value -, it is not considered accountable for the unequal situation of men and women. This is perceived as being grounded in "external processes" over which the firm is not supposed to have any control. In other words, while the equal pay law appears an essential step towards completing the legal establishment of equality between men and women in work and in society, it is not a tool for action strategies in which the firm as such would be likely to play a role.

The recognition of the enduring nature of unequal social processes as obstacles to the effective implementation of equality

Given the inadequacy of classical legal tools to tackle inequalities in the work-place, the next stage in the implementation of equality had to acknowledge the obstacles.

While the 1975 law forbids discrimination on the basis of gender especially in the case of recruitment and dismissal, thereby acknowledging the psycho-sociological nature of the process of discrimination, its sanction-based approach does not allow the indepth modification of sources of discrimination within organisations.

Following the Directive on Equal Treatment[2], which concerns the larger field of recruitment, training, working conditions, and the way that they determine equal treatment of men and women on the job market and within firms, the 1983 French law on professional equality aims at providing firms with tools for diagnosis and for action. It is designed to extend beyond the principles and sanctions whose inability to tackle the unequal nature of the gender structure of the work-place had been revealed. The 1983 French law perceives the organisation and the firm as producing and reproducing gender inequalities through sociological processes and organisational practices which impede equal treatment of equal opportunity for women.

To tackle these situations the law requires that firms report on the comparative status of men and women in terms of recruitment, training, promotion, working conditions and pay. The function of this report is to constitute a basis for social debate and, potentially, for positive actions

174

aimed at the implementation of equal opportunity[3]. Through this compulsory report, the firm's institutional role increases as it becomes accountable for analysing and eventually changing its gender structure, which had been ignored up until then because of external phenomena beyond its control.

What does analysis reveal on the way French firms have integrated this institutional role into their social and human resource policies? Although the symbolic significance of the comparative report on the situation of men and women cannot be under-estimated, it has not led to a true social and economic debate on the status of women within those firms and within the job hierarchy. Most companies have not taken full advantage of this opportunity to examine their employment policies relating to women, even though several companies have exceeded the target set by the law by carrying out general sociological studies on the status of their female employees, or by setting up working groups comprising members of different personnel categories to assess the situation of women within the firm[4].

The implementation of equality through affirmative action

The European Directive on equal treatment expresses the principle that actions aimed at creating equal opportunity between men and women are not contrary to the principle of equality; these "positive actions" are defined as temporary measures necessary to correct the unequal situation of men and women. Positive actions can therefore allow women better access to jobs in sectors where they have been underrepresented, better career and training opportunities, better reconciliation between their family and career responsibilities. However, while the Directive on equal treatment has found its way into all EU national legislation, the legal framework of positive actions is more diversified. Depending on the country, positive actions may be compulsory - for example, in the public sector - or left to the voluntary initiative of firms, or integrated into the bargaining system with unions.

While some degree of legal and administrative constraints exists to implement positive actions, the general setting relies more on negotiation and commitments and on a set of diversified means, including administrative bodies, whose function it is to monitor and evaluate national positive action programs, means of sensitisation of social actors through the diffusion of expertise on positive actions, and last but not least, financial means to support pilot programs or the use of experts whose role is to help organisations develop such programs.

Whatever the institutional setting, this evolution leads firms to acknowledge their contribution to the production of discrimination and of inequalities, and to play an institutional role in the implementation of equal opportunity through the negotiation and/or setting up of positive action plans. Thus, in this sense, the firm is entrusted with a role in the production of gender equality in society.

In France, companies are encouraged to negotiate positive action plans with trades unions to improve the status of women in areas such as recruitment, training, promotion or working conditions. Financial aid can be granted by the state if the proposed measures are judged to be "exemplary".

In the Netherlands, the law on equal treatment of men and women on the labour market allows positive discrimination for women with regard to recruitment, training and promotion, but no compulsory rules have been formulated for the application of positive actions. The government, as an employer, has however taken a more coercive standpoint. As far as the private sector is concerned, the government has made funds available to stimulate positive actions, but has left the realisation of such programs to individual firms' initiative and to the consultation process between employers and employees representatives.

In Belgium, according to the law of 4 August 1978, voluntary schemes can be initiated in the private sector. Following the royal decree of August 1993, companies are also obliged to establish an annual report on equal opportunities between men and women[5].

However, where positive action schemes have been implemented, we are struck by their very pragmatic approach. As far as France is concerned, about 35 firms in various sectors have implemented positive action schemes, the majority of them through negotiating with the trades unions a "plan d'égalité" as defined in the 1983 law. This relatively low figure would indicate that most companies do not feel a need to include equal opportunity among their objectives, or at the very least do no wish to pursue a specific policy as this matter. While in recent years much attention has been given by many firms to improvements in the field of human resource management, most would stress that these should concern both men and women. In other words, despite the 1983 law on positive action, the legitimacy of schemes addressed to "women only" has not gained a wide response among firms in France. The measures covered by these schemes have included recruitment, career development and mostly training.

In recruitment, action schemes have striven to readjust recruitment policies in favour of women executives, engineers and technicians to jobs where they were underrepresented, and to provide more information on vacant positions within the company so as to encourage more women to apply for them.

In the area of career development, action schemes have helped to promote women to male-dominated managerial positions and to define new career paths, for example by enabling women working in administrative functions to enter marketing and sales functions. They have also led to a more systematic inclusion of women in career development programs, and to the setting up of working groups to identify and evaluate the changing content of secretarial functions and its consequences for future secretarial skills.

In the area of training, efforts have been directed towards factory workers and employees. Faced with technological changes and with a growing demand for higher quality in their products or services, companies have taken it upon themselves to transform or upgrade the skills of large numbers of female factory workers and clerical staff who were ill-prepared to confront technological changes or to take on positions requiring initiative and greater responsibility. Thus, in several companies, the schemes have involved between 100 and 200 carefully selected unskilled factory workers in each company, who were able to gain a technical diploma after 400 to 800 hours of training, allowing them to take up jobs on semi-automated assembly and packaging lines. In some other firms, all employees below secondary school level were given courses in economics, banking and communication which could grant them access to further managerial training and allow them to take up managerial positions in the administrative and marketing areas.[6]

Similar strategies can be identified in other European countries. For example, in the Netherlands, actions have concerned proportional representation of women in the recruitment of young graduates, life-career orientation courses for women, or management training for female graduates in the organisation. In Belgium, actions have also involved the recruitment of women into managerial posts which had until then been the preserve of men, or training for women managers in the field of management and career development.

In France, the evaluation of such programs indicates that they allow the best use of the untapped human resources represented by women workers, employees or middle managers. Positive action plans represent an efficient means of selecting those women who are able to fit the characteristics of more qualified jobs or more promising careers. However, the implementation of equal opportunity appears here to be secondary to the usefulness of such programs for changing strategies of firms confronted by technological or economic changes. To improve their competitive position, those firms were often confronted to the choice of either dismissing their low qualified women workers or to develop the skills of their female employees whose aspiration was to stay on the labour market[7]. While society at large assigns to the firm the implementation of more egalitarian values,[8] they have a pragmatic approach to their institutional role. Therefore, it appears legitimate only to the extent that equal opportunity is economically useful. When considering this evolution, two conclusions can be drawn:

1) While the initial conception of changing unequal gender relationships is based on the installation of a proper set of formal legal rules, it evolves as a purely pragmatic approach to organisational change.

2) Given the reluctance of firms to acknowledge fully their institutional role in this area, and given the way they tend to integrate

affirmative action into their pragmatic strategies, one could say that change is only symbolic.

Compatibility of work and family roles and equal opportunity : toward a new approach to organisational boundaries

The debate on the implementation of equality had long left aside the issue of compatibility of work and family roles. While the pragmatic and selective orientation of firms to equal opportunity expresses the limitations of the institutional role they are prepared to play in modifying the gender structure of the organisation, the massive participation of women in the labour force has led to the emergence of compatibility of work and family roles as a central issue in the implementation of equal opportunity for all working women[9].

Equal pay, equal treatment in the various dimensions of the work situation - in recruitment and in access to careers and training - were perceived as both the main issues which had to be tackled and the main objectives in producing gendered equality in the work-place. As a consequence of them, equality between men and women in society would ensue.

Since then, a new debate has arisen which focuses on the issue of reconciling work and family roles as crucial to the establishment of equal opportunity, both in the work-place and in society as a whole[10].

Domestic circumstances and professional commitment are seen as deeply interconnected for women. In this sense, firms' policies on equal opportunity cannot be considered in isolation from the issue of the reconciliation of domestic and professional roles[11]. While the implementation of equality questions the capacity of firms to establish more egalitarian norms, the compatibility issue questions their capacity to produce concrete models which reconcile the productive and reproductive spheres.

In the same way as the debate on equality can be analysed through four stages, the debate on work and family role compatibility can also be analysed from four different points of view - ranging from the traditional model where reconciliation was based on the exclusion of women from the labour force to a pragmatic definition of diversified models of reconciliation. At each of these stages, we shall see that the more crucial issue is the boundaries between company and the rest of society.

The traditional combination model

Traditionally, combining paid and unpaid labour was not an issue given the "natural" assignment of women to domestic roles, at the expense of their right to paid work, or equal access to jobs and careers. The subordination of women was "the one best way" to ensure that family duties were taken care of. In this approach to reconciliation, the spheres of production and reproduction were clearly separated. The boundaries of work organisations were thus clearly defined.

The right to combine paid and unpaid work and the utopia of free choice

The recognition of women's right to work and the increase in the female salaried work force has raised the issue of the conflict between professional and family roles. Women's professional activity has increased greatly in France and in Europe, but it still depends on their family status in a society where domestic and family roles are not yet shared equally.

The increase in the number of working mothers of two children has altered the traditional view of the link between domestic and professional roles which emphasised the "choice" women were obliged to make between work or a career and the family. This "choice" led women either to remain in low-level or routine jobs, as they seemed the only jobs that were compatible with family roles, or to develop a career which conformed to the rules and culture of "masculine" organisations and to the expectations of masculine role models, which involved a sacrifice of family roles. Indeed, top managerial women are still more often single than other working women.

Now that women's rights and aspirations to have a job or a career and a family are recognised, the issue of compatibility between work and family

180

roles had become more of a social issue. There is an increasing awareness that the need to define reconciliation between work and family is an issue of general concern of society, for families and for organisations, rather than as "women's problems".[12]

While organisations are increasingly aware of the necessity to keep their educated and qualified women, demographic issues are also at stake which imply the need for a search for better ways to integrate constraints on both "workers" and "parents".

This new situation first implied a set of formal legal rules which could allow the expression of this new type of integration between the two spheres, for example the 1977 French law on parental leave.

It also implied new organisational policies to fit the needs of a diversified set of workers' aspirations. In France and in other countries positive action schemes have included this dimension of equal opportunity. For example, the inclusion of maternity leave in seniority bonuses and the introduction of an interview with the employees' immediate superior after their return from maternity leave to evaluate their career development have allowed motherhood to be integrated into women's career development in a positive manner. Some firms have included some measures to facilitate the access of women to training which take into account women's family responsibilities.

While compatibility between work and family roles can be enhanced through a variety of means, more flexible working-time patterns form a particularly useful instrument: flexi-hours, part-time jobs and parental leave, different types of time and work organization being more adapted to various types of family constraints or to different steps in personal and professional life.

In the Netherlands, part-time work is very common, but it appears that, as in France, most part-time work is found in the service sectors and in lower and middle-level jobs. In the Netherlands part-time work at the highest managerial level only occurs in the larger public sector organisations, while part-time work at that level in the private sector occurs extremely rarely.[13] In England, more that 50 percent of women part-timers with children aged 0-4 work less that 19 hours per week.[14]

Part-time work has been often presented as a "meeting-point" between the needs of the firm for more flexible working-time patterns and the needs of the female work force. However, if part-time jobs are performed by women only, this could lead to a new type of job segregation which is incompatible with equal opportunity. The issue, therefore, is to allow women to fulfil their professional ambitions and to have a family, but also from an egalitarian perspective, to improve equal opportunity between men and women in terms of access to all types of jobs and careers.

Policies which address both sexes - such as parental leave - are in principle an answer to equal opportunity in terms of combining work and family. However, legal tools as such are inefficient when it comes to modifying the traditional gender division of roles within the family. The Swedish model of paid parental leave is often given as an example of a policy which does prevent family responsibilities from continuing to be a women's "privilege".

Whatever the form of compatibility the firm's time and the family's time appear to be no longer separate but are conceived as mutually interactive and potentially integratable. It becomes the responsibility of the firm to reduce the gap between its needs and the workers' needs by changing the organisation's cultural norms on working-time patterns. All these patterns of compatibility modify the boundaries between the firm and the family.[15]

Compatibility between work and family roles as an issue in the reproduction of inequality

One of the key issues in the search for new forms of compatibility between work and family is "free choice". Legal provisions and organisational policies on combination are now open - in principle - to both sexes, and they are supposed to increase the range of practical choices for both sexes, thereby reducing gender inequality.

From this standpoint the question of compatibility between work and family roles appears as a new way of stating the problem of gender equality. However, the analysis of social processes and practices reveals the rather utopian dimension of such an approach. The notion of "free choice" appears to be utopian for a least two reasons. The first is more specifically related to the reproductive sphere, while the second is more specifically related to the productive sphere.

The first reason to question the notion of free choice is the weight of social constraint and traditions within family patterns and organisations. To assume a "free choice" for both men and women in a given family would imply a pre-established harmony between the choices of both parents, which would ensure that the basic functions of the family will be full filled. This perfectly balanced, flexible, reversible picture of free choice does not take into account the weight of social traditions and constraints on the specificity of men and women's roles, desires and images of themselves, which appear more lasting than previously thought and which contribute to the survival of a traditional model of family organisation. Such an approach to free choice also underestimates the fact that both members of the couple could simply want to have the same thing at the same time. Thus, if a diversification of types of working patterns is favoured in the name of compatibility because these are open to both sexes, in practice it appears that women are usually more concerned with these types of working-time patterns and this can limit their full access to a job or career.

The second reason to question the free choice hypothesis is related to the types of flexible patterns of time and work structures companies want. Up to now, firms have been eager to implement flexible patterns of work organisation mainly for economic and productivity motives. Expansion of opening hours for different types of services, the need to make a more efficient use of costly industrial equipment, the need to adapt the volume of production to the market - these are only a few of the many reasons which cause firms to adapt different kinds of flexible working-time patterns. While it is often emphasised that workers' aspirations and the firm's requirements can find common ground through various types of flexible working-time patterns, questions remain on the way such patterns meet the workers' needs, and whether they transform or do not transform the traditional division of labour, so that their impact on gender relationships can be evaluated.

The two observations draw attention to how the compatibility issue can contribute to reproducing inequality processes, especially when economic or employment and increasing unemployment heighten the risks of women's exclusion from the labour market, or relegation to precarious jobs. Given that the burden of compatibility is unequally distributed, women tend to be assigned more often to precarious or part-time jobs which corresponds to a redefinition of organisational boundaries. Now, gender inequality expresses itself not as much through subordination or exclusion from the labour market, but through the more of less central position that women occupy - in the name of compatibility - with respect to the work organisation and to stable jobs.

As compatibility between work and family roles is no utopian facet of equality, but appears rather to be compromise between conflicting sets of constraints, the question emerges as to how we should evaluate these concrete models of reconciliation.

Compatibility as the production of diversified models of articulation between the firm and society

The evaluation of patterns of compatibility raises two difficulties. If we examine critically some of these patterns from the point of view of equal opportunity as opposed to the "free choice" ideology, we cannot avoid value judgments and we risk underestimating emerging social processes, which may lead some women to "prefer" marginalisation in the work sphere so they can take care of the reproductive sphere.

If we want to avoid a priori value judgments, we have to consider the multiplicity of various patterns of compatibility as diversified types of compromise. One way of analysing these processes "objectively" is to consider each social actor participating in a process of definition and promotion of their preferred models of combining work and family roles.

184

The evolution of compatibility appears, therefore, as an ongoing negotiation process which deals simultaneously with gender relationships in the family and in the work organisation, and one which is centred on the definition of organisational boundaries.

Conclusion

The rise of equality between men and women has revealed the essential role of gender relationships in the structuring of organisations[16].

Through equal opportunity legislation, organisations have become a privileged locus for social and cultural change. However, two main dimensions of such change - a new institutional role for the firm and re-definition of organisational boundaries - cannot be analysed in isolation from the strategies of firms. These strategies tend to favour the search for economic efficiency and to limit the potential impact of equal opportunity change strategies. This situation contributes to reproducing gender inequality and a traditional division of jobs and roles between men and women at least as long as more structural and cultural change in the redefinition of the respective roles of men and women does not take place in society.[17]

Notes

1.   Directive 75/117/CEE February 10th 1975.

2.   Directive 76/207/CEE February 9th 1976.

3.   J. LAUFER, 'Egalité professionnelle: un atout négligé pour gérer les resources humaines', *Revue Française de Gestion*, no.55, Janvier-Février 1986, pp. 18-19.

4.   Women employment in business and equal opportunity - the case of France, *The First international Federation of Scholarly Associations of Management Conference*, Tokyo, September 7-9 1992.

5.   M. Chalude, A. de Jong, J. Laufer : Implementing equal opportunity and affirmative actions programs. The case of three countries: Belgium, France and the Netherlands, in: M.J. Davidson and R.J. Burke (Eds) *Women in management, current research issues*, Paul Chapman Publishers 1994.

6.   J. LAUFER L'entreprise en l'égalité des chances, *La Documentation Française*, 1992.

7.   'L'entreprise et égalité des chances' op cit.

8.   See also V. Sekaran, F.T. Leong (Edit), *Women power. Managing in times of demographic turbulence*, London, Sage publications, 1992.

9.   E.A. Fagerson, *Women in management, Trends, Issues and Challenges in managerial diversity*, London, Sage Publications, 1993.

10. P. Henriot, The career management challenge. Balancing individual & organizational needs. London: Sage Publications, 1992.

11. In France, of every 100 hours, working mothers devote 48 to domestic work and 52 to professional activities, while men devote 28 hours to domestic and 72 to professional activities. In 1985, a father of two children whose life worked outside the home only devoted 15 minutes more to domestic tasks a father in the same situation in 1975. While women's educational level effects their professional activities - 75% of university - educated women with 3 children are in employment compared to 45% of mothers of three without qualifications - their ability to make the most of their training is not as great as that of men or single women without children.

12. J. Laufer, Women in business & management: France, in: *European women in business & management*, M.J. Davidson and C.L. Cooper (Edit), Paul Chapman 1993.

13. J.V. Doorne-Huiskes, 'Women and changing patterns of work : Analysis of the situation in the Netherlands', Paper for the 15th *European Symposium in Social Welfare* - July 2-7 1989, Noordwijkerhout - The Netherlands.

14. L. Hantrais, *Managing professional and family life. A comparative study of British and French women*, Dartmouth Publishing Co. 1990.

15. Egalité professionnelle , conciliation des responsabilités professionnelles et familiales et statut de l'entreprise, *Congrès Mondial de Sociologie* - CR17 - L'organisation, un objet multidisciplinaire (CO-Chairman, R. Sainsaulieu, C: Ballé) Madrid 9-13 juillet 1990.

16. J. Laufer, *La féminité neutraliséee, Les femmes cadres dans l'entreprise*, Editions Flammarion 1982.

17. M. Chalude, A. de Jong, J. Laufer; Op cit.

PART III

Female Management

8   Women on Corporate Boards of Directors[1]

Ronald J. Burke

Faculty of Administrative Studies
York University, Ontario, Canada

Increasing research attention has been devoted to understanding the roles and responsibilities of boards of directors of North American corporations (Gillies, 1992; Lorsch & MacIver, 1989; Fleischer, Hazard & Klipper, 1988). Initially, boards had honorary or at best advisory roles to Committee for Executive Officers (hereafter CEOs) appearing as "ornaments on a corporate Christmas tree" (Mace, 1971). They also have functioned as "old boy's clubs" (Leighton & Thain, 1993). Board members were appointed exclusively at the request of the CEOs. But events of the 1970s and 1980s have brought about changes in both the composition and functioning of boards. A majority of board members now come from outside the corporation (outside directors), board membership has grown, corporate boards have created more committees, corporate directors take their jobs more seriously, and directors bring a greater variety of abilities and skills to the boards on which they serve. Despite these changes, corporate boards of directors continue to be criticized.

Patton and Baker (1987) suggest that board members do not live up to their responsibilities because of a "let's not rock the boat" mentality. They cite several reasons for this. These include: the dual authority often claimed by CEOs as chiefs of management and as Board Chairmen, the large size of corporate boards makes good discussion difficult, many board members are themselves CEOs who value each others friendship and want to keep their seats on the board, board members are too busy to devote enough time to their board responsibilities, and the fact that few directors have large amounts of stock in the companies on whose boards they sit.

One way to deal with some of the concerns raised about the effectiveness and relevance of corporate boards of directors is to appoint more qualified women to them. Why qualified women? First, there are not enough qualified male CEOs to go around. Second, male CEOs do not have enough time to serve on all the boards they are invited to join. Third, many male CEOs do not have enough time to do justice to the boards on which they currently serve. Finally, women are developing the necessary experience, track records and abilities to qualify for board membership, though they are often "invisible" to male CEOs (Schwartz, 1980).

This introduction examines the writing and research that pertains specifically to women on corporate boards. If research on corporate boards has been limited; studies that consider women directors have been few. In fact, the circumstances pertaining to women on corporate boards bear a striking similarity to the larger literature relating to women in corporate management (Burke & McKeen, 1992). These include concepts such as tokenism, stereotypes and the fact that though the number of women serving on corporate boards of directors has increased, it remains stuck at about five percent. Our belief is that increasing the number of qualified women on corporate boards will improve both board and management effectiveness.

Characteristics of Women Directors

Directors were almost exclusively white males until the 1970s. A few token women were then appointed. Women have continued to be appointed to corporate boards, but given the short period of time that has elapsed, the absolute number of women directors is still very small. Several studies have provided a picture of the demographic characteristics of corporate directors (Kesner, 1988; Ghiloni, 1984; *Nations Business*, 1990; *HRM Update*, 1992; *Globe and Mail*, 1990, 1993; *Financial Post*, 1984, 1990; *Wall Street Journal*, 1986; Harrigan, 1981; Kesner, 1988). Although the specific details and numbers vary slightly from study to study, the results are consistent. Corporate directors form a rather homogeneous group. Of all the Fortune 1000 directors, 94% are white males, 67% are over 55 years of age, and 63% of all board members are CEOs of other corporations.

It is not surprising that male CEOs dominate corporate board memberships, given that the recruitment and selection process has relied so heavily on CEOs' suggestions (Patton & Baker, 1987). Male CEOs get to know and feel comfortable with other male CEOs. Lorsch and MacIver (1989) indicate several pluses and minuses in having corporate boards dominated by CEOs. CEOs understand the difficulties of leading complex organizations. CEOs also provide excellent resources, knowledge and information. The negatives associated with CEO dominance of boards is that board members may be too supportive (i.e., not critical enough) of the CEO who appointed them (Patton & Baker, 1987). Most directors still feel they serve at the pleasure of the CEO (Lorsch & MacIver, 1989). CEOs are in limited supply; there are not enough CEOs to fill all board openings so many are overworked and unable to devote enough time to their responsibilities as board members (Patton & Baker, 1987).

Sethi, Swanson and Harrigan (1981) examined descriptive characteristics of corporate board members. They reported that the absolute number of women on corporate boards is small, most having been appointed since 1975. They studied 441 companies in 1979, observing that only 155 women held 188 directorships (3%), up from 2.1% in 1977. The 441 corporations had a total of 6224 directorships. One hundred and sixty-eight corporations had at least one woman director (38%), eighteen organizations had two women directors and one organization had three women directors. Non-industrial organizations were found to have more women directors than did industrial organizations.

They also provide considerable information on the demographic characteristics and board service of the women directors in their sample. A large number of women directors had non-business backgrounds. Women academics (22%) and women with a variety of other non-business back-grounds were common. About 23% of women directors had business/industrial backgrounds, being current or former executives of other firms. Almost 70% were between 46 and 60; 17% were over 61. Most (92%) were outside directors. Women tended to hold more multiple board directorships than did their male colleagues. Eighteen percent of women held only one directorship, 41% had two, 18% had three, and 23% four or more. One explanation they offer for this pattern is that the pool of qualified women (and men) is small. The length of women's tenure with their corporate board was typically short. Seventy-eight percent had served as directors for less than 5 years; twenty-nine percent less than 2 years.

Elgart (1983) reported an increase of female directors in Fortune 500 companies of 2.7% in the past decade. Female directors were more likely to be found in larger firms and firms in the service and financial sectors. Female directors typically had shorter board tenure than did their male counterparts.

In summary, it appears women are increasingly being asked to serve on corporate boards. Their absolute numbers remain small (about 5%), resulting from their low initial base level, the small increase in their appointments, and the limited time that has elapsed. Women serving on corporate boards have more varied backgrounds and experiences than male counterparts, are younger and have shorter board tenure.

Changes in Characteristics of Women Directors

There is some speculation that women directors recently appointed have different characteristics than women appointed earlier and are selected for different reasons (Mattis, 1993). Unfortunately, there is very little data here so any conclusions must be considered tentative. Women directors were found to be younger than their male counterparts. But Mattis (1993) believes that this age difference may be narrowing. She compared demographic profiles of women directors in a 1991 Catalyst study with an earlier Burson-Mosteller study and found that women directors were, on average, 56 years old in the former and 53 years old in the latter. Women directors were less likely to be married and less likely to have children than were male directors. In the 1991 Catalyst study, 15% had never married, 9% had divorced and 25% had no children.

The 1991 Catalyst study also considered levels of education of women directors. It reported that all but 11% had at least one university degree; 25% had three or more university degrees. In a 1976 study, women directors had levels of education generally similar to that of men directors. Less than twenty percent did not have university degrees; thirty-nine percent had a PhD; and a further 16% had specialization in law. The Burson-Mosteller study indicated that few women directors had risen to the highest organizational levels. But many had been highly successful in education and law. In general, women's career fields were more diversified and less business oriented than men's. There seemed to be a different profile in the 1991 Catalyst study. The "new generation" of women directors were more likely to have a focused business-oriented career (42% were corporate). There were fewer women directors having only not-for-profit experience and fewer women directors with a mixture of business and not-for-profit experience.

In summary, it appears that the "new generation" of women being appointed to corporate boards, in comparison with early women board pioneers, are younger, more likely to have business experience and corporate careers, and expected to bring expertise and skill to the board room. They are less likely to be window-dressing.

Selecting and Electing Directors

In the past, the selection of directors had been the exclusive responsibility of the CEO. This situation has slowly changed with the creation of nominating committees on more corporate boards. Lorsch and MacIver (1989) found that 84% of directors in their survey sat on corporate boards that had nominating committees. But despite this trend, CEOs still had the most influence. Fifty-five percent of their respondents indicated that CEOs were the main source of nominations; thirty-three percent indicated that the nominating committee was the main source.

Lorsch and MacIver (1989), among others, have identified a four step process in the selection and election of directors; identifying candidates, evaluating candidates, nominating individuals, and electing them. The first two steps appear to be critical; once a candidate clears them, nomination and election is almost guaranteed. Thus, 68% of Lorsch and MacIver's respondents reported that candidates suggested by the CEO were always elected. Directors felt that they had more influence on the evaluation process than on the nomination process, but that the CEO still had the most influence. As far as election was concerned, in almost one hundred percent of cases, only one slate of directors was proposed. Thus the initial *identification* of potential directors is key.

The Burson-Mosteller survey cited by Mattis (1993) reported that almost all directors were recruited by the CEO or Board Chairman. The more recent 1991 Catalyst survey still found the CEO and/or Board Chairman to be important (54% of women said they were recruited by them), but another 32% of women directors indicated they were recommended by another board member on the nominating committee, someone who knew the CEO or another board member, or by a board member of their own organization. There seems to be evidence of a broader network of personal contacts now being used in board recruitment than previously.

Why do women think they were appointed to serve on corporate boards? Sethi, Swanson and Harrigan (1981) asked a sample of the women directors in their study why they were appointed directors. Five main reasons were identified: they were prominent women leaders with national and international reputations, they had extended family ties and social relationships with CEO/Board Chairmen, and in some cases their families were stockholders, they would add a new dimension to board deliberations, they were experienced managers with good knowledge of business practice, and they were token appointments to satisfy affirmative action requirements. But tokenism was seen by these women directors as positive. They sensed they were recruited *because* they were women, and many were often the first woman appointed to a particular board.

Respondents in Mitchell's study (1984) of Canadian women directors were asked a similar question. They identified up to three reasons why they believed they were selected as directors. In decreasing order of importance, these were: had a community profile (23%), was a woman (21%), had business expertise (14%), provided regional representation (11%), had memberships on other boards (10%), had influential contacts (6%), were corporate officers (4%), because of shareholder's influence (4%), had family connections (3%) and had political affiliations (3%).

In summary, the identification and nomination of women for corporate board appointments is very much dependent on personal contacts with a few key people. This process is undoubtedly similar in many respects to the identification and nomination of men to corporate boards. It probably makes it more difficult for women to be identified than men, however. The process seems to be becoming dependent on a wider variety of contacts which may increasingly operate to women's advantage. Although many women believed they were appointed *because* they were women, they did not see this as necessarily a liability.

Joining and Serving on Boards

Why do directors join boards? Lorsch and MacIver (1989) asked their primarily male respondents to rank the importance of nine reasons for joining a board. These reasons, presented in decreasing order of importance, were; the quality of top management, the opportunity to learn, challenge as a director, prestige of the firm, potential growth of the firm, opportunity to work with other board members, personal prestige, compensation and major stock ownership. The researchers conclude that seeking intellectual stimulation and new ideas are the main motivations for joining and serving on corporate boards. Their study also provided data on reasons why directors refused particular board memberships. In decreasing order of importance these were: lack of time, meeting conflicts, conflicts of interest, feeling they could not play a useful role, no interest in firm's industry, uncertainty about the firm's future and concerns about legal liabilities.

Sethi, Swanson and Harrigan (1981), in interviews with women board members, noted a variety of reasons they offered for joining a particular board. These included: as feminists (activists?) they felt obligated to serve when asked, confidence in the company's leadership, fit with their career objectives; where located geographically - was it easy/hard to get to, time requirements - possible conflicts with responsibilities to spouse and children, and the company's past financial history.

There were also other personal benefits derived from board member-ship. Lorsch and MacIver (1989) asked their directors to state the personal benefits they derived from serving on corporate boards. These benefits, in decreasing importance, were: opportunity to learn, seeing new businesses, establishing contacts to enhance other business relationships, an opportunity to contribute to society and compensation. The last three potential benefits fell far down the list of importance (relatively unimportant).

There is very little information on the motivation of women, and men, in joining corporate boards. There appear to be some differences in sources of motivation but this conclusion must be treated with caution. Both women and men seem to be motivated by opportunities to learn and by challenge, and not motivated by compensation and perks (Mattis, 1993). Women may be more concerned about time demands and conflicts with home responsibilities.

Why Are There So Few Women on Corporate Boards?

Elgart (1983) conducted a survey of Fortune 500 firms inquiring specifically about reasons for not recruiting more female directors. She obtained responses from 143 companies. One hundred and twenty-six companies in her study indicated reasons for not having women directors. Seventy-six firms provided one reason; 36 firms, two reasons, and 17 firms, three or more reasons. The most common reasons were: already filled with qualified candidates, not enough qualified women, and companies were against constituency representation.

Mattis (1993) identified at least three barriers to the appointment of women as directors: the director selection process which relies to a great extent on the "old boy's network", risk aversion by corporate board leadership, and corporate boards not being aware of the roles that women members can play in promoting the advancement of women in their own companies.

Leighton and Thain (1993) argue that the director selection process is fundamentally flawed. Male CEOs and male board chairmen are more comfortable with others like them (other white male CEOs). They are more likely to have other men in their personal networks. Qualified women are less likely to be visible to these men. Organizations are unwilling to take risks by appointing women who are not already serving on corporate boards. Organizations claim they have no empty seats. Organizations state there are not enough qualified women and that they do not know where to look for qualified women. Some writers (e.g., Lorsch & MacIver, 1989; Fleischer, Hazard & Klipper, 1988) even suggest that a homogeneous group of directors can deliberate and arrive at decisions more efficiently than they might if the director group was more diverse. Finally, legal mandates prescribing the role and responsibilities of boards of directors works against the appointment of representatives of excluded or minority groups, though it is hard to argue that 52% of the population is a minority!

Reasons for Having More Women on Boards

There are several reasons why appointing more qualified women to corporate boards has a solid business rationale. First, there are not enough qualified male CEOs to go around. CEOs currently on boards decline three times as many board invitations as do directors from other professions. A Korn-Ferry survey (1982) reported that 62% of all CEOs had declined at least one invitation to join a corporate board compared to only 22% among all other outside directors. The continuing reliance on male CEOs results in lower quality men being appointed. Given this situation, it is necessary that the selection of board members go beyond the traditional search for male CEOs as candidates.

In addition, male CEOs serving on boards indicated a variety of constraints on their contributions (Lorsch & MacIver, 1989). About one-fifth mentioned each of lack of expertise, little time for preparation and lack of information as constraints on their ability to contribute.

Nation's Business (1990) indicated that women serving on corporate boards can serve as role models for company recruits and indicate to potential female recruits that women can be upwardly mobile. That is, the appointment of women can have important symbolic value, both within and outside the organization. In a similar vein, both Mattis (1993) and Schwartz (1980) argue for lots of interaction between women on corporate boards and the managerial women in these organizations. In fact, Mattis argues that the two are interdependent. That is, appointing more women to boards will be associated with having more women in management, and vice versa.

It seems that the early motivations for appointing women to corporate boards involved tokenism and efforts to comply with/or head off employment equity legislation (Mattis, 1993). While this motivation still exists to some extent, other organizations seek such appointments because women directors may bring both business expertise as well as gender-specific perspectives which may be useful (Mattis, 1993). Women directors in Mitchell's study (1984) indicated what they believed were their three major contributions as directors to their boards. The most frequently mentioned contribution was a people perspective (21%), followed by a consumer perspective (14%), general management skills (13%), a regional perspective (13%), human resources skills (10%), public affairs expertise (10%), financial expertise (8%), industry expertise (7%), legal expertise (2%), and technical skills (1%). Thus women directors offered general competence and a variety of specific qualifications and experiences along with potentially useful gender-specific viewpoints.

A survey by Heidrick Partners observed that more women *without* corporate board experience were now being named as corporate directors. These women were selected because of their enhanced business experience and management knowledge, instead of specific board experience. Interestingly these women board members had higher educational qualifications than their male counterparts. This suggests the increasing appointment of women to corporate boards is likely to continue.

Do Women on the Board Make a Difference?

Do women approach directorships differently from men? The answer to this question, according to Mattis (1993), appears to be both yes and no. Women directors do bring new sensitivities and raise issues of greater relevance to women in board deliberations. But women directors, while perhaps calling themselves feminists in some cases, do not want to be branded as feminists. Women directors are often aware that women may have a special responsibility to speak up for women's interests and that others may expect them to do this. While aware of these expectations, the women directors in the 1991 Catalyst study did not necessarily accept responsibility for them.

Most women in the earlier Burson-Mosteller study believed that they could play a role in raising board awareness regarding issues of women in the workplace. But these women, and those in the later Catalyst Study, were aware of the dangers of having a "women's agenda". In fact, some companies look unfavourably on women directors bringing such sensitivities to the boardroom. In general, the vast majority of women directors wanted to be recognized for their general talents and abilities and knowledge as directors not as representatives of the interests of women.

In summary, women serving on corporate boards want to be seen as directors first, women second. They want to be known for their competence on board issues rather than as feminists. It also seems that women may bring particular sensitivities with them on issues important to women. In addition, having women on corporate boards may also influence the tone of board discussions making them less sexist. We do not have an answer to the question of whether women serving on corporate boards have, as part of their implicit mandate, responsibilities for supporting the career aspirations of the managerial and professional women in these organizations. This is not normally specified in the job description of women directors. Some organizations would look on these initiatives favourably, others would not. Some women directors would feel comfortable with these activities, others would not.

There has been relatively little research conducted on boards of directors in general and on women directors in particular. The research on women on corporate boards has been informative, but since so little research has been undertaken, much remains to be done. The only area that has received attention in a few investigations has been the demographic characteristics of women directors, how these compare to men directors, and how these may have changed over time. Almost all the other studies on women directors are idiosyncratic.

Results

The remainder of the chapter presents the results of a research study of the characteristic and experiences of Canadian women on corporate boards of directors. It attempts to both previous research as well as address new questions. More specifically it examines:

1. the personal, educational and career characteristics of Canada women directors,
2. their selection, acceptance and benefits of board memberships,
3. their views on whether having women on boards makes a difference to board processes and functioning,
4. whether women on corporate boards of directors represent forces for change, and
5. their views on why there aren't more women on corporate boards.

Names and addresses of Canadian women directors were obtained from the 1992 Financial Post *Directory of Directors* (Graham, 1991). Each was sent a questionnaire. The final response (N=278) represents about a fifty percent response rate. Some questionnaires were returned as the respondent was no longer at the listed address or with the company, others were not directors but company officers.

An eleven page survey, to be completed anonymously, accompanied by a stamped, self-addressed return envelope, was sent to each woman at either home or office address, depending on the listing in the *Directory of Directors*. A cover letter explained the purpose of the research. A postcard follow-up reminder was mailed out about one month later. All responses were received within slightly over two months of the date of initial mailing.

Characteristics and Background

About ninety percent of the women directors were university graduates. About one-quarter of the women held one or more professional designations. A majority were currently married (71%) with a like number having children, ranged between one and more than five children with an average of 2.4. Ages ranged from 28 to 81, with the average being 45. Respondents indicated their annual level of compensation (base pay plus bonus pay) at their current employment. Pay categories ranged from $50,000 or less (N=21, 8%) to over $400,000 (N=9, 4%). The majority fell in the $100,000 - $200,000 category (N=116, 46%) or the $50,000 - $100,000 category (N=78, 31%).

Respondents indicated, for four types of directorships (private sector, public sectors, not-for-profit, other) the number they held (0 through 5 or more). Most served on private sector boards (N=186, 67%) followed in turn by not-for-profit boards (N=166, 60%) public sector boards (N=121, 44%) and others (N=41, 15%). The sample, as a whole, had more total director-ships in the private sector (N=355), followed in turn by the not-for-profit sector (N=354), the public sector (N=183) and others (N=66). On average, the sample held 1.3 directorships in the private sector, 1.3 directorships in the not-for-profit sector, .6 directorships in the public sector, and .2 other directorships. Among women holding directorships in specific sectors, on average they sat on 1.8 private sector boards, 1.3 not-for-profit boards, 1.5 public sector boards, and 1.6 other boards. When all boards were considered together, women served on anywhere from one (66 women) to thirteen boards (one woman), with the average being 3.5 boards (median = 3; mode = 1).

Respondents were asked, aside from their positions as board directors, whether they had a primary occupation from which they received income. Only 26 (9%) had no other paid employment. The majority were full-time employees of organizations (N=157, 57%), owned their own businesses (N=39, 13%) or functioned as consultants, outside contractors, and freelancers (N=20, 7%).

Among those women with no other paid employment, the majority served either as part-time volunteers (N=13, 41%) were retired (N=10, 31%) or were not retired but worked only on boards (N=11, 34%).

Women directors indicated, for three broad categories of background or expertise (the professions, not-for-profit or public sector, business discipline) those areas in which they had significant background or expertise. Considering the professions first, 54 (19%) had accounting credentials and expertise, 45 (16%) had law training or legal expertise, and 22 (8%) had medical or health care credentials or expertise.

Considering next not-for-profit or public sector expertise, 62 (22%) had not-for-profit knowledge and experience, 58 (21%) had educational institution knowledge and experience, and 47 (18%) had government knowledge and experience.

Finally, considering various functional areas of business and management, almost half the women directors (N=134, 48%) indicated general management expertise, and about one-third (N=99, 36%) indicated financial expertise. About one-quarter reported public relations/advertising/communications expertise (N=72, 26%), market/sales expertise (N=66, 24%) and human resources expertise (N=62, 22%). Few women directors reported production/operations management expertise (N=28, 10%) or engineering/science expertise (N=12, 4%).

The personal and career demographic information indicates that Canadian women directors are an impressive and talented group. Almost ninety percent are university graduates and over forty percent have completed one or more graduate degrees. In addition over one-fifth of them possess one or more professional designations. In addition to these impressive formal credentials, women directors brought a variety of backgrounds and expertise to their director responsibilities. About forty percent had professional backgrounds (law, accounting, medicine or health care). Over half had not-for-profit or public sector experiences. Finally, many areas of business functional expertise were also represented (48%, general management; 36%, finance; 26%, PR or advertising; 24%, marketing or sales; 22%, human resources).

These women were also active on a variety of boards. One woman served on 13 boards; 60 women served on only one board. The typical woman director served on three boards. Most woman served on boards in different sectors (private, public, not-for-profit). Besides serving on boards, the women in the sample also had other employment. Most worked full-time for organizations (57%), were owners of business (13%), or were consultants or independent contractors (7%).

As a consequence of both their skills, education, type of employment and board service, these women received sizeable incomes. Almost half earned between $100,000 and $200,000, and fifteen percent earned over $200,000.

Although most women directors were married (70%) and had children (70%), these percentages are lower than those of their male board colleagues (Gillies, 1992; Lorsch & MacIver, 1989). Women directors in this study also were younger than those described by Mattis (1993) and Mitchell (1984). The women directors in the present study were, on average, 45 years old; the corresponding figures reported by Mattis and Mitchell were 53 and over, 56 respectively.

It is possible to draw some general conclusions about ways in which the demographic characteristics Canadian women directors may have changed during the past decade by comparing findings of Mitchell (1984) with those reported here. The following changes were observed. Current directors were younger, better educated, more likely to have business-oriented backgrounds, were more likely to be working full-time in organizations (as opposed to being homemakers or volunteers).

In the fall of 1976, the Chairman of a major Canadian bank remarked that no women served on his board because none were qualified to do so. It is unlikely such a statement would be publicly made today. Women have and are increasingly acquiring the education, background and experience qualifying them for board service. Women are therefore increasingly being asked to serve on corporate boards, and this trend is likely to continue. There are a variety of reasons for this, as noted by Schwartz (1980). Not only have corporate perceptions of women become more positive, they are under ever-increasing pressure to appoint more women - pressure coming from shareholders, consumers, employees and various levels of government.

Women directors showed considerable agreement on those characteristics ranked first: a strong track record in one's field or occupation was first (N=112, 42%), followed by business contacts (N=56, 21%), and a good understanding of general business principles (N=55, 20%). There was more diversity among the second choice of crucial characteristics but the same three emerged at the top: a strong track record (N=58, 22%) a good understanding of business principles (N=53, 20%), and business contacts (N=34, 13%). There was even more diversity among the third choices. An understanding of general business principles ranked first (N=45, 17%) followed by integrity (N=39, 15%), leadership qualities (N=33, 12%), and communication abilities (N=33, 12%). When the three choices were combined, the most crucial characteristics for attaining directorships were a strong track record in one's own field or occupation (N=196, 70%), a good understanding of general business principles (N=153, 55%) and business contacts (N=113, 40%).

A fairly similar pattern was observed for the three boards. The most common method was being recommended by a board member of the company or recruited by the nominating committee (N=206, 74%), followed by being recommended by the CEO (N=162, 58%), and being recommended by someone who knew the CEO or a board member (N=93, 33%).

Respondents also indicated why they thought there were selected as a director. Nine qualities or characteristics, along with a write-in "other" category, were provided. A fairly similar pattern was once again present across the three boards. The most common characteristic was having the desired area of expertise and responsibility (N=328, 39%), followed by holding appropriate job titles or leadership positions (N=299, 36%), being a women (N=267, 32%) and having high visibility (N=238, 28%).

Women directors then indicated a single item from this list which was the most important factor in their nomination to each board. Once again, a fairly similar pattern was present for each board. Taken the three boards together, the most important factor was having the desired areas of expertise or responsibility (N=158, 34%), followed by holding the appropriate job title or leadership position (N=81, 17%), being a women (N=58, 12%), fitting the desired regional profile for board members (N=44, 9%), having high visibility (N=43, 9%) and having corporate board experience (N=33, 7%).

The most important reason was an interest in the company, followed by wanting to broaden skills and areas of expertise, interest in the industry, would be personally satisfying to make a contribution to a corporate board, wanting to broaden general knowledge of business, feeling it was an honour, wanting to learn about corporate governance and making them more effective in their jobs or helping in their careers. These eight factors were all rated important. The remaining factors (bring a sensitivity about women's issues, income) were not very important.

The most common benefits were: participating in top level strategic planning and decision making, broadening general knowledge of business, other, helped develop new skills and areas of expertise, increased knowledge of corporate governance, and personal satisfaction of making a contribution to a corporate board. Much lower benefits were: giving a source of pride and prestige, more effective in own job or helped advance own career, increasing board sensitivity to issues affecting women, and income.

There was considerable agreement on the most and least important characteristics for attaining directorships. The former included a strong track record, business contacts, an understanding of business and advanced education. These indicate a successful career in traditional business organizations. Somewhat surprisingly, several skills and abilities (leadership qualities, objectivity, diplomacy and tact, communication ability) and character traits (integrity, intelligence) were not seen as very important. It may be that many women at this level have these so the former become the "extras" one needs to attain directorships. Interestingly, not-for-profit experience was seen as unimportant.

The data indicated, as have others (Lorsch & MacIver, 1989; Leighton & Thain, 1993), that being visible to male CEOs, male board chairmen and male board members was the most common route to board nomination. The "old boy's network" is still alive and well. Personal contacts and visibility to these gatekeepers was critical. Somewhat surprisingly, professional search firms seemed to have little impact here.

The reasons given for their selection as directors were somewhat consistent with the critical criteria for attaining directorships already reported. Thus, having the right expertise, holding the appropriate job (business) title, being a woman, having high visibility, and fitting a desired regional profile were important reasons. These women directors, as has already been reported (Mattis, 1993; Sethi, Swanson & Harrigan, 1981) realized they were selected *because* they were women. They also did not see this as a negative. Somewhat surprisingly, having previous board experience was not seen as an important reason for selection. It may be that these women were often the first women to serve on corporate boards, and they had to start somewhere. Once again, not-for-profit experience, having a knowledge of women's issues, or being a minority were seen as unimportant reasons for their selection to corporate boards. The last finding is not surprising since very few of the women in the sample were members of minority groups.

The reasons why women directors accepted board service seemed similar to those offered by men (Lorsch & MacIver, 1989) and involved both interest (company, industry) and efforts to broaden skill and knowledge. Personal satisfaction in influencing board activities was also important. These factors embody professional growth, satisfaction through application of knowledge and skill, and interest. Less important reasons (income, raising women's issues, honour, helping one's career, learning about corporate governance) also seemed similar to those offered by men (Lorsch & MacIver, 1989). These women had already developed successful careers, may be currently earning reasonable incomes, and may have sensed that having a "woman's agenda" would be a negative.

Women directors generally reported considerable benefits from their board experiences. Most of the areas of potential benefit were rated at least somewhat important. The most important benefits emphasized the acquisition and sharpening of skills, applying these skills through participating in strategy development, and learning more about corporate governance. Similarly, less important benefits included income, raising women's issues, helping their own careers, personal prestige and additional business contacts. Many of these women were either beyond those concerns or were aware of the "dangers" of carrying the women's banner.

The pattern of findings contained elements of both optimism and pessimism regarding increasing the numbers of women serving on corporate boards. The optimistic conclusions are based on the importance of a strong track record, business expertise and appropriate business job titles in attaining directorships. More and more women are acquiring these credentials. In addition, being a woman was also seen as influencing their appointments to corporate boards. The reasons women joined boards would also appeal to male board members because they were board and business related. Finally, the many benefits these women reported from their experiences on boards would pass on positive signals to other women interested in board service.

The pessimistic slant on these findings stems from the fact that the nomination process is still pretty much the result of the "old boy's network". Many qualified women would not be visible to this small, important but insulated group of men. Thus it is unlikely that the small percentage of current board members that are women will change appreciably in the short run. But Leighton and Thain (1993) offer useful suggestions for organizations interested in changing the composition of their boards; and Barrett (1993) suggests several motivations for doing so, as does Schwartz (1980).

Impact on Women's Issues

In general, women directors in our sample felt they had limited impact in these areas. The average response across all issues being neither agree nor disagree. Women directors believed they had their greatest effect on making female employees feel more positive about working for the company $(X=3.4)$, followed by increasing board sensitivity to issues affecting female employees $(X=3.3)$, increasing the representation of women in senior management $(X=3.0)$, making shareholders feel more positive about investing in the company $(X=2.7)$, and increasing the company's ability to recruit women $(X=2.6)$.

Women directors felt, perhaps with some justification, that their presence as a woman on the board had greater effects on the board as a whole and on the attitudes of female employees about the company than on external factors. They may have also been better able to gauge their influence on these matters as well.

A related question inquired whether respondents thought they had an impact on their board companies' sensitivity to issues that affect women. Twenty-five (9.0%) thought they influenced companies' sensitivity to a great extent, one-hundred and thirty-eight thought to some extent (52%), and one-hundred and four (39%) thought they had no impact.

210

Types of Impact

Women directors indicating that they had an impact on companies' sensitivity to issues that affect women were then asked to explain the type of impact they had. These write-in comments were content analyzed and twenty-one categories were noted. Up to three responses were coded where appropriate.

Let us consider first responses. The most common impact involved raising issues (N=45, 16%), supporting personnel policies conducive to becoming "women friendly" (N=24, 9%) assisting the career development of managerial women (N=14, 5%), serving as a role model (N=10, 5%), providing another viewpoint (N=9, 3%) and questioning the treatment of women (N=9, 3%). No other impact received more than five mentions. Fewer women provided a second impact. The most common, among those who did, were assisting the career development of managerial women (N=11, 4%), raising issues (N=6, 2%), serving as a role model (N=4 1%) and providing another viewpoint (N=4, 1%). Each of the third responses was offered by only one woman. Taken together, a wide range of areas of impact were indicated.

Women directors indicating that they thought they had no impact on companies' sensitivity to issues that affect women were asked to explain why this was the case. Responses were written and content analyzed. In general, significantly fewer responses were provided by women directors to this question. The most common first responses were: such issues were not discussed at the board level (N=19, 7%) the company was already sensitive to women's issues (N=18, 6%), the company had no women's issues (N=9, 3%), the company was not "tuned in" to women's issues (N=7, 2%) and, gender was irrelevant to the issues that are being discussed by the board (N=6, 2%). Only ten other responses were provided as second and third responses (9 and 1, response, respectively). Only one response, company interested in preserving the status quo, received two endorsements. Once again, a wide variety of limiting factors to having impact on women's issues were identified, but these were few in number.

Women directors indicated whether they currently served on boards on which they were unable to make a substantial contribution. Ninety-one said yes, (34%); one hundred and seventy-seven said no (66%). Respondents indicating yes were then asked why this was the case. Seven responses plus an open-ended "other" category were provided. The most common reason cited (N=46, 51%) were that directors were not fully utilized. This was followed in turn by: being still too new on the board (31%), not having enough time to be prepared to make a solid contribution (N=20, 22%), other (N=19, 21%), directors not provided with enough information (N=18, 20%), lacking the background to make a contribution to a particular board (N=12, 13%), not having an adequate business background (N=8, 9%) and their opinions were not listened to (N=7, 8%).

Women directors do indeed believe they have an impact on their board company's sensitivity to issues that affect women. Sixty-one percent of respondents responded this way. This conclusion was generally supported when specific issues were considered. But women directors believed they had greater impact on internal issues than on external issues (e.g., recruiting women, shareholders feelings).

The specific type of impact identified in the written responses of women directors were also consistent with an inside-the-organization focus. The most common were: raising issues of concern to women, supporting women-friendly policies, helping the career advancement of managerial women and servicing as role models, providing other viewpoints and questioning the treatment of women.

These findings support the conclusion of others (Mattis, 1993; Schwartz, 1980; Sethi, Swanson & Harrigan, 1981; Mitchell, 1984) that women directors can bring unique sensitivities on gender issues, along with general board-related competence and experience, to their board responsibilities. This does not apply to all women directors or all corporate boards however.

Several factors operated to limit the impact of women directors on women's issues. Some of these would also apply to men and issues other than women's issues. These factors would include: directors not being fully utilized, being too new and not having enough time to devote to board responsibilities and lacking the information required to do a thorough job. Only eight percent of women directors felt their opinions were not listened to by male directors and only eight percent felt they lacked adequate business backgrounds to make a contribution.

Other limiting factors were structural and systemic. These included such factors as not discussing such issues at the board level, discussing issues which do not involve gender, and the company not being tied in to women's issues. And as some women directors noted some companies are already sensitive (though it is not clear why this would result in no discussion) and some companies have no women's issues (it is difficult to imagine such circumstances).

The few women serving on corporate boards of directors are already having some impact on board performance on women's issues. And as more women get appointed to corporate boards their impact will undoubtedly be greater and more far-reaching in this area. It is also possible more CEOs/Board Chairmen will realize that appointing more women to their boards has become a business concern with bottom-line implications (Schwartz, 1980). These involve not only enhanced board decision making, creativity and innovation, but also a number of potential effects inside and outside the organization. The former include role-modelling for women managers and professionals, the development of a more women-friendly organizational culture (i.e., policies and practices) and career guidance for high performing women. The latter include becoming, for women, an employer of choice, for clients a service provider of choice, and for potential and current shareholders, an investment of choice.

CEOs and Board Chairmen need to understand the additional purposes women corporate directors can serve, legitimate such activities on the part of women directors, and negotiate such roles and responsibilities when women directors are appointed (Schwartz, 1980).

Appropriate Policy Issues for Board Discussion

Most women directors felt all seven policy issues listed were appropriate for boards of directors to address. Environmental issues (N=269, 98%) ranked first, followed by other social responsibility issues (N=227, 91%), equal opportunity for high performing women (N=216, 85%), equal opportunity for high performing minorities (N=207, 82%) enabling employees to balance work and family (N=203, 81%), additional women on the board (N=189, 76%), and needs of women as consumers (N=148, 62%).

Women directors, however, felt significantly less personal responsibility as women directors to address each of these policy issues. These percentages ranged from a high of seventy-two percent (N=157, equal opportunity for high performing women) to a low of forty-five percent (N=94, environmental issues). Finally, significantly fewer women directors felt it was expected of them as women directors to address these issues. Instead it was a director's role to address such issues regardless whether the director was a women or a man. On average, almost twice as many women directors believed these issues were appropriate for board discussion as opposed to believing it was expected of them to raise and address them. These findings, however do suggest that many women directors were aware of special responsibilities women have on particular issues because they are women.

Women directors indicated whether they had themselves initiated any of these policy issues in general board meetings or committee meetings. Almost two-thirds (N=171, 64%) indicated that they had. They then indicated which of the seven policy issues they initiated. In general, fewer than twenty-five percent of the respondents indicated such initiatives. These ranged from equal opportunities for high performing women (N=81, 29%), enabling work-family balance (N=75, 27%), social responsibility issues (N=69, 25%), environmental issues (N=68, 24%), more women on the board (N=54, 19%), one equal opportunity for high performing minorities (N=41, 15%).

Women directors were asked how frequently they interacted with senior-level women at any companies of which they were directors. About one-quarter (N=73, 27%) had frequent interaction; forty-one percent (N=100) had occasional interaction, ten percent had no interaction (N=27) and almost one quarter (N=60, 22%) indicated that there were no senior-level women at any of the companies of which they were directors.

Women directors who indicated some frequency of interaction with senior-level managerial women at any of the companies of which they were directors, were asked in what ways this interaction occurred. These responses were written-in and content analyzed. Up to three responses were coded for each respondent.

Considering those responses mentioned first, the most common type of interaction occurred at meetings where board issues were discussed (N=52, 19%), serving together on board committees (N=19, 7%), routine board contacts (N=22, 8%), social contacts (8%) and through requests for information (N=11, 4%). Fewer respondents provided second responses. Of these responses, the most frequent were formal social contacts (N=18, 6%) and serving together on board committees (N=9, 3%). Very few women provided third responses; none received more than four endorsements. Those that did included: formal social contacts (N=4, 1%) and support with career development (N=4, 1%). When the distribution of all responses is considered, meetings where board issues were discussed (N=59, 21%), social contacts (N=43, 16%), normal board contacts (N=28, 10%) and through board committees (N=28, 10%) were the most common types of interactions with company women.

Women directors who had no (or little) contact with senior women in the companies at which they were directors were asked why this was the case. Responses were written and content analyzed. Very few responses were provided; no woman wrote more than one. The most common reasons for no contact with senior-level women were: respondent was too busy (N=5,

2%), and these were no (or few) managerial women in these companies (N=5, 2%).

The women directors in this study seemed to be active in raising and/or discussing policy issues of relevance to women. The vast majority believed each of the seven policy issues was appropriate for board discussion (over 80%). almost fifty-eight percent of respondents felt it was their responsibility to address these issues and about forty-three percent felt it was expected of them. Equal opportunities for women and work and family policies were typically ranked among the top three policy issues.

Almost two-thirds of the women had raised one or more of these policy issues for discussion. But the two most widely initiated policy issues (equal opportunity for women, work and family policies) were raised by less than one-third of the respondents. These data indicate that women directors on private sector corporate boards are indeed serving as potential forces for change on issues relevant to women in the broader society.

About two-thirds of the women directors had interactions with senior-level women in the companies on whose boards they served. But these interactions seemed narrowly focused on board-related matters and meetings. These data suggest that women directors are having little direct impact on the managerial and professional women in the companies on whose boards they sit. It is possible that they might serve as role models for such women and benefit them indirectly through the advancement of more "women friendly" policies.

Women serving on corporate boards seemed to be playing an active role in raising and discussing issues of concern to women, both inside and outside of their organizations. This was consistent with observations of others (Mattis, 1993; Schwartz, 1980), and supports the conclusion that women directors are functioning as champions for change on women's issues. This picture is increasingly likely to be the case as more women get appointed to corporate boards, though such progress is likely to be slow.

It may also be possible for organizations to reap additional benefits from women directors once they realize the potential advantages of fostering interaction between women directors and senior-level women (Mattis, 1993;

Schwartz, 1980). Such interaction, beyond routine board-management contacts might impact on career development of senior-level women, reducing their attrition, increasing retention, and influencing the attractiveness of the organization in the recruitment of women. This requires some significant change in the expectations and roles of women directors, and perhaps directors in general.

Why Aren't More Women Directors and on Corporate Boards?

Respondents were asked, thinking about the entire pool of current board members, whether the mix of professional experiences and backgrounds was adequate. One hundred and seven (40%) thought it was; 159 (60%) thought it was not.

Women directors were then asked which types of people should be increased. One hundred and eighteen (42%) believed there should be more women; 51 (18%) believed there should be an increase in board members with different ethnic or racial backgrounds; 50 (18%) thought more members should have business experience; 48 (17%) advocated more heads of small companies; and 45 (16%) wanted more directors who were not CEOs or presidents of organizations. Respondents ranked not-for-profit experience, government experience, and educational experience in lower priority.

Women directors were asked for their views on why more women were not directors of Canadian private sector companies. Eight possible reasons, and another (write-in) categories were provided. Respondents indicated as many reasons as applied. The most common reason given was that companies do not know where to look for qualified women (N=143, 51%). This was followed in turn by: companies are not looking to put more women on boards (N=134, 48%); companies don't think women are qualified for board service (N=126, 45%); companies are afraid to take on women who are not already on boards (N=121, 44%); qualified women are not making it known that they are interested in board service (N=109, 35%); companies are concerned that women will have a "women's issues" agenda (N=98, 35%); there were not enough qualified women for board service (N=70, 25.2); other (N=24, 67); and qualified women are not interested in board service (N=10, 4%).

Women directors believed that the current mix of board members was inadequate. They wanted more women, board members with more varied experience and background (small business, different racial and ethnic backgrounds) and fewer CEOs.

Women directors attributed the absence of women on corporate boards primarily to attitudes of male CEOs and Board Chairmen. Male CEOs were seen as thinking that women were not qualified, were afraid to take on new and untried women, or were fearful that women might have a women's agenda. In addition, women directors believed that organizations were not looking to put women on their boards or did not know when to look for women. Women themselves were seen as shouldering some of the responsibility for their absence by not making their interests known. The women directors in the study seemed to have identified, quite realistically, the reasons why so few women serve on corporate boards.

Recommendations

These findings suggest that women will continue to be absent from the boards of Canadian private sector organizations. There is no obvious punishment from failing to do so. The perceived attitudes of male CEOs and Board Chairmen remain an obstacle to such appointments. For this picture to change, male CEOs and Board Chairmen will have to approach the director selection process differently (Leighton & Thain, 1993; Barrett, 1993). This will obviously involve a more extensive search process. Related to this would be looking at levels below the CEO to find qualified but still invisible women. An important question that remains is what role women currently on corporate boards will or should play in this process.

In order to find more qualified corporate women, CEOs will have to look lower than the CEO level to get talented - but invisible - women. Motivation for this will come, in part, from the difficulty companies say they are having in recruiting nominees for board positions (e.g., conflict of interest, exposure to liability, amount of time involved). Schwartz (1980) identifies two challenges for organizations in this regard: identifying and selecting the best of this "unknown" pool of candidates, and defining and communicating their expectations for women directors. Board chairmen need to articulate a "contract" with women directors. What are their (the board's) expectations on expertise and perspective and her ability to perform? This would include women directors contributions via expertise and perspective, as well as enhancing morale and productivity of women inside the organization. This results from their presence as role models, as well as their active communication with internal women so that their specific needs and problems are addressed. This, of course, needs the consent and encouragement of top management. Women directors may be able to more freely ask questions than male directors, and serve as modest forces for change. Recruiting women to corporate boards then becomes a source of competitive advantage and a bottom-line business issue.

Notes

1. This research was supported in part by the Faculty of Administrative Studies, York University. I would like to thank Mary Mattis and Catalyst for permission to use their survey. Rachel Burke, Doug Turner and Ruth McKay assisted with the collection of the data and Cobi Wolpin helped with data analysis.

References

Barrett, M.W., (1993), Restructuring the board, *Business Quarterly*, 57, 34-40.

Burke, R.J. & C.A. McKeen, (1992), Women in management, in: C.L. Cooper & I.T. Robertson, (Eds.) *International Review of Industrial and Organizational Psychology*, New York, John Wiley, pp. 245-283.

Elgart, L.D., (1983), Women on Fortune 500 boards, *California Management Review*, 25, 121-127.

Financial Post, (1984), Corporate boards are slow to admit women, June 16, 2, 6.

Financial Post, (1990), Women have made modest gains onto boards. May 2, 3, 5.

Fleischer, A., G.C. Hazard, & M.Z. Klipper, (1988), *Board Games: The Changing Shape of Corporate Power*, Boston, Mass., Little Brown & Company.

Ghiloni, B.W., (1984), The corporate scramble for women directors, *Business and Society Review*, 86-95.

Gillies, J.M., (1992), *Boardroom Renaissance*, Toronto, McGraw-Hill.

Globe & Mail, (1990), Despite recent gains, women still a rare breed on company boards, May 2, B7.

Globe & Mail, (1993), Women face closed door to board rooms; No representation, no power, June 30, 131, 14.

Graham, J., (1991), *Directory of Directors*, Toronto, The Financial Post.

Harrigan, K.R., (1981), Numbers and positions of women elected to corporate boards, *Academy of Management Journal*, 24, 619-625.

Human Resources Magazine Update, (1992), Women directors, January, 37, 20-21

Kesner, I.F., (1988), Directors' characteristics and committee membership: an investigation of type, occupation, tenure, and gender, *Academy of Management Journal*, 31, 66-84.

Leighton, D. & D. Thain, (1993), Selecting new directors, *Business Quarterly*, 57, 16-25.

Lorsch, J.W. & E. MacIver, (1989), *Pawns or potentates: The reality of America's corporate boards*, Boston, Mass., Harvard Business School Press.

Mace, M., (1971), *Directors: Myth and reality*, Boston, Mass., Division of Research, Harvard Business School.

Mattis, M.C., (1993), Women Directors: Progress and Opportunities for the Future, *Business and the Contemporary World*, 5, 140-156.

Mitchell, M., (1984), A profile of the Canadian woman director, *Business Quarterly*, 51, 121-127.

Nations Business, (1990), Companies court women for boards, January, 78, 52.

Patton, A. & J.C. Baker, (1987), Why directors won't rock the boat, *Harvard Business Review*, 65, 10-12, 16, 18.

Salmon, W.J., (1993), Crisis Prevention: How to gear up your board, *Harvard Business Review*, 71, 68-75.

Schwartz, I.N., (1980), Invisible resource: Women for boards, *Harvard Business Review*, 16-18.

Sethi, S.P., C.L. Swanson, & K.R. Harrigan, (1981), *Women Directors on Corporate Boards*, Richardson, Texas: Center for Research in Business and Social Policy, University of Texas at Dallas.

Sherman, S.P., (1988), Pushing corporate boards to be better, *Fortune*, July 18, p 58.

Wall Street Journal (1986).

9 Women and Prostitution Management

Lucie van Mens

Faculty of Business Management,
Erasmus University Rotterdam,
the Netherlands

Prostitution has been an issue for public as well as political debate in the Netherlands for the past decade. A small number of prostitutes participate openly in the political discussion, mainly to draw attention to unfavourable working conditions in prostitution enterprises. More importantly, these prostitutes seek ways of organizing their own prostitution enterprises in an effort to create alternatives to the existing suppressive organizational structure of this sector. Profits are divided in a disproportionate manner favouring entrepreneurs. This demand for (a collective of) prostitution enterprises managed by female entrepreneurs who are or have themselves been active prostitutes seems to be inspired by both emancipatory ideals and emotional reasons. Prostitution is a rather particular form of profession. Therefore, emotional complications involved can best be realized by women who have experienced prostitution themselves. On these and other grounds prostitutes argue that managers of prostitution enterprises who have no practical experience are unable to understand levels of aggravation inherent to their job, and thus make on them unreasonable demands on them.

However, in practice a substantial number of the several hundreds of prostitution enterprises in the Netherlands are already managed by female entrepreneurs, and a large number of these female entrepreneurs are (ex) prostitutes. Against this background, the ongoing demand by prostitutes in public and political debate for possibilities to organize prostitution enterprises managed by (ex) prostitutes creates confusion. The question to be answered in this chapter is whether female management of prostitution enterprises is an adequate precondition for the improvement of organizational structures and labour relations in the sex branch?

This chapter is organized in four sections. First, I will develop the conceptual analysis framework. In the second section I will describe briefly the main developments in the organization of prostitution in the Netherlands during recent decades. Furthermore, I will provide a brief overview of the organization of the prostitution branch in Rotterdam - where I collected data during field research - and will analyze whether there is a distinction between nature and size of enterprises managed by women and those managed by men.[1] In section three, the core of this chapter, I will analyze the way female-managed prostitution enterprises are organized and managed using two case studies. The conclusion analyzes whether the fact that a prostitution enterprise is managed by a female manager is an adequate precondition for the realization of acceptable working conditions for prostitutes.

The 'forgotten' managers: a conceptual framework

In organizational studies and more specific studies on female management, the management of prostitution enterprises is totally neglected. This neglect stems from a tangle of reasons. Traditionally, prostitution was seen as an occupation, but more as a crime, a sin or as deviant behaviour. The entrepreneurship of prostitution enterprises has continuously been perceived as a suspicious occupation which generates income from exploitation of female weaknesses.[2] As a result of social condemnation of the prostitution, the taboo on selling sexual services and all kinds of more or less criminal activities which sometimes were developed in prostitution enterprises, brothels have been defined as criminal organizations. In most Western countries nowadays prostitution enterprises are officially forbidden by law and, as a result, are illegal organizations.

In so-called 'normal' or legal organizations, leadership or management has traditionally been a male task. In contrast the management of prostitution enterprises was not an exclusively male occupation. Apart from the above mentioned reasons why prostitution was not accepted as a job or its management as an occupation, the cause seems to be the gendered basis of prostitution, on both theoretical and practical levels. Unlike other jobs, prostitution cannot be defined as gender neutral. Men cannot fulfil the tasks of prostitutes.[3] Joan Acker (1992) claims that at an abstract level other 'regular' jobs can be defined as gender neutral, but that the abstract worker transformed into a concrete worker turns out to be a man. In reality, work is *his* life and his wife takes care of everything else. Acker: 'Thus the concept of a job is gendered, in spite of its presentation as gender neutral, because only a male worker can begin to meet its implicit demands'.[4] In prostitution women are the workers and this is at odds the gendered concept of jobs in which men are the workers. Prostitutes, however, always kept the characteristic 'female' (with adjectives like sinful, criminal, deviant, pitiful, etcetera). In contrast the Madams, who I define as managers of prostitution enterprises, were considered rough and masculine, with little consideration for the feelings of their employees. The question is whether this characterization is based on careful observation or on strong gendered-based assumptions of what a manager should be.

Female managers of prostitution enterprises are, in fact, not the only female entrepreneurs who have to cope with prejudices against their occupation. Entrepreneurship is commonly considered a male activity. In her research on Dutch female entrepreneurs, Anna Aalten (1991) applied an interesting method of studying the manner in which female entrepreneurs reconcile their professional identity with their sex identity. In this context, sex identity must be defined as the ability to be a wife and mother who takes care of the traditional female tasks as a housewife. She found that in spite of commercial success female entrepreneurs did not always define their activities as entrepreneurship. They reconciled their professional identity with their sex identity in redefining entrepreneurship as a form of service industry, and as a kind of 'social motherhood'.[5] Other studies also emphasize that female managers show a high affinity with their workers.[6] The redefinition of the occupation of manager or entrepreneur into 'social motherhood' is perhaps only an attempt to reconcile two 'conflicting' roles as manager and women. The question is whether 'social motherhood' and affinity with employees have positive results for real labour relations and work conditions within the enterprises managed by female entrepreneurs?

Koopman and Walvis (1985) conducted an extensive exploratory study amongst female entrepreneurs in the Netherlands. These entrepreneurs claimed that the biggest difference between male and female entrepreneurs is their management style. Their relationship with their employees was considered more personal than in male-managed enterprises, and employees received more training. Again the question must be whether employees consider favourable this difference in management style and the personal relationship with their employer.

Koopman and Walvis also developed a typology of female entre-preneurs: The 'conventionals', the 'hobbyistic', the 'innovative' and the 'alternative'. The 'conventional' entrepreneurs have a positive attitude towards both traditional ideals of entrepreneurship and traditional male-female relations. The 'hobbyistic' entrepreneurs are not greatly concerned with entrepreneurial values, but cure about traditional male-female relations. The 'innovative' entrepreneurs are sceptical about the traditional male-female relations, but take a very severe approach to entrepreneurial values. For the 'alternative' entrepreneurs the decision to start an enterprise resulted from political conviction. They have no faith in traditional entrepreneurial values and attacked traditional male-female relations. The labour conditions of (female) employees where considered more important than the enterprise itself.

Female entrepreneurs interviewed by Aalten claim that their decision to become an entrepreneur was not always a conscious choice, but more an outcome of their (personal) circumstances. For example, husband's early death forced them to take over his enterprise. Others claim that their businesses were started as a hobby and grew unexpectedly. In all cases empathy with their employees was a reason to continue their occupation.

From this perspective the questions to be addressed are: how female entrepreneurs in prostitution define their professional identity? Do they consider themselves 'conservative' or 'alternative'? Do they try to reconcile their professional identity with their sex identity by redefining their tasks as 'social motherhood'? The next question is whether their potentially female managerial style has positive results for the labour conditions of their workers?

The management style of female entrepreneurs in the prostitution branch can not be analyzed in isolation from a broader knowledge of the sexual services in common and more specifically, the position of the 'madams' and their enterprises in that market. Several studies on 'regular' enterprises headed by women showed that the number of employees in these enterprises is lower than in enterprises managed by men.[7] Furthermore, women tend to start enterprises in branches which are defined as traditionally female, such as personal services and in the textile and care industries. Prostitution should also be defined as a personal service and as part of the leisure industry. The first question to be addressed is whether the size of female managed prostitution enterprises is smaller or larger than those managed by men. Secondly, whether female managed enterprises can be found in all segments of the prostitution market?

Developments in the market and segmentation

Laws, regulations and market developments

In the Netherlands prostitution is not forbidden, but prostitution enterprises as such are illegal. In practice however prostitution enterprises are tolerated. One of the reasons for this tolerance is that the content of the laws regulating prostitution enterprises is vague which makes it difficult to prove that these laws, which stem from 1911, have been violated. In addition attitudes towards prostitution in society have changed over time. In most contempor-

227

ary Dutch cities prostitution is more or less accepted as a part of city life and an active prohibition of prostitution enterprises is seen as not realistic.

The change in attitude towards prostitution has given more space for organizational changes in the prostitution branch. For example, until the nineteen sixties prostitution was nearly exclusively located in areas in old quarters, or near the city centres, popularly known as red light districts. However with the sexual liberation of the nineteen sixties there were less inhibitions regarding prostitution. As a consequence the 'supply' from the red light district became broader and new types of prostitution enterprises appeared. The diversification of the supply seems not only to be caused by a growing tolerance towards sex and sexuality but also due to increase in general economic prosperity.[8] Visitors of sex enterprises could now pay higher prices and accordingly the prostitution branch reacted by fulfilling new demands and more luxurious wishes. Since the nineteen sixties new enterprises appeared, not only in the alleys of the red light districts but also along stately avenues and canals. The uniformity in the supply, which was characteristic of the prostitution branch in the first half of this century, disappeared and the sex market increasingly became segmented.

The prostitution branch in Rotterdam - the biggest harbour in the world and the second biggest city in the Netherlands - consists mainly of ninety enterprises. In addition there are a few escort services, and more or less independent working prostitutes who meet clients at home or in pubs. According to the laws in practice street prostitution is concentrated on one street. The number of prostitutes that works daily in Rotterdam is estimated 1220.[9] The daily number of prostitutes working in the enterprises is around 750. Around forty percent of these prostitutes are of non-Dutch origin.

The ninety enterprises can be roughly divided into two types namely sexclubs and private houses. The difference is that the service package in the clubs is broader than in the private houses. The clubs not only offer sexual services but also floor shows, liquors and bath facilities which are more extensive than in private houses. Clubs charge higher prices for the sexual services than private houses.

The number of prostitutes working in clubs is on average higher than in private houses where only a few women, around two till five, work together. In the biggest club in Rotterdam there are more than thirty women.

The entrance as an entrepreneur

The managers of all the thirty sexclubs in Rotterdam are without exception men. In some of the clubs however wives or girlfriends are also actively involved in the management. Most of the private houses on the contrary are led by female managers. The female entrepreneurs are mostly experienced prostitutes. Some of them combine their managerial tasks with active prostitution, but most of them withdraw gradually from their old occupation in favour of the managerial tasks.

Reason for the different market position between by male and female managed enterprises can partly be explained by the way in which they enter the market. The women start their enterprise at a stage in which they still may be successful as prostitutes, while at the same time realizing that they can not continue for longer. As their age increases, clients' interest in them will decline.

In many cases the women start their enterprise in their own living house. They may have had already the habit to receive once in a while clients at home and they start to rent the 'facilities' at home to colleges. The entrance as a manager is a gradual process. When the business is not flourishing or when the new entrepreneur is not able to cope with all kind of organizational problems which arise inevitably, she can easily close the enterprise. Her investments are small and she is not confronted with a big loss. If the business runs well and the new manager is able to attract both clients and prostitutes who work for her, she plans to expand or to make investments in her house in order to create a more market-oriented atmosphere. At this stage the managerial activities are no longer experimental.

To set up a club initial investments are needed, especially when the club is to be located in a building which previously had another function. In order to buy the building managers take a loan and must be able to prove that they are trustable entrepreneurs and debtors.

For prostitutes it is difficult to obtain a mortgage.[10] In case they have an ambition to start a club they usually have to convince some creditor to invest in their business. Since prostitutes do not have either much experience in entrepreneurship or even working experiences, investors do not always consider them as worthy debtors, particularly when the nature of their job is revealed. Not all the clubs however are owned by the managers. Most of them are hired. New managers who are considered able to manage the club and have enough cash to pay the (high) premiums, are usually acquaintances or sometimes even relatives of the owner of the clubs.

Two case studies

Expansion of the enterprises

The start as an entrepreneur and manager of a small enterprise, located in the own living apartment and a few employees/prostitutes, by no means implicate that it is impossible to expand the business. In this third part of the article I will describe the way in which two female entrepreneurs organized and expanded their businesses. I choose to make an in depth study of these two enterprises because they were typical for the way in which private houses in Rotterdam are organized.[11] I will pay special attention to the question whether their approach to business was similar to other female entrepreneurs in other branches. How do they reconcile their professional identity with their sex identity? Are they able to create favourable working conditions for their employees?

In the following paragraphs I will briefly describe their backgrounds, the way in which they approach their business, and strategies in which they attempt to attract more clients, and the working conditions and circumstances of the prostitutes.

The two entrepreneurs, who I address as Jane and Caroline, are both in their middle age. They have both worked more than ten years as prostitutes, and than started their enterprise in their apartments. Jane and Caroline are not mutual acquaintances but this doesn't mean that there is no awareness regarding each others existence and even work style. Most managers of private houses know each other at least by names and at times have substantial information about each others enterprises. Source of such information are usually prostitutes who in the process of shifting work place, inform their new bosses about previous experiences.

Before Jane joined prostitution she was administrative worker at a commercial enterprise. She has been married and has a daughter. After her divorce she had sexual contacts with several men. Disappointment in her relations and lack of money were main reasons to become a prostitute. At the age of thirty nine Jane remarried and had a second child. Since then she stopped working as a prostitute and only manages her enterprise.

Caroline had worked as a saleswoman in a shoe shop before entering prostitution. Financial constraints were also the main reason for her to enter prostitution. Caroline is not married but has a steady relation with one man. She decided to stop working as a prostitute, since she is too occupied running her enterprise.

Both women have expanded their enterprises over the years. Jane manages four private houses, where in total around fourteen prostitutes, most of them part-time, are employed. She is the owner of the apartments. Apart from these private houses Jane also owns a house which she rents to students. Her 'official occupation' is landlady. Jane plans to withdraw from the prostitution totally in a few years time and to rent her four private houses in a 'regular' way. Reason being that she does not want to confront her second daughter with the fact that she is a sex madam. Besides that Jane wants to move to a suburb far away from her private houses. Whether and when her plans to close her business will become reality is yet to be seen.[12] Caroline does not think about retirement. On contrary, she tries to expand her business continuously. In 1989 she managed six private houses and in 1991 eleven. However, she disposed of four houses due to difficulties in managing them and now restricts herself to the management of seven houses. She hires the apartments in which the private houses are located. During the period Caroline managed six houses she had around eighteen prostitutes working for her on full time basis. The analysis of Carolines management style and approach to her business presented in the next paragraphs, refers to the period during which she 'only' managed six private houses.

Jane and Caroline approach and organize their businesses in a different style. Jane clearly defines herself as an entrepreneur: "Originally I belong to the business world. I continuously made investments from my own earnings. I have worked until I was forty.[13] My business is a small enterprise and one has to approach it like that. I have started some business and I have responsibility towards the bank, and business is running quite efficiently. But I also had good luck. I bought the first house in 1981, the second in 1982 and the next one in '83. It was possible in those days. My bank had an easy administrator. Now I have six premises. When I bought the last one, I could not get a mortgage. They said that a loan for a prostitution enterprise was not allowed any longer".

Contrary to Jane, Caroline does not define herself as an entrepreneur. She describes herself as a mother of a group of rather afloat girls, who needs her constant interference and education. Caroline: "I have six houses but for years I don't do anything else than helping the girls. I help them with their saving accounts.[14] I go with them to the bank to teach them how to manage their monetary affairs. And if they have problems, they can always rely on me. But not all the girls like to work for me. Some of them leave, that's because of me. They find my rules to strict. Yes, I am demanding, but you have to bring them up. They are all children. Although it might be strange, but these girls are like my children, irrespective of the fact that they work one or eight years".

The different approach and opinion towards business, results in a different style of personnel management. Jane wants her employees to work as independent as possible, she does not exercise control on them continuously. She advises them how to approach for example clients, but these advises are not binding. Her task is much less labour intensive than that of

Caroline, all the more because Caroline supplies food daily to her employees. Lunch and dinner are prepared in every house by Caroline or ex prostitutes who guard her houses. Jane does not supply food to the prostitutes and it is also not possible for them to stay in her houses. On the contrary Caroline provide the facility to stay overnight without payment. Jane considers it dangerous for the development and independence of prostitutes to bind them too much to the enterprise and to the prostitution business in common. As a result of social condemnation of the profession many prostitutes tend to isolate themselves from the 'regular' society, and might loose their old ties. Jane: "It is important to keep social contacts outside the prostitution world. I always tell them so and that is why I do not allow them to work continuously but from Mondays to Fridays only. During the week-ends the second group takes over and this is better. These young girls are exhausted after having entertained ten or fifteen clients a day. I do not allow them to work full time and half a day is enough. I do not interfere much but I give them some advises. For example to keep a cashbook, in order to get a better understanding of their income. They create their own job and do not work for the boss. But some of them can not cope with this independence. With me you have to become independent. I do not cook for them and they have to take their own food".

The market strategy

Both Jane and Caroline manage houses on cheaper market segment. The prices are determined by the nature of the sexual services offered. In both enterprises the cheapest services cost fifty guilders and the most expensive hundred twenty five.

For Jane the cheap prices are a result of a conscious strategy. She is aiming at a larger number of customers who are not able or willing to pay too much for a sexual encounter. She is aware that her houses - as a result of price and the limited services - do not appeal to the taste of customers with more luxurious demands. Jane: "When one aims at only fifteen percent of the population, one cannot offer diverse services on cheaper prices. It is better to keep the prices low, than you receive more customers. But there are always men who are attached to the atmosphere of clubs and they do not come here again".

In relation to the furnishing of the houses the prices are low and in this respect Jane offers more than her direct competitors like Caroline. Caroline hardly made any investments in her houses. The furnishing is old. In relation to the surrounding it is not possible to ask higher prices for the services and from this point of view she does not have an advantageous market position.

As managers and ex-prostitutes Jane and Caroline have their own answer to the question of why men visit prostitutes. Jane about this topic: "I never gave it a deep thought to why they come. It can be the result of a bad relation, but that is not necessarily so. However one trend is clear. When he starts, he continues to use prostitution according to his budget and desire. If he starts in his twenties, he continues to use it until his eighties. In such a case the nature of his relationship is irrelevant. It is the sensation of another female body. It does not matter whether it was satisfactory the first time or not. When it was pleasant, he thinks, I go again. If it was disappointing, than he goes again to see whether it is always going to be like that". And Caroline: "Nine out of ten clients have a wife and children. They live in a house where they have to be silent. The children will notice when the parents do 'it'. That's why they come, because here they can do 'it'. They have a good marriage, that's not the problem. They love their wives".

The clients' choice

Both Caroline and Jane advertise several times a week in daily newspapers, mentioning some characteristics of their employees like their outlooks, characters or sexual possibilities. The text of the advertisements is however not always in accordance with the reality. Especially the age differs from the real age of the prostitutes, which is usually several years older than stated in the advertisements, because most clients feel attracted to younger girls.[15]

Managers try to distinguish their enterprise from others through the advertisements. It is not easy to be original in a few lines and good advertisements are more or less copied by others. For example, when Jane worked as a prostitute, she promised 'twice a climax' in her advertisements. She was the first to use these words, which are often used by others now. When a new girl works in one of the houses it is always mentioned. 'New' appeals to the curiosity of the customers and new or unknown prostitutes attract a lot of clients. After a few weeks however the new comer is not considered new any longer and the number of customers may decrease.

The income of prostitutes is closely related to the amount of customers they have. It can be assumed that it is not complicated to 'educate' prostitutes to become customer friendly workers. Prostitutes however are aware of the attractiveness of being 'new'. In spite of the fact that they may be rather old workers they can choose for strategies in which they are repeatedly considered to be new. In order to do so they continuously shift working place and as new-comers attract a lot of customers. They do not invest too much energy in their clientele. Since they plan to shift work place they are not so interested in the question whether the clients were satisfied with their services or not. This approach is not advantageous for the houses were they work. A disappointed customer may not come back, while the pillar of both Janes and Carolines enterprises is a stable clientele. For this reason Jane and Caroline consider it both as their task to emphasize regularly the importance of a customer friendly approach. They often tell the prostitutes to be kind and polite towards the customers in spite of the low prices.

The work conditions

In order to bind the prostitutes to their working place the managers try to create an attractive working surrounding and conditions for their employees. In a lot of enterprises the distribution of the amount of money which the customers pay is traditionally fifty - fifty. Both manager and prostitute get fifty percent of what the client paid. Caroline divides the income on this basis and she is dependent on the turnover of prostitutes.

Jane choose for another system. She hires her houses to the prostitutes for a fixed amount of money a day (250 guilders for a full day and 125 guilders for half a day). As a result the income of Jane is rather stable and not dependent of the turnover of prostitutes. This different style of income generation has consequences for the way in which their enterprises are organized. If Caroline wants to be really sure that she gets her legitimate amount of money she must continuously control how many clients her employees have received and how much money was paid for their services. She manages this by employing ex-prostitutes who work for a small amount of money as porter and guardian in the private houses. Besides this Caroline daily visits all her houses for at least one hour to keep in contact with the prostitutes. Jane doesn't need this type of control. The prostitutes own her daily 250 guilders, whether they were visited by clients or not.

Prostitutes who must make the choice to work for Jane or for Caroline must try to weigh for themselves where they will earn better. Women who attract a lot of clients may prefer the system of Jane. With a high number of customers the 250 guilders rent for Jane will be less than the fifty percent they have to pay to Caroline. Prostitutes who do not attract many clients may get financial problems in the houses of Jane. The 250 guilders they have to pay may be the same or only a bit less than their total daily turnover.

The number of clients who visits the enterprises of Jane and Caroline is not only dependent on the prostitutes working there. I already mentioned that the houses of Jane are furnished better and more luxurious. For this reason the houses of Jane are more attractive for clients. In order to earn an acceptable amount of money Janes' employees must attract a relatively big number of customers, but Jane created an infrastructure which makes this more easy for them.

The recruitment of employees

One of the tasks of managers of enterprises for prostitution is the recruitment of new employees. The wastage of prostitutes is high and attracting new women is a continuing activity. The new prostitutes must fit in with the atmosphere in the enterprise and they must also agree with the labour conditions. Several methods for recruitment are used. Candidates are firstly recruited through advertisements in news papers. Secondly they are recruited through intermediation of brokers. These brokers mostly 'offer' foreign women from developing countries of Southeast Asia, the Caribbean and Africa. Since the fall of the iron curtain a growing number of the foreign prostitutes now comes from former communists countries in the Central and East Europe.[16] A few managers of prostitution enterprises in Rotterdam use a third method. They regularly travel abroad to recruit new prostitutes. Apart from this it also happens that prostitutes spontaneously approach an enterprise to offer their services.

As a result of a system of indebtedness with brokers and brothelkeepers, who lend money to the women for, for example, transport costs or intermediation charges, foreign prostitutes are tied to their creditors and have little freedom of movement. Besides this foreign prostitutes lack knowledge about the Dutch (prostitution) culture and language. They stay temporarily in the Netherlands on a tourist or artist visa which expires after three month and there is no possibility to get acquainted with the situation. When they decide to stay longer, they become illegal inhabitants which makes them more vulnerable for blackmail and exploitation. The conditions under which foreign prostitutes live and work differ, but in general these are worse than for Dutch prostitutes. The latter can choose their own working place and are better placed to negotiate with both managers as well as clients.

Jane and Caroline both want to attract the same 'type' of employees namely, women who are willing to offer their services for a relatively low price and who are willing and able to receive a big number of clients.[17] Furthermore they prefer women who exercise adequate Dutch. Although the main goal of their clients is to obtain a sexual encounter, simultaneously they appreciate it better if there are less language barriers. Moreover both Jane and Caroline prefer younger prostitutes.

In spite of these similarities there are important differences in the preferences of Jane and Caroline. Jane prefers women who can cope with independence and self responsibility. According to Caroline prostitutes need protection and care. She prefers more or less obedient workers who do not oppose her.

To recruit new prostitutes both Jane and Caroline advertize in news papers. In case non-Dutch speaking candidates apply, Janes houses might be undermanned for a certain period. Caroline prefers full complement. Even when candidates are not according to the profile, she employs them. When there are no reactions to her advertisements, she gets new employees through brokers and pays several thousand guilders for the intermediation. The prostitutes, mostly of foreign origin, have to pay back these costs. Since prostitutes are bound by debt, they loose freedom of choice and obedience towards for example Caroline, is more or less enforced.

The rules of the house

The rules of the house are explained to new prostitutes. These rules include the prices, agreements regarding working hours, hygienic measures, and the grounds to refuse clients. Both Jane and Caroline pay extra attention to prostitutes who newly enter this business. They stay around more than usual and try to make them understand them the required sexual, social and hygienic behaviour of the job.

In both enterprises the prostitutes are bounded to the fixed prices. Reason for this fixed but low prices are to attract more clients. Furthermore the fixation of prices also contributes to a better relation amongst the prostitutes. If employees were allowed to set their own prices, competition might become too severe.

The possibility to refuse clients is an important topic in the Dutch debate on prostitution. As - non-official - employees these women have to obey certain rules of the enterprise but this does not imply that they have to give their services to every paying client. If they are to obey the boss without limit, their physical integrity is endangered. Prostitutes who openly participate in the debate emphasize that prostitute themselves ought to decide whether or not to serve a client. If they are forced to do so, it should be considered as rape.[18]

Jane and Caroline approach this issue differently. Jane allows her employees to refuse, on the only condition that immediate colleges know the type of clients to be refused. Jane: "The prostitutes decide themselves whether they take a client or not. If they see some weird or dirty John, they are not forced to serve him. It is their own body. But they have to know from each other what types they do not like. A man who is not preferred by one prostitute is normally also not popular with the others. It's not pleasant when one has to do the dirty jobs for others".

In the houses of Caroline it is not allowed to refuse clients. An exception is made for prostitutes from Suriname - the former colony of Dutch Guyana - , who are allowed to refuse compatriots. Reason is that family and ethnic relations amongst the Surinamese in Rotterdam are very close. If a Surinamese client meets a Surinamese the word about her profession will soon spread. The clients however are not aware that they are being refused because Surinamese prostitutes are warned by the guardian of the house and are withdrawn for a while, in case a Surinamese client enters.

In relation to the danger of AIDS the necessity of taking the right precautions in changing sexual relations, like the use of condoms, has been emphasized during the last decennium. In prostitution the use of condoms was already relatively widely spread before the danger of AIDS. Jane claims that she never worked without a condom and considers it a part of her professional attitude. She sees a positive aspect of AIDS. She does not need to spend much time and words to convince the prostitutes about the necessity of the use of condoms. She strongly advises her employees never to have sex - manual, oral nor intercourse - when clients do not agree to use condoms. In relation to the use of condoms Caroline is much less strict and for instance oral contacts can be obtained without condom and this feature is mentioned in her advertisements also.

Carolines' employees have to visit a physician weekly for a check-up on venereal diseases. When they are contaminated they are not allowed to work until cured. During this period these women have no income. Jane let her employees decide whether and when they should visit a physician. She advises them to go there once in a while and considers it unnecessary to go every week since these women take adequate precautions.

Female managers in prostitution

Both Jane and Caroline claim that it is important that a prostitution enterprise is managed by a woman and even better by a (ex) prostitute. They should understand the specific physical and emotional aspects of the job as well as the social dangers of the profession better. Jane: "A woman approaches this profession different than a guy. He does not know what it means to lay on your back day after day. He neither knows nor understands the physical and mental pressures".

Caroline emphasizes that she understands the social behaviour of prostitutes outside the working floor better than male managers as a result of her own experiences: "The women seldom join prostitution through force. They choose themselves for this job. It hardly ever occurs that they were forced by a pimp to join prostitution. But once they are in, they get a pimp very soon. There are men with a sense for these things. This is because all of a sudden the girls start to earn and spend a lot of money. In this way they automatically attract a certain type of people. I experienced the same".

In spite of, or maybe as a result of their understanding for the profession both Jane and Caroline earn a good living from their business. I estimated that the yearly gross income of Jane from her 'renting of rooms' is minimum 520,000 guilders (around 250.000 US dollar). The estimated minimal gross income of Caroline is 618,800 guilders (around 300.000 US dollar). The yearly turnover in Janes enterprise must be estimated at minimally 1,040,000 guilders and in Carolines enterprise at 1,237,600 guilders. Of course they both have expenditures: to pay mortgage, advertising, cleaning and reparations of apartments, taxes and in the case of Caroline the food supply, et cetera. Being a Madam might be not always be seen as a respectable profession, but it is certainly a profitable job.

Conclusions

Conservatives versus alternatives

Women who enter this entrepreneurship are aware that they can expect better earnings than a prostitute. They may start their own business more or less as an experiment, they do not know whether they will succeed, but in contrast to female managers described by Anna Aalten (1991), they enter the scene willingly and consciously. Like entrepreneurs in 'regular' branches, however, they try to reconcile their professional identity with their sex identity. Caroline clearly defines her activities as a mother for the prostitutes. She wants to educate and protect 'her children'. In reality she is possessive and cannot distance herself from them. Jane defines herself clearly as an entrepreneur, but she also defines her task as educational. She wants her employees to grow independence and self-responsibility.

In terms of clients, Caroline emphasizes the service character of the job more than Jane. Caroline defines the clients as more or less pitiful characters who are in sexual need as a result of personal circumstances. Jane is more commercial about the description of her clients' needs: they want sex and their background or circumstances are irrelevant. They do not earn pity, or disrespect. Both managers try, of course, to direct the prostitutes in a customer-friendly approach, because their income is largely dependent on revisiting clients. There can be a gap between definition and reality. In spite of her sympathy for the pitiful clients, Caroline does not create an attractive surrounding for them. Jane does. As an entrepreneur she realizes that environment and interior have an added value appreciated by the clients.

It is hard to place either Jane or Caroline into Koopman and Walvis'(1985) typology of female entrepreneurs. Jane has a clear positive attitude towards traditional ideals of entrepreneurship. From this point of view she can be defined as conservative or innovative. Caroline should be characterized as hobbyistic. Their appreciation of traditional male-female relations is a complicated affair. In their professional life as prostitutes they 'disobeyed' all monogamous rules imposed on women. On the other hand, they fully accepted the 'myth of the polygamous nature of men' and during interviews, never showed any hatred or disgust for men in general.[19] In their present private lives they both have steady relationships with one man. Jane considers leaving the business all together for the sake of her child, thus revealing a somewhat ambivalent approach to her enterprise. In a traditional male-female relationship - with Jane in the role of responsible mother and housewife - there is no place for a prostitution enterprise. She is not fully able to reconcile her professional identity as a sex madam with her sex identity; in her private life she shows a positive attitude towards traditional male-female relationships.

Attempts to push Jane and Caroline in a typology are less important than the answer on the question whether the fact that they are female entrepreneurs is an adequate precondition for the improvement of organizational structures in the sex branch. The answer is no. The simple fact that they are women bears no relation to the circumstances in which their employees work, in spite of the fact that they show similar characteristics to female entrepreneurs of regular businesses. Prostitution enterprises may need an entrepreneur who is characterized as alternative by Koopman and Walvis. They consider labour conditions as the most important topic. In my research I did not find any entrepreneur who can be characterized as alternative.[20]

The tradition of prostitution

Prostitutes demand a higher share of the turnover. According to them, the entrepreneurs get a disproportionate high percentage of the fees clients pay for their services. From this point of view, the situation in enterprises managed by women enterprises is no different from that in male-managed enterprises. From this perspective their demand for led by women enterprises is not always understandable. The question, however, is why female managers who as prostitutes themselves were confronted with this 'injustice' continue with the same system of money division. One explanation can be that the entrepreneurs enter the business with an expectation of high profits and not for idealistic reasons. Structural changes cannot be expected from them simply because they are women. In addition, they work according to tradition, the fifty - fifty share is an old custom in Dutch prostitution. Jane does not work on fifty - fifty basis, but the huge rents she asks means the end result does not differ much from the old system.

Ex-prostitutes may understand the specific nature of the job better than others, but this does not lead automatically to a more emphatic approach to the prostitutes. Knowing the job can also result in an attitude in which the madams urge working girls not to complain too much about the aggravating nature of the job. After all, they endured it themselves, and survived.

Caroline reveals this view more clearly than Jane. She is unconcerned about one of the basic demands of prostitutes the right to decide themselves whether to offer services to a client or not. The prostitutes simply cannot refuse unpleasant customers. She is, however, concerned with their personal well-being. She wants to protect them from pimps and encourages them to save money. On the other hand, Caroline's behaviour towards foreign prostitutes is somehow pimp-like. They are confronted with huge debts and lose their freedom of decision and negotiation. Nor can the supply of food be interpreted as considerate behaviour only. In spite of probable good intentions, Caroline makes her employees dependent. They spend 12 hours a day - they have 60-hour working weeks! - in her houses and the danger of loosing ties with the outside world is great. The conclusion is that prostitution is no longer a way to earn money but has become a way of life. After a period of this type of internment it is very hard for the prostitutes to enter regular society again.

Jane approaches prostitution as a real job performed by responsible adults. Her style of work bears more resemblance to the wishes of prostitutes who demand more independence and possibilities to develop their own way of working. She does not attract prostitutes with a priori weak negotiating position, such as those who need the 'help' of brokers, and she does not want to cut off the prostitutes from society in general. According to her, prostitution is a real profession and not a way of life. She emphasizes the importance of social ties outside prostitution. Prostitutes get 'old' relatively sooner and therefore must plan and prepare for a life and career afterwards.

The way ex-prostitutes manage a sex enterprise is diverse and it cannot be concluded that being an ex-prostitute is an adequate precondition for acceptable working circumstances and conditions. Prostitutes who demand better working conditions and circumstances must try to develop a new philosophy and strategy about how to run a sex enterprise. Traditionally working conditions in prostitution do not reveal strong examples of how to run the business in a more favourable way, as these relationships have always been highly exploitative. Solutions may lie in cooperatives owned by prostitutes who work them or in facilitating enterprises where prostitutes can develop their own working style, and where the rents are more related to the real value of the space and facilities. This does not mean that prostitutes are motherless orphans. The way in which other branches are managed and organized may reveal examples for a better and more just organization of this branch.

Notes

1. Data on which the analysis is based were collected during field research in the city of Rotterdam which I conducted in preparation of my Ph.D. Thesis on management, organization and labour relations in prostitution enterprises. To study these issues 34 enterprises were visited where either managers or their employees like bartenders or porters were interviewed. In total, 92 prostitutes were approached out of whom were made in-depth interviews with 30. In addition interviews were conducted with 130 clients, and also with representatives of several organizations which have contact with the prostitution branch, such as doctors, social workers, police-officers and taxi drivers (Van Mens, 1992, p. 49 - 60).

2. Ever since the Middle Ages laws against brothelkeeping were developed. The activities of the brothelkeeper or madam was defined as a criminal as they took advantage of weaknesses and sin. Prostitutes themselves were not to be punished as they behaved according to female nature. (Bullough and Bullough [1987], p. 119). Current Dutch laws on prostitution reveal a similar train of thought. These laws prohibit brothelkeeping, but prostitution itself is not against the law. This construction - the laws stem from 1911 - results in the first place from a moral aversion to prostitution. Secondly, the laws aim at protection of prostitutes against the exploitative activities of brothelkeepers (Van Mens, [1992], p. 4).

3. Some prostitution is of course, directed at clients with homosexual demands. The majority of prostitutes, however, are women and in this article I refer to heterosexual prostitution only.

4. Acker, [1992] p. 257.

5. Aalten, [1991] p. 174-175.

6. An overview of this studies is given in Brouns and Schokker, [1990] p. 217-226.

7. For example 'Door vrouwen opgerichte bedrijven' (1985), see also the contribution of Jungbauer-Gans in this book.

8. Van Mens [1990], p. 205.

9. The number of prostitutes on yearly base is much higher. A part of the prostitutes moves from one city or even country to another and there is a constant 'renewal' of the population. Another part only works temporary in the business, while others only work a few days a week.

10. For women in general it can be more hard to obtain a mortgage or a loan in order to start an enterprise. See for example the contribution of Jungbauer-Gans in this book.

11. Furthermore I choose these enterprises because their entrepreneurs had shown the capacity to remain on the market. Besides that it was important to make a study of companies with a somehow comparable size.

12. The income which Jane has out of her prostitution enterprises is considerably higher than an income as regular landlady. She seems to be longing for a regular life as house wife and mother, but at the same time she got used to her huge income which she will loose when she withdraws.

13. In this context the word work means that Jane was a prostitute.

14. She manipulates the prostitutes to save money in a joint account in her own and the prostitutes name. For a few prostitutes from the Dominican Republic who didn't have the appropriate visas, the fact that they did not own their money in cash had a sad result. The were suddenly repatriated by the police, and their money stayed behind in The Netherlands.

15. When they read advertisements the mentioned age of prostitutes is for many clients a discriminative element in their choice for a certain enterprise. Once they already entered the enterprise and have to make a choice for one of the several prostitutes working there, age is not a very discriminative element any longer. The behaviour of the prostitutes and their ability to make social contact with the clients and to make them at ease becomes more important. (Van Mens [1992], p. 135 - 143).

16. In Rotterdam an office for publicity managers is established which attracts artists from developing countries and from Central and East Europe. The artists - mostly striptease dancers - get a low salary and improve their income through prostitution in the clubs were they perform. In some cases they are forced to prostitute themselves. (De Stoop, 1992: Van Mens 1992)

17. Offering services to a big number of clients daily doesn't implicate automatically a more heavy work load. Having sexual encounters with for example three clients who each paid for a time unit of one hour can be considered more heavy and exhausting than for example eight short encounters with visitors who only stay five till fifteen minutes.

18. The law against brothelkeeping had as purpose to protect prostitutes against forced sexual encounters with clients.

19. A lot of prostitutes revealed very negative feelings towards men in general and clients in particular. By being moderately positive about the nature of the clients. Caroline and Jane maybe proved to be very professional entrepreneurs in a service business.

20. From a commercial point of view, the question remains whether an alternative enterprise is able to survive for a longer period. As in most other branches competition in prostitution is severe which may have consequences for an organization, even in enterprises with an 'alternative philosophy'.

References

Aalten, Anna, (1991), *Zakenvrouwen*, Over de grenzen van vrouwelijkheid in Nederland sinds 1945, Amsterdam.

Acker, Joan, (1992), Gendering Organizational Theory, in: *Gendering Organizational Analysis*, (ed: Albert J. Mills and Peta Tancred), Newbury Park p. 248 - 261.

Brouns, Margo and Alie Schokker, (1990), *Arbeidsvraagstukken en Sekse*, trendrapport, Den Haag.

Bullough, Vern L. and Bonnie Bullough, (1987), *Women and Prostitution*, A Social History, New York,

Hazewinkel, Fernanda, (1982), *Prostitutiebeleid in Rotterdam (1828 - 1982)*, De naakte feiten over mislukte pogingen de prostitutie te concentreren en te kanaliseren, Rotterdam.

Koopman, G. and C. Walvis, (1985), *Vrouwen en Ondernemen*, Den Haag.

Mens, Lucie van, (1990), De seks-consumenten, in: *Het Verlies van de Onschuld*, Seksualiteit in Nederland, (ed: Ger Hekma), Groningen, p. 193-207.

Mens, Lucie van, (1992),*Prostitutie in Bedrijf*, Organisatie, Management en Arbeidsverhoudingen in Seksclubs en Privéhuizen, Delft.

Stoop, Chris de, (1992), *Ze zijn zo lief, meneer*, over vrouwenhandelaars, meisjesballetten en de bende van de miljardair, Leuven.

10 Chances of Survival and Success of Male and Female Businesses[1]

Monika Jungbauer-Gans

Institute of Sociology
University of Munich, Germany

Growing numbers of women are entering the labour market in all industrialized countries, but the desire to participate does not always match opportunities. Compared to men, women have part-time jobs and are in marginal occupations more often, and their unemployment rate is higher. Becoming self-employed is sometimes regarded as a way of overcoming an unsatisfactory labour-market position: a way out of unemployment or a possibility to create a job with freedom of decision-making. This chapter will investigate whether founding a business is a way women can overcome labour-market disadvantages. To this end, success and survival chances of businesses founded by men and women are compared. The study is based on empirical data. The main questions are: Do businesses founded by men and women differ significantly? Which factors determine success and survival chances of businesses? And the most important question is: are businesses founded by men more successful than those founded by women?

In order to answer these questions some theoretical approaches are sketched to hypothesize on possible determinants of success (section 2). Both economic and sociological theories are used. Data and methods are described in the subsequent section. Characteristics of male and female founders and their businesses are then compared. The question on whether female businesses are as successful as their male counterparts will be answered next. The analysis is based on three indicators of success: survival chances, growth of the number of employees, and prospects for the future. The conclusion at the end of the chapter will sum up the most important results.

Theory

We can start from the assumption that there is no single approach which can explain sufficiently gender specific differences in the success of newly founded businesses. It is necessary to review a number of theories dealing with the different positions of men and women in the labour market. Four theoretical approaches originating in economic and sociological gender studies seem to be fruitful perspectives.

Human Capital Theory

Human capital theory was developed by Schultz (1960), Becker (1964) and Mincer (1974). The central idea is that workers will invest in their 'human capital' (education, vocational training, professional experience) in order to receive higher wages. The higher the human capital, the higher the productivity, which in return represents the higher wages employers are willing to pay.

A great number of empirical studies shows that human capital resources affect the income of workers. Human capital theory was used to explain income differences of men and women (Mincer/Polachek 1974; Mincer/Ofek 1982; Diekmann 1985). There are three reasons for the fact that women usually accumulate lower human capital than men. First, women expect fewer years of employment and therefore the "pay-off-time" of investments in human capital is shorter (Becker 1981). Second, by interrupting their working career in order to bring up children, women reduce their professional experience, and their knowledge may become obsolete during their absence from work. Third, because women cannot spend additional time or because of employers' unwillingness to finance additional training, women participate less often in career-contributing courses. Women normally accumulate less human capital than men due to all of these reasons.

Although human capital theory was developed primarily to explain income differences between employees, it also can be applied to self-employed men and women (Preisendörfer/Voss 1990; Brüderl et al. 1992). The founder's knowledge and skills are important for the performance of small and medium-sized businesses. Preisendörfer and Voss (1990) argue that there is a positive relationship between the earnings capacity of entrepreneurs, measured by their human capital, and the risk of organizational mortality. Taking the founder's age as a proxy for human capital they expect a concave relationship between entrepreneur's age and organizational mortality analogous to the common age/earning profile.

The following working-hypothesis is based on human capital theory: Businesses founded by women are less successful than businesses founded by men, because women regularly have lower levels of human capital. To test this hypothesis two types of human capital will be distinguished: general human capital (education and professional experience), and specific human capital (prior experience in the sector and prior self-employment experience).

Female Working Capacity

The second approach used here concerns the concept of "female working capacity". It has been developed to explain the structure of the female labour market and has been widely discussed in German gender studies (Beck-Gernsheim/Ostner 1978; Beck-Gernsheim 1981). The main argument is that women's lives are characterized by a fundamental tension between house-keeping and occupation. Both types of work have different, often opposite demands. Housekeeping is characterized by a wide variety of tasks, and a lack of foreseeability, and a natural as well as cyclical conception of time. Working time and leisure time are not separated. Professional work serves a double purpose by satisfying the needs of society and by earning the worker's living. It consists of a single task, is mediated in the labour market and underlies an economy of time. Full-time jobs often rely on a second, unpaid person running the household. The historical development of the division of labour in the family resulted in a situation in which women are responsible for housekeeping. Due to carrying out this kind of work and due to socialization, women acquire typical qualifications and values (caring for others, emotional virtues and dependence). Personality features suited to household tasks are reinforced. Skills, behavioral patterns and values appropriate to housekeeping are not usually those needed to further a career. However, these qualifications are useful in specific professions and jobs (e.g. nursing), but they are hardly ever rewarded.

Some implications for the situation of women who set up businesses can be drawn from this approach. As they are not used to competition and fighting for success, women should be underrepresented here. Women are not as ambitious as men, and they can be expected to set up smaller businesses employing only a few, if any other people. They should choose trades that mesh with typical working capacity in branches where they have experience. The investigation of the data will show whether these implications remain true.

Social Networks

The theory of social networks investigates the utility of social contacts. Social relations can be useful resources and therefore are named "social capital" (Coleman 1990). Social capital is a kind of exchange relationship. Within a social network people give and receive information, help and even finance. Early empirical research in this field conducted by Granovetter (1974) distinguished between weak and strong ties. According to Granovetter, weak ties are more important in job finding than strong ties. During the last five to ten years this approach has been applied to entrepreneurship research (Aldrich/Zimmer 1986; Johannisson 1986; Birley 1985; Alrich et al. 1986). Social networks have two functions for entrepreneurs: detecting business opportunities (ideas, information and support), and receiving resources (borrowing money from family members, winning colleagues as partners, clients or customers; Aldrich et al. 1987). Some studies confirmed the usefulness of social networks for the success of businesses (Aldrich et al. 1986; Johannisson 1986; Birley 1985).

Are there any differences in the way men and women use of social networks? Women may have less access to weak ties, especially if they do not participate in the labour market. The quality of social relations may also be different: Women emphasize emotional aspects more than men; men use social networks more as a means to further their plans (Dachler/Hoskin 1991).

Organizational Ecology

This theoretical approach, which looks at populations of organizations, investigates success and survival of organizations. The evolution of populations is seen in terms of founding and mortality rates. Populations are groups of organizations which depend on the same environmental segment (both socially and materially) (Hannan/Freeman 1977). Populations gain environmental fitness via a selection process (Carroll 1984). Organizational ecologists believe successful organizations are characterized by structural inertia. Organizations acquire reliability and accountability by developing routines and specific knowledge and by external legitimacy. Because of structural inertia, organizations are not able to adapt quickly to changes.

An important thesis taken up by organizational ecology is the 'liability of newness' notion formulated by Stinchcombe (1965). Newly-founded organizations have higher mortality rates than older ones because routines must be developed and relations with the environment must be established. This thesis was modified by Brüderl and Schüssler (1990) into the 'liability of adolescence' thesis. They proved an increasing mortality rate during the first months. After nine months the risk of failure reached a peak and declined afterwards as the 'liability of newness' thesis predicts. During the first few months new organizations can spend their resources, which prevents them from early death. The 'liability of smallness' thesis says that small organizations with only few resources face higher mortality rates than large organizations (Aldrich/Auster 1986). In addition, environmental conditions, such as seasonal variations and economic circumstances at founding time, play a central role for founding and for mortality rates.

Although no direct implications for the success of female businesses can be derived from this theory, there are some indirect connections. If women start businesses with fewer resources, they have smaller chances of survival and success.

Four different approaches have been discussed in order to hypothesize the chances of female businesses. No approach should be favoured, because they complement each other and each can provide useful insights. The theoretical concept of this paper is summarized in figure 1. Planning, financing and business characteristics are indicators of the amount of resources the founder was able to bring into the new firm. Characteristics of the market are an important factor in organizational ecology. Individual attitudes concerning the objectives of the business may be influenced by gender specific personality traits and work capabilities. The list of theoretical arguments is completed by human capital and social network indicators.

Before the results of the empirical investigation of these arguments can be discussed, some information about data and methods is provided.

Data and Methods

This article is part of a study called the "Munich Founder Study". Data were collected through interviews with business founders in 1990.[2] A stratified sample from the founding cohort of the years 1985 and 1986 in Upper Bavaria was taken from the Chamber of Commerce of Munich and Upper Bavaria's register. Therefore, there are no craft businesses in the study. The stratification criteria were: (1) business in operation or closed,

Figure 1: Determinants of Success and Survival Chances

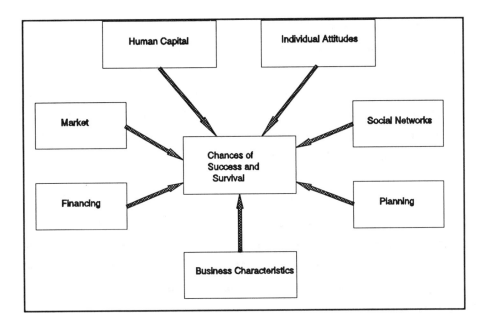

(2) legal form of the founding, and (3) branch of industry. Closed businesses were overrepresented, because of higher unavailability; registered businesses, and manufacturing and construction were overrepresented, because of small numbers. 1,849 business founders were interviewed. As over 100 never got off the ground, only 1,726 are included into the following examination of success and survival.[3]

Event history analysis is applied to investigate the survival chances of newly-founded businesses. The event to be investigated is the business's death. The stochastic models account for the dynamics of the process. Central concept are the hazard function and the survivor function. The hazard rate reflects the probability of having an event, under the precondition that it had not occurred before the considered point of time. The survivor function describes the proportion of businesses surviving until time t. Censored data are given when the event had not occurred before the observation period was finished. Event history analysis takes this information into account, although nothing can be said about the further length of the episode. In this study a proportional log-logistic rate function is used (Brüderl 1992).

Multivariate regression analysis is used to analyze the determinants of growth of the businesses under investigation. The parameters α and β are estimated using the ordinary least square regression. The β coefficients differ significantly from 0 if the t-value (=coefficient divided by its standard error) is larger than 1.96 (5%-significance) or 2.58 (1%-significance). The coefficient of determination R^2 gives information about the explained amount of variance (and thus about the fit of the model).

OLS-regression can only be used for a metric dependent variable. If there is a dichotomous dependent variable, the logistic regression model will be applied (Aldrich/Nelson 1984). The probability of $Y=1$ is a logistic function. It is not possible to compute R^2. McFadden's pseudo-R^2 is then used instead and is computed using the log-likelihood functions of the models with and without covariates.

Founders and Businesses

More than one quarter of the businesses were founded by women (26%). If the stratification of the sample is taken into account, 31% of all businesses in Upper Bavaria were established by women in the years 1985. and 1986. But for further analysis unweighed data are used. The proportion of female business founders is still lower than the female labour force participation (38%) in Germany.

In this chapter the determinants (independent variables) of success and survival chances will be described which have been derived from our hypotheses. The most important question is whether men and women differ in respect to these variables. Whether success and survival of businesses is actually influenced by these aspects will be investigated in the next section.

The motivation for founding a business is one of the best documented fields in entrepreneurial research. Sometimes the motivation or objective is considered important for the success of the business. Most research on entrepreneurial motivation is based on McClelland's famous analysis (1961, 1965). He said that successful entrepreneurs have a higher need for achievement than unsuccessful entrepreneurs. Besides the need for achievement, need for independence and for higher occupational satisfaction are basic motivations (Hisrich 1989; Carter/Cannon 1992; Klandt 1984). These 'pull factors' are often distinguished from 'push factors' (unemployment, job dissatisfaction; Bögenhold/Staber 1990, Evans/Leighton 1989). In many studies women and men list similar aspects (Rehkugler/Voigt 1990; Assig et al. 1985; Holmquist/Sundin 1986; Schwartz 1976; Cromie 1987).

Table 1: Characteristics of Founders and Their Businesses

Characteristics	Men Percent/Mean (Absolute/ Standard Deviation)	Women Percent/Mean (Absolute/ Standard Deviation)	All Percent/Mean (Absolute/ Standard Deviation)
**Objectives ** **			
Sufficient Income	61%	72%	64%
	(762)	(319)	(1081)
High Profit	39%	28%	36%
	(496)	(124)	(620)
Entrepreneurial	85%	80%	83%
Attitude *[a]	(1061)	(348)	(1409)
**Education ** **	10.83	10.37	10.71
Years	(1.72)	(1.54)	(1.68)
**Work Experience ** **	15.55	13.25	14.94
Years	(10.73)	(9.70)	(10.51)
Industry-specific	63%	48%	59%
**Experience ** **	(806)	(217)	(1023)
Self-Employment	39%	19%	34%
**Experience ** **	(486)	(86)	(572)

Characteristics	Men Percent/Mean (Absolute/ Standard Deviation)	Women Percent/Mean (Absolute/ Standard Deviation)	All Percent/Mean (Absolute/ Standard Devi- ation)
Support by Weak Ties[b] Index, Range [4,20]	6.16 (2.89)	5.98 (2.84)	6.11 (2.88)
Planning ** Months	5.23 (7.79)	3.87 (6.77)	4.88 (7.56)
Purpose ** Additional Occupation	28% (352)	40% (182)	31% (534)
Main Occupation	72% (921)	60% (271)	69% (1192)
Legal Form ** Small Trade	62% (793)	84% (380)	68% (1173)
Registered in commercial register	38% (480)	16% (72)	32% (552)
Start-up Capital ** DM Median	30,000	5,000	25,000
DM Mean	169,000	47,000	137,000
Market * No Change	60% (759)	66% (297)	62% (1056)
Dynamic Change	40% (504)	34% (151)	38% (655)

a) "Economy works only, if the entrepreneurs have high profits"
b) Sum of support from four groups: acquaintances, business partners, former
employer, former colleagues; 1 = no support at all, 2 = little support, 3 = some
support, 4 = a lot of support, 5 = full support.
Significance: * < 0.05; ** < 0.01.

The first topic in this study are the objectives of business founders. There
are significant differences between men and women: More men (39%) than
women (28%) want to make large profits, whereas more women are satisfied

with an adequate income (table 1). The statement "Economy only works if entrepreneurs have high profits" serves as an indicator of whether the founders have entrepreneurial attitudes. This statement is accepted by 85% of the male business founders and by 80% of the female business founders and is much more common among business founders than among employees (see Jungbauer-Gans 1993).

Human capital resources are acquired during education and professional work. It increases the productivity of people. Entrepreneurs, too, may have advantages if they have a higher stock of human capital. Some studies found that human capital increases the survival chances and success of businesses (Klandt 1984; Bates 1985; Preisendörfer/Voss 1990; Brüderl et al. 1992). In this chapter general human capital is measured by the years of education and the years of work experience. On the average, men attended 10.8 years of education, women 10.4 years. Before founding the business, men collected more than 15.5 years of experience in the labour market, either employed or self-employed. The number is significantly lower among women with only 13.2 years of experience (table 1). Furthermore, specific human capital can be analyzed. Two-thirds of the male founders have experience in their branch, whereas only half of the female founders have this kind of human capital. Whether self-employment experience is a positive or negative sign of the success of a business will be investigated in the next section. For 39% of men this business is not their first one, but only 19% of women had founded a business before (table 1).

Social networks may contribute to acquiring resources and information necessary for a successful founding (Aldrich/Zimmer 1986; Aldrich et al. 1987; Birley 1985; Balkin 1989). In this context, weak ties will be investigated (Granovetter 1973, 1985). Support from acquaintances, business partners, former employers and colleagues was rated (from 1 = 'no support at all' to 5 = 'full support') and a sum index was calculated. The higher the value of this index, the stronger the support from persons connected to the founder by weak ties. The values of men and women do not differ significantly. For men the index is 6.2 an average for women 6.0 (table 1).

Before analyzing the main features of the businesses, planning efforts of the founders are scrutinized. Successful entrepreneurs collect more information before starting the business than unsuccessful entrepreneurs (Picot et al. 1987; Jungbauer-Gans/Preisendörfer 1991). Although more detailed information about planning efforts was available, the time spent on the preparation of the business is used as indicator. Men planned their businesses for 5.2 months. This time is significantly longer than the time invested by women (3.9; see table 1).

The reason may be that men established larger businesses. The business is their main occupation for 72% of the male founders. Only 60% of the women rely on the business to earn their living; 40% of them use the business as additional income (table 1). The proportion of registered firms is much higher among men than among women. And men also invested a higher capital stock. The start-up capital of half of the businesses founded by men amounts to more than DM 30,000; 50% of the female founders invest up to DM 5,000.[4] The above-mentioned criteria are taken as indicators for the amount of resources the business founder was able to invest. Organizational ecology considers resources as an important determinant of survival chances. Market constraints are considered important, too. The rapidity of changes in market conditions is the last point of interest. 40% of the male founders forecast dynamic changes in their markets, as opposed to only 34% of the women (table 1). The influences of these aspects on the success and survival chances of newly-founded businesses are analyzed in the following section.

Success and Survival of Male and Female Businesses

The most important measure of success are the survival chances of newly-founded businesses. In organizational ecology several theses dealing with the survival of organizations have been stated. The 'liability of newness' thesis has been modified into the 'liability of adolescence' (Brüderl/Schüssler 1990). The 'liability of smallness' thesis argues that the survival chances of organizations depend on their resources. The survival chances of businesses have already been investigated (Preisendörfer et al. 1989, Brüderl/Jungbauer-Gans 1991, Brüderl et al. 1991, Brüderl et al. 1992). Only few papers deal with the survival chances of female businesses (Kalleberg/Leicht 1991), although the founder's sex is always used as standard variable. All studies confirmed that female businesses do not die sooner than male businesses, in as far as characteristics of the business and of the person are controlled for.

First, the survivor functions of male and female businesses are taken into consideration (figure 2). The function of male founders is higher than the function of female founders, i.e. male businesses live longer than female businesses. After 60 months (five years), two-thirds of the male businesses are still in existence, opposed to only half of the female businesses.

Figure 2: Survivor Functions

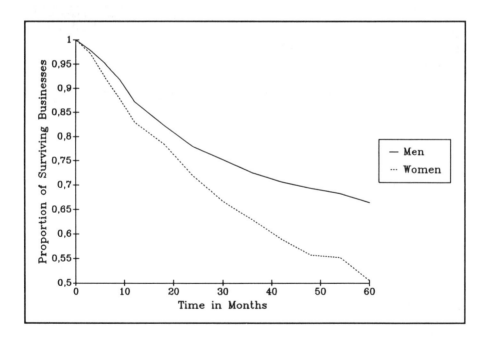

Whether this difference is due to the founder's sex or due to other determinants of survival chances is the next point of investigation. The proportional log-logistic regression model is used. With this model the shape of the hazard rate may decline monotonically, as proposed by the liability of newness thesis, or may have a non-monotonic shape, as suggested by the liability of adolescence thesis (Brüderl 1991; Brüderl et al. 1992). By using a parametric rate model it is possible to integrate covariates. Two models are estimated. In the first model (table 2, model 1) only the sex of the founder is included. Similar to the survivor functions it indicates that the death rate of female businesses is significantly higher. However, in the second model (table 2), in which all determinants of success are integrated, male and female businesses no longer differ. This means that, if women and their businesses had the same characteristics as men there would be no differences in survival chances.

Table 2: Success and Survival Chances

Success and Survival Chances	Death Rate (Proportional Log-Logistic Regression)		Development of Employees (OLS-Regression)		Prospects for the Future (Logistic Regression)	
Coefficent (t-Value)	(1)	(2)	(3)	(4)	(5)	(6)
Sex (1=Woman)	0.447** (5.06)	-0.040 (0.42)	-0.074** (5.91)	-0.055** (4.08)	-0.737** (5.13)	-0.478** (2.87)
Objectives (1=High Profit)		0.043 (0.46)		0.031** (2.78)		0.344* (2.47)
Entrepreneurial Attitude (1=Yes)		-0.378** (3.71)		0.015 (0.90)		0.281 (1.39)
Education (Years)		-0.135** (4.50)		-0.001 (0.32)		-0.043 (1.00)
Work Experience (Years)		-0.050** (3.55)		-0.002 (1.01)		-0.018 (0.75)
Work Experience^2/100		0.088* (2.49)		-0.000 (0.11)		-0.061 (1.04)
Industry-specific Experience (1=Yes)		-0.449** (4.70)		0.040** (3.16)		-0.112 (0.70)
Self-Employment Experience (1=Yes)		0.073 (0.66)		-0.015 (1.30)		0.033 (0.22)

Success and Survival Chances	Death Rate (Proportional Log-Logistic Regression)		Development of Employees (OLS-Regression)		Prospects for the Future (Logistic Regression)	
Coefficient (t-Value)	(1)	(2)	(3)	(4)	(5)	(6)
Support by Weak Ties (Index)		-0.043* (2.37)		0.004* (2.20)		0.022 (0.95)
Planning (Months)		-0.022** (2.76)		0.000 (0.58)		0.032** (3.27)
Purpose (1=Main Occupation)		-0.138 (1.38)		0.032* (2.23)		0.550** (.14)
Legal Form (1=Registered Firm)		-1.956** (5.72)		0.046** (3.39)		0.479** (2.85)
Start-up Capital (natural log)		-0.022* (2.22)		0.004** (2.85)		0.055** (3.23)
Market (1=Dynamic Change)		-0.156 (1.66)		0.010 (0.95)		-0.131 (0.96)
Number of Employees at founding (natural log)		-0.264** (3.48)	-0.019** (3.70)	-0.047** (7.39)		-0.075 (0.88)
Lambda-Parameter	0.101** (14.10)	0.082** (13.55)	-	-	-	-
Shape-Parameter	1.672** (11.35)	1.655** (11.19)	-	-	-	-
Constant	-4.331** (11.55)	-0.962** (3.29)	0.093** (11.55)	-0.008 (0.16)	0.518** (7.46)	-0.069 (0.22)
Number of cases	1726	1609	1167	1097	1140	1074
Model Fit Degrees of freedom	Chi²=24.7 df=1	Chi²=3-72.4 df=15	R²=3.5%	R²=10.7%	Pseudo-R²=1.7%	Pseudo-R²=8.5%

Significance: * < 0.05; ** < 0.01.

Businesses of persons with an entrepreneurial attitude have better survival chances. The human capital indicators show the expected effects: Education and experience in the branch diminish the death rate, and general work experience shows a curvilinear relationship (better survival chances with a medium number of years and worse chances with a small or a large number of years). Support from the social network enlarges the survival chances, as

263

does the planning-time before founding. Registered companies, firms with higher start-up capital and with a larger number of employees at founding live longer than smaller businesses. The market conditions, the purpose and the objectives of the founding and self-employment experience have no effect on the death rate. In both models the shape-parameter is larger than 1. This confirms the 'liability of adolescence' thesis.

Summarizing, it should be pointed out that the difference of survival chances of male and female businesses is due to different types of businesses and to different qualifications and attitudes. If women set up the same businesses or have the same personal requirements, their businesses would have the same survival chances. Whether the determinants of survival have the same effects for both groups of founders was again tested (Jungbauer-Gans 1993). At first glance, more similarities than differences appear. Only the purpose of founding has different effects for men and women. Founding a business as main occupation means better survival chances for male businesses. Running a business as additional occupation has a lower death rate among women than that of a main occupation. This result may be interpreted in respect to the growth rate of the businesses. If the development of the business is not as good as expected, women interested in earning their living by founding a business as main occupation may be forced to close down quickly.

The next question to be investigated is whether the number of employees and the development of this number differs between male and female founders. Job creation by businesses is a relevant topic. Birch (1987, p. 16) discovered that 88% of all new jobs are created by small businesses. He distinguished four components of the job-creation process: creation of jobs by foundings, loss of jobs by the closing of businesses, expansion of businesses, and contraction of businesses.

The question of whether businesses founded by women grow more slowly than businesses founded by men, has not yet been answered. Some studies looked at the size structure of businesses. In most cases women are owners of small or medium-sized businesses (see Rehkugler/Voigt 1990, Kirsch/Lühder 1990, Ambos 1989, Hisrich/Brush 1987 and 1984). But no study compares systematically the number of employees in male and female businesses.

Businesses founded by men are significantly larger than businesses founded by women. But this difference disappears if other factors are controlled for (see Jungbauer-Gans 1993, p. 120). The size of businesses at the time of founding is influenced by the objective for founding a business and the purpose of establishing a full job, the legal form and the amount of capital. The sex of the founder is not important.

Figure 3:   Number of Employees During ... Year after Founding (Mean; incl. founder)

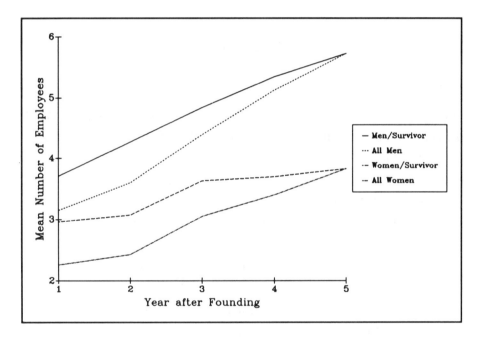

The development of the number of employees is shown in figure 2. Men start with an average of approximately three employees. In the fifth year after founding the businesses have almost doubled their number of employees. However, the growth of the businesses is not as high as this number may suggest, since many small businesses have closed. Therefore, the average number of employees may rise without the creation of further

265

jobs. A second graph shows the growth of those businesses surviving through the whole period ('Men/Survivor'). There is considerable growth, even among these businesses. The same development can be observed in businesses founded by women. But because their initial size is smaller, the development takes place at a lower level.

In a next step, we are interested in the determinants of the growth rate. As suggested above, some of the growth of the population in general may be due to selective death of small businesses. Therefore, only the surviving businesses are used to investigate the growth rate. Dependent variable in an OLS-regression is the average growth rate during the first four years:

$$Y = \frac{\ln g_5 - \ln g_1}{4} = a + \beta' X + \gamma \ln g_1 + u$$

Because the distribution of business sizes is right-skewed, the logarithms of the number of employees are used.[5] The size of the business in the first year is integrated as a covariate in the model to control for different starting size. The coefficient of this variable can be interpreted as elasticity.[6]

The results are summarized in table 2. In the third model only the sex of the founder and the number of employees are included as covariates. The fourth model also contains the theoretically-derived determinants of success. There are significant differences between men and women: The growth rate of female businesses is lower than that of male businesses, even if it is controlled for important determinants. The growth rate of businesses increases due to the high-profit target high rather than sufficient income. Among the human capital indicators only experience in the branch of founding is important for growth rate increase. Support from people through weak ties and the features of the businesses are also influencial. Registered companies and businesses with higher start-up capital increase their number of employees more than small trades and businesses with low start-up capital. So do firms which serve as main occupation for their founders. The negative coefficient for the number of employees means that the smaller the number of employees at the time of founding, the larger the relative increase. Entrepreneurial attitude, planning time and market conditions have no effect on the growth rate.

Whether the growth rates of male and female businesses are influenced differently by different determinants was investigated by estimating separate models (see Jungbauer-Gans 1993). There are hardly any differences. Entrepreneurial attitudes tend to lower the growth rate among female businesses, but increase it among male businesses. Both coefficients do not differ significantly from zero. This also applies for support from persons through weak ties and registered firms, where only male businesses show the expected effects.

The expectations for the future of existing businesses is used as a last indicator of success. Almost two-thirds of the male business owners expect their business to grow, but fewer than half of the women do so. This difference between men and women remains if the determinants of success are included (table 2 models 5 and 6). Judgement of the future is influenced by the objectives. Persons who want high profits expect a better development than persons satisfied with earning their livelihood. As far as the human capital indicators, the market conditions and the number of employees in the first year are concerned no effects are indicated. However, the other features of the business are important. The longer the planning period and the higher the founding capital, the better the prospects for the future. This is also true for businesses founded for main occupation and for registered companies.

Conclusion

Success and survival chances of newly-founded businesses were investigated. Three indicators of success were used: survival chances, growth of the number of employees, and prospects for the future. The central measure of success are the survival chances. The growth rate can only be analyzed for surviving businesses. The estimation of future expectations is subjective, but those expectations may influence the development of the business through the owner's decisions.

There are considerable growth rates of the number of employees. However, female businesses do not grow as fast as male businesses, even if other determinants are controlled for. During the first four years, the growth rate depends on the objective of the founding, experience in the sector and support from the social network. The following business attributes are of central importance: purpose of founding, legal form and amount of start-up capital. Smaller businesses grow faster than larger ones. If all these factors are taken into account, the number of employees at founding does not depend on the sex of the founder (see Jungbauer-Gans 1993), although the further development does.

In bivariate analysis the survival chances of female businesses are worse than the chances of male businesses. But if the differences in founder's human capital and in other resources are taken into account, the sex effect disappears completely. If women have the same experience, or if they found the same businesses, the survival chances of their businesses would be as good as the chances of male businesses. The most important determinants of business survival chances are: the objective of the founding, education, general work experience (with a curvilinear relation), experience in the branch of founding, social support, planning the time and the characteristics of the business. The death rate of male and female businesses is influenced mostly by the same factors. Only the purpose of the founding has different effects. The liability of adolescence thesis could be confirmed.

More men than women expect their businesses to expand. The prospects for the future are determined by the objectives of the business, the planningtime, the purpose, the legal form and the capital stock.

The most crucial determinants of success and survival chances are characteristics of the business. 'The more, the better' should be the device of business founders. Nevertheless, support from acquaintances, former employers and colleagues and, especially experience in the branch promote the success of businesses. Survival chances are additionally improved by general human capital.

268

The conclusion of this study is that female businesses do not expand as widely as male businesses, even if women have the same requirements and set up the same kind of businesses. However, there are no gender differences in the survival chances of businesses. Businesses founded by women consolidate at a lower level. To evaluate female businesses, success should be measured by other criteria. One reason for the differences observed may be that women often have to bear in mind their family obligations. Another reason may be that women lack acceptance as business owners. The initial question of whether founding a business is a way out of the secondary position in the labour market cannot be answered positively or negatively; however, being self-employed should not be preferred. When important prerequisites are present, allowing the establishment of a firm of considerable size (with high start-up capital, as main occupation and registered company), the decision to found a business can be right. Experience in the branch of founding is also of great importance. Women should not be reluctant to hire employees.

Women do not comply with these requirements as often as men. Two processes may be the reason for this: First, a self-selection of women choosing female-dominated branches only and founding small businesses and, secondly, the effects of prejudices in the labour market. Women interrupt their employment more often and are in lower positions in the hierarchy. Thus, they cannot accumulate the amount of human and financial capital in the same way men do. In the future, the interest of women in self-employment will probably rise, because of an increasing occupational orientation. Younger women have better opportunities for starting a business, have better education and higher qualifications. Improved material conditions will hopefully ease the initial position of women in the future.

Notes

1. This is the summary of a thesis on female business founders, written out at the Ludwig-Maximilians-University in Munich. The research was supported by the Deutsche Forschungsgemeinschaft with grant Zi 207/7. I am grateful for the helpful comments given by Josef Brüderl, Peter Preisendörfer, Gabriele Wiedenmayer and Rolf Ziegler.

2. The study was conducted at the Institute of Sociology, University of Munich by Prof. Dr. Rolf Ziegler and was granted by the Deutsche Forschungsgemeinschaft (DFG) with grant number Zi 207/7.

3. For more information about the data see Jungbauer-Gans (1993).

4. Due to some outliers, the means of start-up capital are much higher. Therefore it is better to interpret the median. Almost 25% of all founders had no start-up capital.

5. The logarithmic number of employees in the first and fifth year after founding are named $\ln g_1$ and $\ln g_5$.

6. This strategy is used to take into account heterogeneity among the population. The advantage is a very clear interpretation. What would happen if a shorter period of time is chosen, it was also tested. The effects of the determinants are almost the same when a period of two, three or four years is considered (see Jungbauer-Gans 1993).

References

Aldrich, Howard/Auster, Ellen (1986), Even Dwarfs Started Small, Liability of Age and Size and Their Strategic Implication, in: Aldrich, Howard (Hg.), *Population Perspectives on Organizations*, Uppsala, Acta Universitas Upsaliensis, 29-59.

Aldrich, Howard/Rosen, Ben/Woodward, William (1986), Social Behavior and Entrepreneurial Networks, *Frontiers of Entrepreneurship Research* 6.

Aldrich, Howard/Rosen, Ben/Woodward, William (1987), The Impact of Social Networks on Business Foundings and Profit: A Longitudinal Study, *Frontiers of Entrepreneurship Research* 7, 154-168.

Aldrich, Howard/Zimmer, Catherine (1986), Entrepreneurship Through Social Networks. In: Aldrich, Howard (Hg.): *Population Perspectives on Organizations*. Uppsala, Acta Universitas Upsaliensis, 13-28.

Aldrich, John H./Nelson, Forrest D. (1984), *Linear Probability, Logit and Probit Models*, Beverly Hills, Sage.

Ambos, Ingrid (1989), *Frauen als Unternehmerinnen und die Charakteristik ihrer Betriebe*. Bielefeld, Kleine.

Assig, Dorothea/Gather, Claudia/Hübner, Sabine (1985), *Voraussetzungen, Schwierigkeiten und Barrieren für Existenzgründungen von Frauen*, Untersuchungsbericht für den Senator für Wirtschaft und Arbeit, Berlin.

Balkin, Steven (1989), *Self-Employment for Low-Income People*, New York, Praeger.

Bates, Timothy (1985), Entrepreneur Human Capital Endowments and Minority Business Viability, *Journal of Human Resources,* 20, 540-554.

Beck-Gernsheim, Elisabeth (1981), *Der geschlechtsspezifische Arbeitsmarkt*. 2. Ed. (1. Ed.: 1976). Frankfurt, Campus.

Beck-Gernsheim, Elisabeth/Ostner, Ilona (1978), Frauen verändern - Berufe nicht? Ein theoretischer Ansatz zur Problematik von "Frau und Beruf", *Soziale Welt,* 257-287.

Becker, Gary S. (1964), *Human Capital. A Theoretical and Empirical Analysis With Special Reference to Education,* New York, Columbia University Press.

Becker, Gary S. (1981), *A Treatise on the Family,* Cambridge, Massachusetts, Harvard University Press.

Birch, David (1987), *Job Creation in America. How our Smallest Companies Put The Most People to Work,* New York, Free Press.

Birley, Sue (1985), The Role of Networks in the Entrepreneurial Process. *Journal of Business Venturing* 1, 107-117.

Bögenhold, Dieter/Staber, Udo (1990): Selbständigkeit als Reflex auf Arbeitslosigkeit? Makrosoziologische Befunde einer international-komparativen Studie, *Kölner Zeitschrift für Soziologie und Sozialpsychologie* 42, 265-279.

Brüderl, Josef (1991), *Organizational Mortality and The Liability of Adolescence: Further Evidence.* München (unpublished).

Brüderl, Josef (1992), *Bell-Shaped Duration Dependence in Social Processes. A Generalized Log-logistic Rate Model,* Bern (unpublished).

Brüderl, Josef/Jungbauer-Gans, Monika (1991): Überlebenschancen neugegründeter Betriebe, Empirische Befunde auf der Basis der Gewerbemeldungen in Oberbayern im Zeitraum 1980-1988, *Die Betriebswirtschaft* 51, 499-509.

Brüderl, Josef/Preisendörfer, Peter/Baumann, Axel (1991): Determinanten der Überlebenschancen neugegründeter Kleinbetriebe, *Mittab* 1/91, 24. Jg., 91-100.

Brüderl, Josef/Schüssler, Rudolf (1990), Organizational Mortality: The Liability of Newness and Adolescence, *Administrative Science Quarterly* 35, 530-547.

Brüderl, Josef/Preisendörfer, Peter/Ziegler, Rolf (1992): Survival Chances of Newly Founded Business Organizations, *American Sociological Review 57,* 91-100.

Carroll, Glenn R. (1984), Organizational Ecology, *Annual Review of Sociology* 10, 71-93.

Carter, Sara/Cannon, Tom (1992), *Women as Entrepreneurs,* London: Academic Press

Coleman, James (1990), *Foundations of Social Theory,* Cambridge, Mass., Belknap Press of Harvard University Press.

Cromie, Stanley (1987), Motivations of Aspiring Male and Female Entrepreneurs, *Journal of Occupational Behaviour* 8, 251-161.

Dachler, H. Peter/Hoskin, Dian-Marie (1991), *Organizational Cultures as Relational Processes: Masculine and Feminine Valuations and Practices.* 10th EGOS Colloquium 15-17 July 1991, Wien.

Diekmann, Andreas (1985), *Einkommensunterschiede zwischen Frauen und Männern. Theoretische Perspektiven und empirische Ergebnisse zur Einkommensdiskriminierung von Arbeitnehmerinnen,* Teil A und B. Forschungsberichte H. 212 und 218 des Instituts für Höhere Studien Wien.

Evans, David S./Leighton, Linda (1989), Some Empirical Aspects of Entrepreneurship, *The American Economic Review* 79, 519-535.

Granovetter, Mark (1973), The Strength of Weak Ties. *American Journal of Sociology* 78, 1360-1380.

Granovetter, Mark (1974), *Getting a Job: A Study of Contacts and Careers,* Cambridge, Mass., Harvard University Press.

Granovetter, Mark (1985), Economic Action and Social Structure: The Problem of Embeddedness. *American Journal of Sociology* 91, 481-510.

Hannan, Michael T./Freeman, John (1977), The Population Ecology of Organizations, *American Journal of Sociology* 82, 929-964.

Hisrich, Robert D. (1989), Women Entrepreneurs: Problems and Prescriptions for Success in the Future, in: Hagan,Oliver/Rivchun, Carol/Sexton, Donald (Hg.), *Women Owned Businesses,* New York, Praeger, 1-32.

Hisrich, Robert D./Brush, Candida (1984), The Women Entrepreneur. Management Skills and Business Problems, *Journal of Small Business Management* 22/1, 31-37.

Hisrich, Robert D./Brush, Candida (1987), Women Entrepreneurs: A Longitudinal Study, *Frontiers of Entrepreneurship Research* 7, 187-199.

Holmquist, Carin/Sundin, Elisabeth (1986), Female Entrepreneurs: A Newly Discovered Group, in: Donckels, Rik/Meijer, Jane N. (Hg.), *Women in Small Business. Focus on Europe,* Assen, Van Gorcum, 33-44.

Johannisson, Bengt (1986), New Venture Creation - A Network Approach, *Frontiers of Entrepreneurship Research* 6.

Jungbauer-Gans, Monika (1993), *Frauen als Unternehmerinnen,* Erfolgs- und Überlebenschancen neugegründeter Frauen- und Männerbetriebe, Frankfurt, Lang (forthcoming).

Jungbauer-Gans, Monika/Preisendörfer, Peter (1991), Verbessern eine gründliche Vorbereitung und sorgfältige Planung die Erfolgschancen neugegründeter Betriebe? *Zeitschrift für betriebswirtschaftliche Forschung* 43, 987-996.

Kalleberg, Arne L./Leicht, Kevin T. (1991), Gender and Organizational Performance: Determinants of Small Business Survival and Success, *Academy of Management Journal* 34, 136-161.

Kirsch, Claudia/Lühder, Katrin (1990), *Gründerinnen. Hoffnungen, Erfahrungen und Perspektiven von Frauen, die sich ihren eigenen Arbeitsplatz schaffen,* Hamburg: Frau und Arbeit e.V.

Klandt, Heinz (1984), *Aktivität und Erfolg des Unternehmensgründers. Eine empirische Analyse unter Einbeziehung des mikrosozialen Umfeldes,* Bergisch-Gladbach, Eul.

McClelland, David C. (1961), *The Achieving Society.* Princeton, N.Y., Van Nostrand.

McClelland, David C. (1965), N-Achievement and Entrepreneurship: A Longitudinal Study, *Journal of Personality and Social Psychology* 1, 389-392.

Mincer, Jacob (1974), *Schooling, Experience and Earnings,* New York, Columbia University Press.

Mincer, Jacob/Ofek, Haim (1982), Interrupted Work Careers: Depreciation and Restoration of Human Capital, *Journal of Human Resources* 17, 3-24.

Mincer, Jacob/Polachek, Solomon (1974), Family Investments in the Human Capital: Earnings of Women, *Journal of Political Economy* 82, 76-108.

Picot, Arnold/Laub, Ulf-Dieter/Schneider, Dietram (1989), *Innovative Unternehmensgründer,* Berlin: Springer.

Preisendörfer, Peter/Schüssler, Rudolf/Ziegler, Rolf (1989), Bestandschancen neugegründeter Kleinbetriebe, *Internationales Gewerbearchiv* 37, 237-248.

Preisendörfer, Peter/Voss, Thomas (1990), Organizational Mortality of Small Firms: The Effects of Entrepreneur Age and Human Capital, *Organization Studies* 11, 107-129.

Rehkugler, Heinz/Voigt, Martina (1990), Unternehmerinnen. Zehn Thesen zu einer von der Wissenschaft vernachlässigten Personengruppe, *Die Betriebswirtschaft* 50, 355-363.

Schultz, Theodore W. (1960), Investment in Human Capital, *American Economic Review* 51, 1-17.

Schwartz, Eleanor Brantley (1976), Entrepreneurship: A New Female Frontier, *Journal of Contemporary Business* 5, 47-76.

Stinchcombe, Arthur L. (1965), Social Structures and Organizations, in: March, James G. (Hg.): *Handbook of Organizations,* Chicago, Rand McNally, 142-193.

J